Edward A. Charlesworth is President of Stress Management
Research Associates, Director of Willowbank Psychological
Associates, and on the faculty of Baylor College of
Medicine, all at Houston in Texas, where he also lives. He
has written and co-written many books, and recorded
education programmes and scientific papers.
Dr Charlesworth's primary interests are stress in adults and
children, habit disorders and hypnotherapy.

Ronald G. Nathan is Director of the Biofeedback Clinic and
Associate Professor of Psychiatry and Family Medicine at
Louisiana State University. He has co-written several books,
teaching monographs and journal articles. Dr Nathan has
conducted stress management workshops for such diverse
groups as police officers, nurses, lawyers, housewives,
secretaries and dentists, and has lectured and consulted for
many large firms. He lives in Shreveport, Louisiana.

Stress Management
A Comprehensive Guide to Wellness

Edward A. Charlesworth, Ph.D.
*Willowbrook Psychological Associates
and Baylor College of Medicine*

Ronald G. Nathan, Ph.D.
*Departments of Psychiatry and Family Medicine
Louisiana State University
Medical School in Shreveport*

CORGI BOOKS

STRESS MANAGEMENT

A CORGI BOOK 0 552 99269 0

Originally published in Great Britain by Souvenir Press Ltd.

PRINTING HISTORY

Souvenir Press edition published 1986
Corgi edition published 1987

This book is an extensively revised and updated edition of the
work originally published in 1982 by Atheneum, New York

This book is set in 10/11 pt Plantin
by Colset Private Limited, Singapore.

Corgi Books are published by Transworld Publishers Ltd.,
61–63 Uxbridge Road, Ealing, London W5 5SA, in Australia
by Transworld Publishers (Australia) Pty. Ltd., 15–23 Helles
Avenue, Moorebank, NSW 2170, and in New Zealand by
Transworld Publishers (N.Z.) Ltd., Cnr. Moselle and
Waipareira Avenues, Henderson, Auckland.

Made and printed in Great Britain by
The Guernsey Press Co. Ltd., Guernsey, Channel Islands.

TO
Robin, Myra,
AND
Our Parents

Special recognition is given to the following scientists and writers – original contributors to the foundations of stress management training.

Robert E. Alberti
Herbert Benson
Barbara B. Brown
Kenneth H. Cooper
Albert Ellis
Michael L. Emmons
Meyer Friedman
Thomas H. Holmes
Edmund Jacobson
Alan Lakein
Arnold Lazarus
Wolfgang Luthe
Neal E. Miller
Richard H. Rahe
Ray H. Rosenman
Johannes H. Schultz
Hans Selye
Joseph Wolpe

Contents

vii

What is Scanning?
Your Body's 'Mirror'
Cues for Using Your Body's 'Mirror'

SECTION III: OVERCOMING YOUR SPECIAL STRESSORS

SECTION VII: ENHANCING HEALTH AND PREVENTING DISEASE: WHEN YOUR BODY WEARS OUT, WHERE ARE YOU GOING TO LIVE?

Preface

This book is part of what may become the most important health care revolution of this century. People want to do more with their lives than merely cope with the overwhelming cost of ever-mounting stress. They are seeking new and effective ways of taking control of their lives, preventing disease, and enhancing their health.

Those who are successful seem comfortable in almost any situation. Their lives are full and yet unhurried. They look relaxed and confident, even when they are making critical decisions or meeting important people. Physically fit and seldom tired, they project a sense of quiet strength. These stress management pioneers are also preventing the very diseases that pose some of the greatest challenges to modern medicine.

More and more twentieth-century illnesses have been shown to be related to the smoking, drinking, eating, and hurrying behaviors of patients. It is estimated that as many as 75 percent of all medical complaints are stress-related. The list of these disorders is long and growing: ulcers and stomach disorders, migraine and tension headaches, high blood pressure, rapid and irregular heartbeats, insomnia, back pain, muscle aches, and skin diseases, as well as many psychiatric disorders. Fifty percent of the people living in the United States report suffering from at least one psychosomatic symptom on a regular basis. These disorders and symptoms are reaching near epidemic proportions.

One of the great paradoxes of modern medicine is that improved health technology and living conditions have been accompanied by an increasing demand for medical services. Health care costs in the United States increased from $190 billion in 1979 to $229 billion in 1980. These figures are expected to nearly double by 1985. Unfortunately, you cannot buy good health.

A recent study conducted at the University of Tennessee showed that more than half of all hospital admissions could be prevented by changes in lifestyle. One way to contain skyrocketing costs and prevent stress-related diseases is to find ways of helping people adopt health-promoting behaviors, rather than find ways of operating, medicating, or radiating away the effects of unhealthy lifestyle. Behavioral medicine is the revolutionary new, multidisciplinary field devoted to understanding and changing these and other health-related behaviors.

This is an exciting time to practice medical psychology, which is one of the major branches of behavioral medicine. As teachers in medical schools, we have found a refreshing openness to the behavioral sciences among both students and faculty. Industry has also become aware of the costs of stress and the potential savings when employees learn stress management skills. These savings include reduced personnel turnover, alcoholism, absenteeism, lateness, premature employee death or disability, and other symptoms of burnout. The Mental Health Association of America has recently received a grant from several large industries to create a clearinghouse for information about stress and employee assistance programs.

Both of us have been involved in stress management training for many years. Edward A. Charlesworth, Ph.D., began developing an educational tape series in 1972, and in 1980 we completed an extensive manual to share with clinicians several effective techniques for treating stress-related disorders. Working with hundreds of patients, executives, homemakers, police officers, teachers, students, factory workers, dentists, secretaries, nurses, doctors, and others from all walks of life, we have learned a great deal about stress management. But perhaps the most exciting thing we have learned is that stress management can not only by successful, it can also be fun. In fact, wellness behaviors are known to be positively addicting.

Many stress management programs emphasize how to treat a disease, prevent illness, or lengthen one's life. We prefer to emphasize the pleasures of good health, as well as the consequences of high-risk living. Donald R. Dell, a leader in the wellness movement, makes a frank, comic appeal to vanity. 'I like to tell people that wellness is fun, romantic, hip, sexy, and free. People who practice it are stronger, better looking, have higher morale, superior bowel movements, and more antibodies against disease. They also become widely popular, tax-exempt, and get elected to office.' Although we cannot guarantee these changes, we hope to go well beyond stress management for your physical health.

Our goal is to help you achieve maximum well-being and enjoy a richer and more rewarding lifestyle. Many of our patients come to us for psychosomatic problems and leave not only symptom free but with a far greater sense of self-confidence, self-esteem, and involvement in life. They are no longer the victims of stress but victors over stress.

This book provides ways to assess your stress so that you can begin to understand and change your stress response. Stress and tension can be used in creative ways to make use of energy that would otherwise be lost through distress and disease. For example, when we are tense and anxious, we may find it difficult to enjoy the world around us, and we may develop physical disorders. It is important to learn new ways of coping, but it is also important to enjoy a renewed sense of self-sufficiency and to begin living life more fully.

We will present techniques that can be learned through self-guided exercises in a short period of time. To this end, we have provided self-assessment forms, charts, and case examples.

Part of this book will help you to establish goals and rehearse their attainment. We will teach you how to be more relaxed in even the most stressful situations. But we want you to go beyond simply lowering your level of tension. You will learn how to overcome fears or phobias and reach out for experiences you might otherwise avoid. We also want you to find new and rewarding goals, such as those of Dag Hammarskjold, a past president of the United Nations, who wrote, 'If only I may grow firmer, simpler, quieter, and warmer.'

In one chapter, you will learn the hazards to your heart of time-urgent living. There is more to life than increasing its speed or slowing it down. The process of discovering these rewards can become a source of great pleasure. For example, when we discuss time management with an executive, he may think of greater productivity and efficiency on the job. But our goal is a much larger one. We hope that he will not only be able to increase his work productivity but also will have more quality time with his family and children. Again, the goal is to enhance not only your health but also your life.

Two of the chapters in this book involve exercise and nutrition. The basic fitness behaviors and sources of nutrition for health are fairly well established in scientific circles. We have outlined these findings, but we have also shared how to begin making them a permanent and pleasant part of your lifestyle. We hope that rather than willpower, you will learn enjoyable ways of more fully developing and maintaining your body. Doing so may well add years to your life and most certainly will add life to your years.

Another part of this book will help you to learn about assertiveness training. Too often we clamp a lid on our true feelings until we are ready to explode. Assertiveness training provides new skills for expressing yourself to others honestly and without fear.

It has been said that life is like playing a violin solo in public and learning the instrument as one goes on. Although this is true for most of us and is part of the adventure of life, this book will provide some effective ways of approaching the instrument and finding more of the joy in playing it well. Men and women are the most adaptive creatures on the face of the earth. We can live in any environment, even in space or under the sea. To survive happily and successfully, the next generation will have to find enjoyment in adapting to a rapidly changing world.

Some writers have proposed that happiness involves having more pleasant thoughts and images than unpleasant ones. If this is true, then happiness is available to each and every one of us at almost any time. We cannot and would not want to promise you unending bliss, but this book will help you learn new, healthier ways of perceiving and dealing with events. As Shakespeare wrote, 'Things are neither good nor bad, but thinking makes them so.' For example, a crisis or mistake may be stressful but can be thought of as an opportunity to learn and grow from the experience of life. Thus, by taking on the challenge of stress in our lives and approaching life in new ways, we can learn about ourselves, accept our strengths and weaknesses, and grow from both our successes and our failures.

The responsibility for much of your health and happiness rests squarely on your shoulders. We hope that you will use this book to feel new emotions, think new thoughts, and undertake new activities that will not only reduce distress and disease but also bring you pleasure and wellness.

Houston, Texas Edward A. Charlesworth
Shreveport, Louisiana Ronald G. Nathan
February 1984

Acknowledgments

Many people have contributed to this book and helped to bring it to press. We wish to thank Nema Frye, M.S., R.D., who shared her expertise and collaborated with the authors in writing the chapters about exercise and nutrition. Special and deep appreciation is extended to William Braud, Ph.D., and Eugene Doughtie, Ph.D., for their early inspiration, research, and academic guidance in exploring the physiological and psychological aspects of stress management.

Both Paul Baer, Ph.D., and Ben Williams, Ph.D., gave countless hours of time in developing early research and clinical materials that allowed us to explore the effectiveness of our techniques. The basic outline of this book reflects their contributions, which deserve full acknowledgment and are sincerely appreciated. Beverly Graves, R.N., and Carol Loggins, R.N., were also highly instrumental in helping to test our materials in a corporate setting.

We are truly in debt to Shirley Hickox for her painstaking editing and proofreading of several drafts of our manuscript. If this book is readable, much of the credit belongs to Shirley, who generously volunteered hundreds of hours to help our readers. Various drafts were also read and critiqued by Robin Charlesworth, M.A., Sue Crow, R.N., William Day, M.D., Sharon P. Davidson, M.S.W., Marilyn Gibson, M.A., Fred Kotzin, Ph.D., Mary Lou McNeil, M.D., Bill Myerson, Ph.D., Art Peiffer, Ph.D., and Dean Robinson, M.D. Thank you for your valuable comments.

We would like to thank Ruby Harris for her dedication and hard work in typing and retyping early drafts of the manuscript. Danell Gable and Sherry Hardin of Silent Secretary, as well as Rhonda Thomas, deserve special recognition for composing and typing later drafts of this guide. We are also grateful for the creativity and flexibility with which Bob and Peggy Cooper of Graphics South designed and typeset the illustrations and charts for this guide.

A few words of acknowledgment are hardly sufficient to indicate the importance of the many hundreds of participants in our stress management groups. These people are the true authors of this book. They have been some of our best teachers. Only through their work have we been able to sift through the effective and ineffective techniques and suggestions that we have presented over the last decade. A sincere 'Thank You' to each and every one of you.

This book would still be a workshop manual if it were not for the perceptive reading, expert guidance, and knowing persistence of our literary agent, John Ware. We have also enjoyed the blessings of two top-flight editors, Neil Nyren and Susan Leon.

Finally, a very special thanks to our families for their consistent support, encouragement, and love: to our parents, who worked so hard to give us a head start on the road of life, and to our wives, who have endured many long weekends of 'work without play' and insulated each of us from other demands when we needed a rest. They have sacrificed much, and we are grateful. We also wish to thank Jennifer, William, Travis, and Webster for the long thoughtful walks they eagerly accompanied us on.

Part One

*Learning about Stress
and Your Life*

1 How Do You Respond to Stress?

Stress and Our Ancestors

The twentieth century has been called the Age of Anxiety. The history books that our grandchildren read will speak of the alarming increases in health problems related to tension and anxiety in what may be called the Century of Stress. You may well ask, Has man always been nervous and anxious? The plays of Shakespeare included many examples of the stress response. One of the most respected medical textbooks of the 1600s gave excellent descriptions of anxiety states. In fact, our nervous responses can be traced to the prehistoric caveman.

Imagine a caveman sitting near a small fire in the comfort of his cave. Suddenly, in the light of his fire, he sees the shadow of a saber-toothed tiger. His body reacts instantly. To survive, the caveman had to respond by either fighting or running. A complex part of our brains and bodies called the autonomic nervous system prepared the caveman for 'fight-or-flight.' This nervous system was once thought to be automatic and beyond our control. Here is a partial list of the responses set up by the autonomic nervous system and how you may recognize them from your own experience.

1. Digestion slows so blood may be directed to the muscles and the brain. It is more important to be alert and strong in the face of danger than to digest food. Have you ever felt this as 'butterflies' in your stomach?
2. Breathing gets faster to supply more oxygen for the needed muscles. Can you remember trying to catch your breath after being frightened?
3. The heart speeds up, and blood pressure soars, forcing blood to parts of the body that need it. When was the last time you felt your heart pounding?

4. Perspiration increases to cool the body. This allows the body to burn more energy. Do you use extra deodorant when you know you are going to be under stress?
5. Muscles tense in preparation for important action. Have you ever had a stiff back or neck after a stressful day?
6. Chemicals are released to make the blood clot more rapidly. If one is injured, this clotting can reduce blood loss. Have you noticed how quickly some wounds stop bleeding?
7. Sugars and fats pour into the blood to provide fuel for quick energy. Have you ever been surprised by your strength and endurance during an emergency?

The caveman lived in the jungle or the wilderness and faced many environmental stressors. Often these were immediate, life-threatening events involving dangerous animals or human enemies. For the caveman, this fight-or-flight response was very valuable for survival.

Stress and Modern Man

Modern man has the same automatic stress responses that the caveman used for dangerous jungle situations, but now man is seldom faced with a need for fight-or-flight. If a cat is threatened, it will arch its back. A deer will run into the bush. When civilized man is threatened, he braces himself, but he often struggles to contain his nervous reactions because the threat is not usually one of immediate, physical harm. Bosses, budgets, audiences, and examinations are not life-threatening, but sometimes we feel as though they are.

Smaller stressors and briefer stress responses can add up to hundreds a day. These can be parts of our lives that we hardly notice and almost take for granted. If you work in an office, stress may accumulate with every ring of the telephone and every meeting you squeeze into your already busy day. If you are a homemaker, all the endless tasks you must do can mount up just as quickly and take just as much of a toll as those faced in the office.

Man's ability to think of the past and imagine the future is still another way in which stress responses can be triggered at any time and in any place. In addition, distance is no longer a buffer. Turning on a television set makes us instantly aware of wars, famine, disasters, political unrest, economic chaos, and frightening possibilities for the future.

The rate of change in our lives is accelerating. We need only to read Alvin Toffler's *Future Shock* to realize that the unexpected has become a part of our everyday lives. These unexpected situations are not ones we can overcome physically. Tigers are seen primarily in zoos, but it is as if we see their stripes and saber teeth manifested in many ways in our everyday world.

Not only do we seem to trigger our stress response more often, but most situations do not provide an outlet for the extra chemical energy produced by our bodies. The fight-or-flight response is not useful for most of the stress situations in modern life because we have few physical battles to fight and almost nowhere to run. In the past, the demands for fulfilling basic needs for food, shelter, and safety made good use of our heightened arousal. Today, few of these outlets are available.

Physical Stress Versus Emotional Stress

When we think about what has happened or what might happen, we cannot run from our anxieties or physically fight our fears. We are undergoing emotional stress. The body has only limited ways of using the output of its various stress reactions to cope with emotional stress.

Physical stress is different from emotional stress. Even exercise triggers a stress response. In fact, until recently, scientists relied on the research in exercise physiology as a basis for understanding the effects of both psychological and physical stress upon the body. Although the effects of physical and emotional stress are similar, we now know that there are differences between them.

Many hormones are elevated during the stress response. Three of them are norepinephrine, epinephrine, and cortisol. Norepinephrine and epinephrine are more commonly known as adrenalin. In response to a physical stressor, such as extremes in environmental temperature or the stress induced by exercise, there is primarily an increase in norepinephrine. In addition, there is a small increase in epinephrine. In response to a psychological stressor, there is also an increase in cortisol. To understand the effects of stress, we need to study the effects of each hormone that is secreted in response to a stressor.

In general, norepinephrine has the greatest effect in increasing heart rate and blood pressure. Epinephrine has the greatest effect in releasing stored sugar. All of these actions tend to aid in preparation for vigorous physical activity.

23

Cortisol also acts to aid in preparation for vigorous physical activity. But unfortunately, one of its functions is to break down lean tissue for conversion to sugar as an additional source of energy. Cortisol also blocks the removal of certain acids in the bloodstream. When cortisol is elevated in the blood for prolonged periods of time, it causes ulcerations in the lining of the stomach because of increased acid formation.

Some of the results of increased cortisol secretion are higher levels of fatty acids in the blood, breakdown of lean tissue, and increased gastric acidity. Because of the potential for ulcerations in the stomach lining and the breakdown of healthy, lean body tissue, it is clear why emotional stress responses with excesses of cortisol have led scientists to claim that man, once the victorious predator, is now preying upon himself.

Other Effects of Emotional Stress

Even if we could exercise or somehow 'burn off' all the chemicals produced by emotional stress, upsetting psychological distress can interfere with productivity, learning, and interpersonal relationships. If our stress reactions increase, we become less and less able to handle even minor stress. Usually our ability to interact with and understand other people is also disrupted. We can exhaust our adaptive energy reserves and become more susceptible to diseases. It is clear that, for life in the twentieth century, our fight-or-flight and emotional stress mechanisms are often both unnecessary and harmful.

Balancing Emergency and Maintenance Systems

The autonomic nervous system has two divisions. One division is called the sympathetic nervous system. The word 'sympathetic' has two parts. 'Sym' means *before* and 'pathetic' means to *arouse the feelings*. Thus sympathetic means *before feelings are aroused*. Let's return to the caveman sitting in front of his fire. The caveman's response to the tiger included increased heart rate and breathing. These responses were automatic and occurred *before* the tiger aroused the caveman's *feelings* of fear.

The parasympathetic nervous system is also part of the autonomic nervous system. This system influences the body in ways that are almost the exact opposite of those of the sympathetic nervous system.

'Para' implies a modification. The parasympathetic nervous system may be thought of as modifying the sympathetic nervous system response. For example, the parasympathetic nervous system decreases heart rate, slows breathing, retards perspiration, and accelerates stomach and gastrointestinal activity for the proper digestion of food.

If the sympathetic division can be thought of as an emergency system, the parasympathetic division can be thought of as a maintenance system. This maintenance system is responsible for the conservation and replenishment of energy. Scientists have evidence to suggest that our parasympathetic nervous system can be activated through relaxation procedures such as are used in stress management training programs. Maybe we can all learn to replace fight-or-flight responses with what have been called stay-and-play responses.

Hans Selye and the General Adaptation Syndrome

Dr. Hans Selye is often referred to as the 'father of stress research.' His pioneering work demonstrated that every demand on the body evokes not only physiological responses specific to the demand but also the nonspecific and uniform stress responses we have already discussed. Selye classified reactions to stress as the general adaptation syndrome. The general adaptation syndrome has three stages: (1) alarm reaction, (2) resistance, and (3) exhaustion.

The Alarm Reaction

During the alarm reaction, the stressor activates the body to prepare for fight-or-flight. Both electrical and hormonal signals are involved in mobilizing the energy needed for an emergency. Heart rate, breathing, and perspiration increase. The pupils of the eyes dilate. Adrenalin and cortisol are released. Stored energy floods the bloodstream. According to Selye, if the stress is strong enough, death may result during the alarm reaction.

The Stage of Resistance

During the resistance stage of adaptation to stress, the signs of the alarm reaction are diminished or nonexistent. Resistances to noxious stimuli and illnesses such as infectious diseases increase above their normal level.

25

The Stage of Exhaustion

If the stressful stimuli or responses are not diminished, the stage of resistance is followed by a stage of exhaustion. During this stage, the exposure to a stressor has nearly depleted the organism's adaptive energy. The signs of the initial alarm reaction reappear, but they do not abate. Resistance is decreased, and illness or death may follow.

The general adaptation syndrome has great importance as an early theory of stress and disease. It stimulated much research contributing to our understanding of stress and resistance as factors in every illness. Stress may interfere with our ability to resist most diseases, but we now also know that the ability to manage stress adaptively can be learned. When this skill is used, stress is enjoyed as a challenge rather than dreaded as a threat.

Stress and Disease

If your doctor has recommended that you relax or take it easy, you may be suffering from a stress-related disorder. It is estimated that up to 75 percent of all visits to physicians are made by people with a stress-related problem. Stress may be a major factor in causing hypertension and coronary heart disease, migraine and tension headaches, ulcers, and asthmatic conditions. Stress may lead to harmful habits such as smoking and overeating, which have been shown to cause or intensify still other diseases. Stress is also suspected to aggravate chronic backache, arthritis, allergies, hyperthyroidism, vertigo, and multiple sclerosis.

Dermatologists find that stress is a factor in many skin disorders such as hives, eczema, and dermatitis. It has also been strongly associated with many gastrointestinal disorders including irritable colon and gastritis. Some of the excess hormones that the adrenal glands release during repeated stress responses can interfere with your body's immunity to infection. You then may become more susceptible to bacteria and viruses such as the flu virus.

Stress and Mental Health

Stress not only affects our bodies, but it also affects the way we think and feel. Have you ever come home after an unusually stressful day at the office feeling irritable and thinking about problems at work? At such times, your family already knows without asking that you had a hard day.

Sometimes we pass our irritability along to others. The stock market drops, for example, and the boss blows up at his secretary for not doing enough work. She goes home and screams at her children for being too loud. Her children scold the dog for being bad, when he just wanted to play. Do you have any idea what happened to the cat when the dog finally caught it? Stress can disrupt our lives as it ripples from person to person and even person to pet. This is just one of the many ways daily stress affects our mental health and our relationships with others.

The effects of long-term stress can be devastating. Most of us can bounce back from a bad day at the office or at home, but we may be unable to do so if stress continues day after day. Under long-term stress, our personalities may seem to change. We may suffer from depression and feel hopeless and helpless. Occasionally we may feel tense and explosive. Sometimes we find ourselves compulsively repeating meaningless tasks in an attempt to control our lives. At times, we act impulsively without thinking about the consequences. At other times, we have exaggerated fears of such simple acts as leaving our house, traveling by airplane, or riding in an elevator.

The changes we experience after long-term stress may have many causes. These causes may be very complex or as simple as learning an unhealthy response. Whether the cause is simple or complex, the problem physical or mental, stress can intensify our difficulties.

The Current Score in the Stress Arena

Although we have begun to conquer the Age of Anxiety, we still have an enormous task ahead. Stress is clearly winning at this time. Here are some of the current scores in the arena of stress. They may be categorized as the three D's: disorders, drugs, and dollars.

Disorders

30 million Americans have some form of major heart or blood-vessel disease.

1 million Americans have a heart attack every year.

25 million Americans have high blood pressure.

8 million Americans have ulcers.

12 million Americans are alcoholics.

Drugs

5 billion doses of tranquilizers are prescribed each year.
3 billion doses of amphetamines are prescribed each year.
5 billion doses of barbiturates are prescribed each year.

Dollars

$19.4 billion are lost by American industry each year because of premature employee death.

$15.6 billion are lost by American industry each year because of alcoholism.

$15 billion are lost by American industry each year because of stress-related absenteeism.

$700 million are spent each year to recruit replacements for executives with heart disease.

These numbers may seem impersonal. They do not reflect the pain and suffering of the victims of stress and their loved ones.

Healthy Stress

All stress is not harmful. As a source of motivation, stress can spur us on to creative work and it can enrich our pleasurable activities, as Hans Selye made clear in his book *Stress without Distress*. There is an important difference between life's stimulating thrills and its overwhelming anxieties. This is why it is best to manage stress responses rather than try to remove them.

2 The Challenge of Stress and the Benefits of Wellness

Have you ever wondered why some people seem to be comfortable in almost any situation? They seem calm and collected even when they make the most important decisions. They project a sense of quiet confidence and seem to have overcome the fears most of us associate with modern life.

Many of these people have felt the same anxiety that others feel, but they have cultivated ways of relaxing in the most difficult situations. Instead of focusing on the fears or anxieties of life, they view life as an opportunity for more than just coping. They see it as a challenge but one to be enjoyed.

These are the winners in the game of life. There are signs that more and more people are enhancing their enjoyment of life and not just coping with the status quo. Men and women are the most adaptive creatures on the face of the earth. We can live in almost any environment, even in space and under the sea.

The people who are most likely to survive and succeed in this and future generations will be those who can find enjoyment in adapting to a rapidly changing world. Before we talk about the skills of the winners in life, let's talk about some of the approaches that have failed to work.

Bottled Tranquilizers

To help overcome excessive and chronic stress responses and to relieve feelings of being uptight, many people turn to a variety of tranquilizing medications, narcotic drugs, and alcohol. These external agents have helped many through periods of trauma, but they do not modify the fight-or-flight response mechanism.

Over time, many users actually increase their stress by fighting the sedative side effects of the drugs in an effort to maintain alertness.

Instead of increasing their internal control over stress, they become more and more dependent on drugs to offset its effects.

These drugs and chemicals cannot think for us. They cannot decide what stress is good and what stress is bad. A tranquilizer cannot decide if a stress response comes from healthy excitement or debilitating anxiety.

The Benefits of Wellness

Because of the shortcomings of drug therapy, much scientific research has been directed toward finding alternative means of stress management. From this work, a number of effective procedures have emerged. Some of these teach you ways to relax and gain control over stress, tension, and anxiety. Other techniques teach you how to change stressful attitudes, beliefs, and actions. There are also procedures that help you release the emotional and physical effects of stress.

As a nation, we have begun to face the challenge of the Age of Anxiety and the Century of Stress. Consumption of fats and cholesterol is on the decline. Cigarette use has decreased over 25 percent since 1964. An estimated 400 percent more people with hypertension have successfully lowered their blood pressure since 1970 through improved medical care. More and more people are exercising and practicing relaxation and stress management skills. Large companies are building 'wellness' centers for stress release, physical fitness, and relaxation.

When companies build wellness centers and promote lifestyle changes, their costs can be repaid through improved employee health and decreased health care costs, as was demonstrated in a major study reported this year by Dr. Charlesworth and his colleagues at Baylor College of Medicine. After ten weekly lunch-hour sessions of stress management training, using the techniques in this book, a group of forty hypertensive employees had significantly reduced their blood pressure beyond the results of standard medical care. Three years later, their blood pressures remained lower or, in some cases, had decreased even further. In addition, the program decreased the costs of their health insurance claims by over 60 percent. More and more studies are showing the many benefits of wellness.

Wellness: Enhancing Your Health

These changes are signs of progress, but we are just beginning to understand the psychology of stress. There are truly vast frontiers to explore in regard to the physical and psychological health-enhancing properties of stress management and relaxation. Thus techniques such as the ones you are about to learn have the potential to go beyond the treatment or the prevention of disease and into the frontiers of health enhancement. If these techniques can truly enhance health, a stress management program could not only help prevent some diseases but also make you healthier and more productive. This is what we mean by 'wellness.'

The beauty of nonpharmacological approaches to the management of stress and the enhancement of health is that such techniques are nonaddictive. They can be set aside until they are needed and can readily be called up as situations demand. For many people, this program will help replace tranquilizing pills with calming skills.

Enjoying Life

Thousands of people have learned to relax in potentially difficult situations. These people can view stressful situations as opportunities to learn and use new life-enhancing skills. Stress management training will show you ways of learning these skills. With practice, you will be able to enjoy life rather than feeling uptight, overwhelmed, and unable to cope. Most people report not only healthy physical changes but a new appreciation for the richness of life. After all, when one is anxious, it is difficult to 'take time to smell the roses.'

One successful stress management student compared her new skills to the wax on a well-kept car. When it rains on a waxed car, the water beads up and runs off. She said stressors in her life still rain on her, but now she can relax and watch their effects roll off.

Stress Management Can Be Fun

Learning to enjoy the challenge of stress will take practice. It can also be fun, as you see yourself becoming more and more able to cope with and enjoy life. With daily use, you will fully benefit from this program of stress management. The skills are much like other physical skills in that they take some time to learn. Home practice will be helpful when learning these exercises, but soon you will be able to relax and take action calmly without written or spoken instructions.

Stress management is very much like learning to ride a bicycle. At first, you need training wheels or someone to guide you. Later, after practice, you are able to take the training wheels off and ride the bicycle alone. It is also similar to learning to drive a standard shift car. At first, the car probably jolted forward. Then you talked yourself through the procedure: 'Slowly push the gas pedal down. Now, gently let the clutch up.' If you are currently driving a standard shift car, it is probably an automatic habit to depress the gas or clutch pedal and move the gear shift. The same is true when you master stress management skills.

The first part of this program would be of some help if it taught you to relax when following instructions at home in a reclining chair. But its greatest value is allowing you to be relaxed in the face of real-life stressors. Take the example of riding a bicycle one step further. In learning to ride a bicycle, the goal is to use it not only in your driveway or on the sidewalk but also on streets and busy bike paths. Likewise, the goal of stress management training is to use it whenever you need it.

Stress management training is not a cure-all. Instead, it is a change in lifestyle and a new way of viewing the world. You acquire the habit of relaxation and trade the stress and strain of daily living for a relaxed and enjoyable way of seeing and doing things. You might be able to reduce your stress by dropping out of society, but you would be throwing out the good with the bad. Stress management is another alternative. You can learn to manage your stress and enhance your wellness by changing your responses to modern society.

How This Book Is Organized

Each chapter in this book introduces information or a technique that research or clinical work has shown to be an effective way to understand or manage stress. We have selected stress management concepts and skills that people have been able to learn in relatively short periods of time. In fact, the skills you will learn were chosen by the hundreds of people whom we have helped to become successful stress managers. Some skills are more difficult to learn than others and are best learned after some easier ones have been mastered. We have arranged the material to help you build on skills that are found in the earlier chapters of this book.

How to Use This Book

Most of the individuals and groups that we counsel and train are taught one technique each session. We explain the method and give participants instructions so they can practice the skill during the session. Most of the relaxation procedures, such as those in Part II, have immediate positive effects. After the session, the participants are encouraged to practice the new technique every day during the next week. This practice usually enables them to learn the skill and begin receiving some of its benefits by applying it in stressful situations.

To get the most from this book, we recommend that you progress through it like a workbook and practice one procedure at a time. Many hospitals and clinics now teach stress management to individuals or groups. You may be using this book as part of such a program. If a psychologist or other qualified professional is guiding your training, follow his or her recommendations. Basic mastery of this stress management program from start to finish takes several weeks to several months of practice. Very few people can learn to use and enjoy stress management skills effectively in less time.

On the other hand, as psychologists, we know that people vary widely in the way they learn and change. Perhaps you have already learned ways through earlier training or experimentation to recognize your stressors and to relax your body quickly and deeply. If so, you may want to skim the next chapter as well as the chapters in Part II and start learning some of the skills in the remaining chapters.

Some people will want to practice a few skills while reading through this book and come back to master the skills they found most useful. If you decide not to follow our recommendations to practice one skill at a time, try to look back over what you have learned successfully in the past and use the same approach in learning to manage stress.

Some people may prefer to read this material as a book rather than using it as a workbook. If you enjoy reading a book from cover to cover, we invite you to do so. In some ways, this would be like reading a good cookbook. Perhaps you would try out some of the recipes for stress management or save one for a special occasion. Maybe you would put some of the recipes in a convenient place and at a later time plan your strategy for coping effectively with a stressful situation.

33

3 Discovering Where Stress Comes From

'Stress' has become a household word, but what is it? How does it affect you? How can you recognize stress in your life?

Stress has many meanings, but most people think of stress as the demands of life. Technically, these demands are called 'stressors,' and the actual wear and tear on our bodies is the stress.

The demands or challenges of life can come from people and events around us, as well as from our inner thoughts and struggles. When these demands increase, people often feel that they are under excessive stress.

One of our goals is to present better ways not only to help you learn to live with stressful situations but also to help you find more enjoyment in meeting and mastering the challenges of our changing world. You should not have to give up the challenges of life that you enjoy and want to keep. You might be bored if you were forced to spend your days sitting in an easy chair. When you live successfully in a stressful world, you will be neither overstressed nor understressed.

Most people are not aware of their minute-to-minute stress responses. For better or worse, we learn to ignore, overcome, or accept them as part of living. What are these important stress responses?

Short-Term Stress Responses

At times, we are all too aware of how stress affects us. Have you ever felt that your stomach was jittery or 'full of butterflies'? Maybe you had a lump in your throat or your chest felt tight. Perhaps your pulse raced and your heart pounded. You may have felt pain in your neck and shoulders from tension. Maybe you felt sweaty or 'all wound up.' Thoughts may have raced through your mind, but when someone asked a question, your mind went blank. You may have 'flown off the handle' at the drop of a pin. Can you remember getting upset and having any of these responses? Most of us have experienced some of these feelings at one time or another.

Long-Term Responses to Stress

The short-term stress responses are physical or behavioral warning signs. If the stress becomes chronic and incessant, the short-term warnings become more serious stress responses. Some people work longer and harder but actually become less productive. For many, the words 'I don't have time' become a way of life. Dangerous stress disorders can follow changes in the way we feel and in the way we act. For example, some people become withdrawn or depressed.

Smoking and drinking may become problems. One's sexual life may suffer. Pain associated with headaches, arthritis, and other chronic diseases may increase. Some people eat more and gain weight, while others eat less and lose weight. Sleeplessness and sleepiness may become problems. Day-dreaming and difficulties with concentration are common. Feelings of suspiciousness, worthlessness, inadequacy, or rejection may become prominent.

Too many of us have some of these experiences too much of the time. We find ourselves anticipating the worst and being nervous before anything has happened. We may not recognize how our personality has changed. Even if the change is pointed out to us, we may not believe we have changed.

The following explanations and diagrams will help you to understand what your stressors are and how you respond to them. Notice that no matter where stress comes from, if the short-term effects occur intensely and frequently, the long-term costs are the same – the quality of your life suffers. On the other hand, if you increase and refine your coping skills, your life and health actually improve.

Stressors: Where Does Stress Come From?

We broadly define stressors as the external demands of life or the internal attitudes and thoughts that require us to adapt. Stressors can include traffic jams, pollution in the city, that fifth cup of coffee, the pushy salesman who will not take no for an answer, or the angry boss. Stressors can also include the work that never seems to get done, the

35

children who never seem to listen, or the way some people put themselves down for their shortcomings. Notice that some of these stressors come from our surroundings and others from our inner struggles. Some stressors come from both sources.

Many elements contribute to a stressor being stressful. There are certainly individual differences among us. Hans Selye says, 'You can't make a racehorse out of a turtle.' How much control we have over the stressor and whether we feel we have a choice in our exposure to it will determine our response. If you 'have to' work late because your boss 'made you,' for example, you will respond differently than if you 'choose to' work late because you want to finish the project and take the weekend off. The compatibility between a person's background, aspirations, and interests and his or her work will also determine how stressful the work seems.

Thinking of stressors in different categories will help you become more aware of the varieties of stress in your life. As you read the brief descriptions that follow, think about an average day and consider how each stressor may be reducing your enjoyment of life.

Emotional Stressors

Emotional stressors include the fears and anxieties with which we struggle: Can we prevent nuclear war? What if we run out of gasoline? What if I lose my job? Additional emotional stressors include worrying about unpaid bills, fretting about your children, or taking an exam.

The messages we silently give ourselves about our actions and the actions of others are also emotional stressors. Telling ourselves how 'awful' we are going to do in some activity is an emotional stressor that may lead to poor performance. On the other hand, consistently denying that we need to be prepared and 'do our homework' may also be an emotional stressor and can lead to failure. Both 'awfulizing' about tomorrow and procrastinating about today's activities can trigger stress responses.

Each individual has a unique set of emotional stressors. Some of them may seem contradictory. One person may not be concerned if bills are paid late but may be very concerned if his girl friend is not on time. Another person may be very upset about paying a bill late but hardly concerned if his girl friend is not on time.

Family Stressors

Interactions with family members can be stressful. The family structure has been changing drastically. The institution of marriage was once a strong, supportive force that could help family members cope with other stressors. Now, nearly half of all marriages end in divorce and an estimated 40 percent of children born in the last decade will spend at least part of their youth in homes with only one parent.

The percentage of people aged twenty to thirty-four years who have never married has increased by nearly 20 percent in the last twenty years. In the last twenty-five years, the number of unmarried couples living together has more than doubled.

Families go through various stages of stress even if divorce is not a factor. The birth of a child places new demands for adaptation on a family. The striving of teenagers for independence can lead to struggles between parent and child. In addition, families must adapt as the teenagers become adults and move away. Finally, families must cope with aging parents and grandparents.

Social Stressors

Social stressors involve our interactions with other people. Asking a person for a date, giving a speech, and expressing anger are common social stressors. Attending parties may be stressful for the person who likes quiet evenings at home. On the other hand, the outgoing person may find staying at home every night stressful.

Social stress is also related to feeling that we have no place in the social order. Often when communities toiled together, people drew strength from awareness and interactions with other members of the same community and social class. Now, many people feel isolated and chronically strive to find a feeling of community.

Social stressors vary widely from person to person. What brings relief from stress for one person may contribute to the stress of another person.

Change Stressors

It has been said that there are discoverable limits to the amount of change that humans can absorb. Since 1900, the rate of change has been accelerating at a speed previously unimagined. We may be subjecting masses of people to changes that they will not be able to tolerate.

THE TWO STRESS CYCLES:

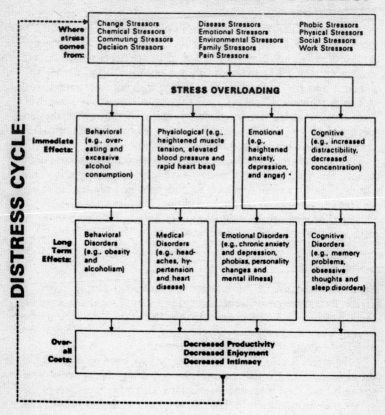

DISTRESS CYCLE

Where stress comes from:

Change Stressors	Disease Stressors	Phobic Stressors
Chemical Stressors	Emotional Stressors	Physical Stressors
Commuting Stressors	Environmental Stressors	Social Stressors
Decision Stressors	Family Stressors	Work Stressors
	Pain Stressors	

STRESS OVERLOADING

Immediate Effects:

- Behavioral (e.g., over-eating and excessive alcohol consumption)
- Physiological (e.g., heightened muscle tension, elevated blood pressure and rapid heart beat)
- Emotional (e.g., heightened anxiety, depression, and anger) *
- Cognitive (e.g., increased distractibility, decreased concentration)

Long Term Effects:

- Behavioral Disorders (e.g., obesity and alcoholism)
- Medical Disorders (e.g., headaches, hypertension and heart disease)
- Emotional Disorders (e.g., chronic anxiety and depression, phobias, personality changes and mental illness)
- Cognitive Disorders (e.g., memory problems, obsessive thoughts and sleep disorders)

Overall Costs:

Decreased Productivity
Decreased Enjoyment
Decreased Intimacy

38

DISTRESS AND WELLNESS

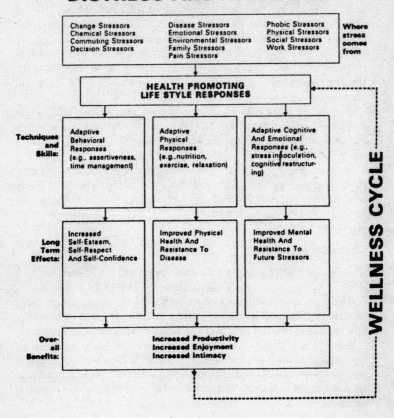

Change Stressors	Disease Stressors	Phobic Stressors	Where
Chemical Stressors	Emotional Stressors	Physical Stressors	stress
Commuting Stressors	Environmental Stressors	Social Stressors	comes
Decision Stressors	Family Stressors	Work Stressors	from
	Pain Stressors		

HEALTH PROMOTING LIFE STYLE RESPONSES

Techniques and Skills:

Adaptive Behavioral Responses (e.g., assertiveness, time management)

Adaptive Physical Responses (e.g., nutrition, exercise, relaxation)

Adaptive Cognitive And Emotional Responses (e.g., stress inoculation, cognitive restructuring)

Long Term Effects:

Increased Self-Esteem, Self-Respect And Self-Confidence

Improved Physical Health And Resistance To Disease

Improved Mental Health And Resistance To Future Stressors

Over-all Benefits:

Increased Productivity
Increased Enjoyment
Increased Intimacy

WELLNESS CYCLE

We experience change stressors when we alter anything important in our lives. When we leave a job, a house, or a relationship, part of our adjustment to our loss or to our new situation involves stress. When we move from one part of the country or city to another, we experience the change of uprooting. The loss of our social network and supports can be very stressful. Technological advances and the shifting framework of traditions and customs are also stressful changes.

If we do not make enough changes in our lives, we can feel stagnant and bored. This feeling can also be a source of change stress. Even the alleviation of pain or disease can be a change that demands readjustment.

Stress management training is a change stressor because training requires giving up old habits and thoughts. Stressful ways of living are harmful, but they are also comfortable and hard to exchange for healthier ways of managing stress.

Chemical Stressors

Chemical stressors may include any drug a person abuses, such as alcohol. Chemical stressors also include the pesticides or sweeteners in foods we eat. Caffeine is a common chemical stressor. Nicotine in tobacco is another. Most drugs, both those that are sold by prescription and those that are sold over the counter, are chemical stressors.

We choose to ingest most chemical stressors. We may ingest excessively large quantities of alcohol or smoke. Some chemical stressors are less under our control. For example, we may live in a city where we drink chemicals in the water. Likewise, many foods have chemical additives.

Work Stressors

Work stressors are the tensions and pressures we usually experience between nine and five o'clock at our place of work. If you are a homemaker, your hours may be longer. Asking the boss for a raise, trying to meet impossible deadlines, explaining an embarrassing mistake, disciplining your children, or cleaning the floor a second time to remove fresh mud tracks are all work stressors.

Work stressors, like social stressors, differ from individual to individual. One person may work well under the pressure of deadlines and find slow periods boring and stressful. Another person may get uptight and stressed when given a deadline.

Some occupations generally involve more work stressors than others. Did you know that secretaries suffer more from stress than executives do, as measured by the incidence of such stress-related problems as heart and artery disease, high blood pressure, ulcers, and nervous disorders? The U.S. National Institute of Occupational Safety and Health compiled a list of the twelve occupations most susceptible and least susceptible to stress-related diseases. The following two lists are given in order of susceptibility and may offer some surprises.

Most Stressful Occupations	*Least Stressful Occupations*
Laborer	Seamstress (hand-stitcher)
Secretary	Checker
Inspector	Stockhandler
Clinical lab technician	Craftsman
Office manager	Maid
Foreman	Farm laborer
Manager or administrator	Heavy-equipment operator
Waitress or waiter	Freight handler
Machine operator	Child-care worker
Farm owner	Packer, wrapper
Miner or machine operator	College or university professor
Painter (not artist)	Personnel or labor relations worker

This list of stressful occupations does not reflect one of the common components of work stress. We believe the changing nature of our working world is a major contributor to stress. Even in 1900, J. P. Morgan commented that he no longer knew everyone on his staff by first name. Since that time, businesses have mushroomed and frequently have hierarchies of managers. Most of us have little personal contact with our 'real' boss, and we may find it frustrating to meet or even communicate our needs. The 'home office' or the 'corporation' often acquire identities of their own; but how do you discuss your needs with the 'home office' or the 'corporation'?

The sexual composition of the work force is also changing. Nearly 50 percent of women over sixteen years of age are now in the labor market. This group includes half of all the mothers with school-age children. Economists predict that over the next ten years, the number of working women will increase, and six women will enter the work force for every five men.

Other changes have occurred in the working world. Fifty percent of the labor force is white-collar. Fewer jobs are linked to end products such as merchandise, food, or the consumer. It has become more and more difficult to see the value of our individual contributions.

The importance of work stress in predicting life span was demonstrated in a government task force study on longevity and the work force. The study found that 'more so than any measure of physical health, the use of tobacco, or genetic inheritance, the number one predictor of longevity in this country is work satisfaction.'

Decision Stressors

It has become more and more difficult to make decisions both on and off the job. Rational decisions depend on our ability to predict the consequences of our actions. Now our ability to make the best predictions is often compromised by more alternatives and less decision time. A good example of vocational decision stress is reflected in the occupational alternatives available to us. There was a time when a man became an apprentice to his father and a woman became a mother. Now the number of choices we have is overwhelming. A brief look at the thousands of jobs in the *Dictionary of Occupational Titles* confirms the potential confusion.

Decision stress on the job is also increasing. Certain jobs carry too much responsibility with too little authority. People experience role ambiguity and conflicting job demands. Predictability and control in our rapidly changing world are increasingly unattainable. There are more possibilities to consider, but humans have only a limited capacity to receive, process, and remember information. If you push beyond certain limits, your stress response may sound an alarm.

Commuting Stressors

Many people commute long distances to work. Some people drive in rush-hour traffic daily. Others spend hours on a bus or train. Depending on your distance from work, the amount of traffic you encounter, and your mode of travel, commuting may or may not be a major stressor.

Phobic Stressors

Many people have exaggerated fears of certain animals, places, objects, or situations which they know pose no immediate danger. These intense and recurrent fears are called phobias. The range of phobias is unlimited, and there are Greek names for almost anything a person can fear.

Some of the common ones and the objects of the unreasonable fear include claustrophobia (small enclosed spaces), acrophobia (heights), aquaphobia (water), and, in children, school phobia. Social phobias can be specific fears of activities such as speaking in front of large groups or meeting new people.

Some of the more unusual and esoteric phobias include ergasiophobia (work), gymnophobia (nudity), cibophobia (food), phobophobia (phobias), and even onomatophobia (names or terms).

One of the authors was bitten by a dog at the age of six. For eighteen years, he was afraid of dogs – not just the dog that bit him but most dogs, chained or unchained! This is an example of a conditioned fear. Many people have learned their phobia through such conditioning. Many of these people do not remember the connection or link that caused the phobia. The author realized that his fears were exaggerated and how they started, but by carefully avoiding dogs, he had never learned to overcome his phobic anxiety.

The author fell in love with a woman whom he wanted to marry. But there was a problem. She not only loved him but also Irish setters. She wanted to raise one of these beautiful dogs when they could afford a home with a yard. This did not stop the author from marrying the woman he loved because buying their own home seemed very far off in the future. Time passed quickly, however, and a few months before the day of reckoning, the doctor looked in the mirror and recalled the words 'heal thyself.' Using the techniques that will be presented in this book, the author was able to overcome his phobia and enjoy the companionship of 'man's best friend.' This is an example of how a stressor can become a source of pleasure and recreation.

Physical Stressors

Physical stressors are demands that change the state of our bodies. Physical stressors can be the strain we feel when we physically overextend ourselves, fail to get enough sleep, lack an adequately nutritious diet, or suffer an injury. Pregnancies and menstrual discomforts are examples of physical stressors that are specific to women.

Physical stressors often involve increased physical demands. Working eighty hours each week without getting adequate rest can place a physical demand on the body. An abrupt change from high, sustained activity to the boredom of low activity can also be a stressor. For example, some heart attacks occur immediately after a busy period of time when a person finally has a chance for rest.

Disease Stressors

Disease stressors are those we experience as a result of long- or short-term disorders. Many disease stressors are short-term and place us under immediate but time-limited stress.

We will concentrate here on chronic diseases, particularly those that may have been inherited and last a lifetime. For example, some people are born with a predisposition to develop headaches, arthritis, asthma, allergies, ulcers, high blood pressure, diabetes, dermatitis, hyperthyroidism, multiple sclerosis, or hyperkinesis.

These conditions may or may not be caused by stress. Nonetheless, they can be aggravated by stress. With stress, the disease may increase in intensity. The attacks of the disease may last longer, and the frequency of the episodes may increase.

There is a theory that each person genetically has one or more weak systems within his or her body. For example, a young man may find that one or both of his parents had hypertension. He should monitor his blood pressure more frequently than a person without a family history of hypertension. He may have a predisposition toward manifesting stress through increases in his blood pressure. Knowing your weak system could enable you to use your body as a barometer of stress.

Pain Stressors

Pain stressors are the aches and pains of new and old injuries, accidents, or diseases. Pains that cause people stress over a long period of time are particularly important. Old traumas to the joints, for example, can leave a person with a painful osteoarthritis. This condition, like a chronic disease, can flare up in times of stress.

A person with headaches may be plagued by chronic pain. In

periods of stress, the pain may become more severe, last longer, and occur more frequently.

Part of the stress of any chronic pain may result in a decrease of both physical and social activities. Thus the stress of chronic pain may lead to still more stress through isolation and inactivity. Ultimately, it may lead to depression.

Environmental Stressors

Environmental stressors include aspects of our surroundings that are often unavoidable, such as noisy typewriters, smoke-filled rooms, cramped offices, choking exhaust fumes, the glare of the sun, and the burning heat of summer or the chilling cold of winter.

The extreme conditions to which we are exposed can be either too much or too little. Loud noise is stressful, but studies in special sound-insulated rooms called anechoic chambers have demonstrated that total silence is also highly stressful. In such sensory deprivation, people may experience boredom, perceptual distortions, and even hallucinations.

Stressors That Are Better Reduced Than Managed

This book will help you to learn exciting and effective ways to live more successfully with many of the stressors we have just defined. Some stressors, however, are better approached in direct ways to help reduce or eliminate them rather than learning ways to cope more effectively with them. If drinking too much coffee makes you jittery or irritable, it is more efficient to reduce this chemical stressor by substituting water or caffeine-free drinks than to use the techniques in this book to attempt to be less irritable or shaky.

For many people, such changes are easier said than done. For them a number of the techniques in this book may be useful in helping to reduce the urge for coffee and adjust to life with less caffeine. This is also true for other chemical stressors such as alcohol or nicotine. The use of these chemicals is often related to difficulties in coping with other stressors that we will explore in this book.

The majority of environmental stressors can be managed most efficiently by making environmental changes. For example, if you work in an excessively noisy environment or live next to noisy neighbors, some of the techniques you can learn from this book would help to reduce the muscle tension you experience in response to the noise. A more direct approach might be to use earplugs. Other techniques in this book might help you if you were afraid to ask your boss or neighbors for a change in the level of noise. Thus some of the relaxation or assertiveness techniques presented here could help you indirectly to make an environmental change; but making the change would be your real goal.

To help you make such changes, think of yourself as an environmental engineer or architect. Some of your ideas and blueprints may come from the chapter on time management. To avoid expressway traffic jams, for example, a growing number of executives are changing the times they arrive at and leave their offices. Others 'van-pool' and enjoy reading a newspaper or talking with friends on the way to work. Still others listen to prerecorded books on tape. Thus they change the drudgery of commuting to the enjoyment of recreational 'reading.' Take a good look at your work and play. If you are creative, the rewards are many.

4 Beginning to Manage Your Stress

You now know something about the stressors in your life, the stress responses of your body, and the long-term effects of chronic stress. With this knowledge, you may want to eliminate stress from your life. This goal seems worthwhile, but it brings to mind two thought-provoking cartoons.

The first shows a man in flowing robes who is sitting cross-legged on an isolated mountaintop. Three physicians are standing in front of the man. They are dressed in white coats and hold stethoscopes in their hands. One doctor says to the others. 'Well, at least we know it's not stress-related!'

The second cartoon pictures a glassy-eyed beggar in a gutter calling out to a well-dressed man carrying a black bag. 'Don't you remember me, doc? I'm the man you told to slow down and let my business take care of itself!'

Let us assure you that we are not going to teach you how to escape to mountaintops or eliminate all stressors in your life. Nor are we suggesting a stress-*reduction* program. Rather, we are offering you a stress *management* program. Stress can be stimulating and can make your life exciting. Our goal is to help you learn how to live with your stressors without letting them interfere with the quality of your life. We want you to reduce the wear and tear on your body, but we also want you to enjoy life.

Stress Hygiene and You

What you will learn is not a cure-all. It will not be a pill that you can take and then feel forever young. We hope that what you learn about the management of stress will be what soap and water are to dirt. Most people wash themselves to feel clean and refreshed. If you let dirt and grime build up, you begin to feel uncomfortable, and you may develop infections. You may need to wash more at some times than at others.

At times we make washing our bodies a chore. Another way to wash is to recline in the tub for a slow, warm bath. The same is true of the stress management skills you will learn here. You will want to use regularly what you learn. But there will also be times when you will need to use the procedures more frequently, slowly, and deliberately.

No one forces you to bathe daily or to wash your hands throughout the day. The same is true with stress management skills. When you give yourself permission to improve the quality of your life and to decrease the wear and tear on your body, you may choose to practice the suggestions in this book. Only you can decide when you are ready to take better care of your needs. We hope you will choose to try these techniques and find ways to make your life a more relaxing and rewarding experience.

It may help you to list your personal reasons for beginning stress management training. At times during this program, as in any new venture, you may get discouraged or feel that it is not worth the effort. Have you ever started to learn a new sport and wondered how anyone could ever enjoy it? At such times, it may be helpful to review your list of reasons for learning how to manage stress better.

If you do not have a list of reasons that are convincing to you, you may want to study the last chapter of this book. It may help you to become aware of what is keeping you from getting started. Then come back and write a new list of reasons for learning how to manage stress.

Barriers to Beginning

We hope that everyone who reads this book will continue using it and will become a successful stress manager. But, we realize that some people may decide that they don't have the time, don't have the interest, or don't need to relax. The problems people mention most often are difficulties finding a quiet place and enough time to practice stress management training. The following example illustrates some of these common difficulties.

Ms. Aptaker is a highly successful executive secretary and a single parent. She was referred to us for a mild ulcer and frequent tension headaches. She complained of neither having the time nor a quiet place to practice relaxation.

After examining these problems more closely, Ms. Aptaker discovered that she could use her coffee and lunch breaks at work to practice relaxing in a room that was not in use. She also discovered that her eight-year-old son Sean was curious about her new activity and wanted to try it.

Ms. Aptaker and Sean began practicing relaxation together in the afternoon when he came in from playing in the park and before she prepared supper.

After scheduling these practice times and finding quiet places, Ms. Aptaker said, 'One of the reasons I complained so much about neither having the time nor the place to practice was that I felt guilty about doing this for me. I felt that I always had to be productive at work or showing attention to Sean at home. Now I'm doing something that's good for me. My work is better, and Sean and I are closer.'

There are many reasons why people find problems difficult to overcome. The obstacles may be very real, but they can be exaggerated by our guilt over a feared loss of productivity should we take the time to relax. It may be reassuring to know that most of our patients find their productivity increasing with stress management training.

As you begin to examine your personal barriers to beginning stress management, keep in mind what motivates you. There are only two major motivators in life. One is fear, and the other is desire. Fear constricts us and impairs our ability to reach our goals. Desire, on the other hand, pulls us like a magnet to our goals. Focus on your desire to be a successful stress manager, but be aware of your fears or obstacles. Obstacles can be the fertilizer for creativity once you recognize and begin to overcome them.

Most people find it helpful to list personal obstacles and problems that interfere with their learning and practicing stress management skills. Knowing what your obstacles are will help you plan ways of overcoming them. List your personal obstacles to beginning stress management training and the potential solutions for these problems.

Example. Problem: *I have a tendency to give up too soon when I try something new.*

Solution: *I'll practice with someone else and remember that some habits take time to change.*

Discuss your personal reasons for beginning stress management training and the potential obstacles that you may face with close friends or relatives. Do not make your decision to begin stress management lightly.

The stress in most of our twentieth-century lives will not decrease. Just as animals evolve and adapt to new environments, the survivors of our generation will be the individuals who learn to adjust to and enjoy the 'future shocks' of our changing world. We cannot change all the future stressors that we will probably face, but we can change our responses to them.

An additional suggestion that we would like to make is that you find a partner to train with. This is particularly important if you are not working with a professional. Finally, once you have decided to start, it may be helpful to discuss your plans for practice with a family member or close friend. Such people can offer valuable suggestions and encouragement. In addition, a public commitment to practice is often more difficult to break and a better source of motivation than a private one.

Professional Help

More and more psychotherapists are learning how to conduct stress management training and adding it to the services they provide. Psychotherapists can be psychologists, psychiatrists, social workers, nurses, or counselors. These professionals can also help you assess the appropriateness of stress management training for your problems.

Some of the long-term psychological effects of chronic stress, such as depression and personality changes, may require other forms of treatment. Intense and recurrent fears of things that are not dangerous are called phobias. Many phobias such as fear of airplane travel or public speaking respond well to the stress management training described in this book. Others may require treatment that only a psychotherapist can provide. A professional can help you decide on the best treatment for you.

If you have a stress-related disorder but always seem to find reasons why you cannot slow down and practice stress management, read the time management chapter and the last chapter in this book. If you are still having difficulty a psychotherapist may help you to understand it and decide if you want to change your lifestyle. If you want or need additional guidance, the last chapter will help you choose one of these professionals.

Biofeedback Training

Some mental health professionals offer biofeedback training as part of stress management training. Biofeedback machines measure and display some of the physical changes that occur when we use certain stress management skills. Just as a bathroom scale is useful if you are dieting, a biofeedback machine can be useful in learning stress management. If you are interested, you may want to refer to some of the suggested readings at the end of this book.

Warnings and Precautions

If there is any possibility that the problems you are experiencing relate to a physical illness, read no further – see your physician. Poor diet, hormonal imbalances, and other physical problems can wear the masks of stress or anxiety symptoms. If you have not had a physical examination recently, we recommend that you have one.

If you are currently under a physician's care for diabetes, hypertension, a thyroid disorder, or a serious depression, consult with your physician before starting this stress management training program. The dosages of the medications your physician prescribes for these conditions may need to be monitored as your skills in stress management increase. Finally, if you have heart disease or severe headache, your stress management training should be conducted under professional supervision.

Relaxation Training

Part II emphasizes relaxation training. Relaxation is a very important part of stress management. The ability to relax quickly in any situation will serve two purposes. First, as soon as you begin using it, it will help you decrease daily wear and tear on your body. Next, it will give you the self-control to decide how you want to handle stressful situations so as to decrease anxiety, anger, or fight-or-flight responses and enjoy the experience. Being able to stay calm, relaxed, and in control is an important part of being able to change stressful situations in positive ways. Without this ability, you can be at the mercy of your stressors and you may react to them rather than acting on them.

You may wish to use relaxation tapes to help learn stress management skills. There are several cassette tape relaxation programs available commercially. In Appendix III, we recommend compatible prerecorded instructions. Some of these have instrumental and environmental backgrounds to enhance the relaxation training. Also, many psychologists and other health care professionals have recorded relaxation exercises for use by their clients.

You may want to use the detailed relaxation instructions in this book to record your own relaxation tapes. Appendix I lists musical and environmental selections that are compatible with relaxation practice. If you record your own relaxation, you may want to use some of these selections. Many of the selections have a calming effect on mood, as well as heart rate and respiration. Select the musical or environmental background that you find especially relaxing.

Recommended Books and Recordings

In Appendix III, we have listed prerecorded relaxation tapes and other recommended listening materials for many of the chapters in this book. The recorded materials can help you to practice new techniques or learn related information.

We have also included recommended books in Appendix III to accompany most chapters. These readings can also help to expand and deepen your knowledge of the topics covered in this book.

Part Two

*Relaxing Ways
for a
Stressful World*

5   Progressive Relaxation: How Can I Relax by Tightening My Muscles?

How often, when we are stressed and worried, do we hear someone say, 'Just relax'? Perhaps a friend makes this suggestion when you are feeling uptight about job frustrations or other demands. Maybe your dentist says, 'Just relax,' when the drill begins to hum. When patients complain of nervousness, headaches, backaches, or just plain exhaustion, physicians often tell them to relax. Many people tell us to relax but never tell us how.

For most people, relaxation is the best skill to learn at the beginning of stress management training. Progressive relaxation is a technique for muscle relaxation which was developed by Dr. Edmund Jacobson. As a medical student, Dr. Jacobson realized that, even when he was relaxed, his muscles were still somewhat tense. He became aware that this muscle tension might reflect the increasing pace of life.

In the 1920s, Dr. Jacobson was beginning his career as a physician. Even then, almost every individual was facing ever-growing demands that were almost unknown to earlier generations. The average businessman was striving for greater and greater achievements in hopes of security. Businessmen often fought off fatigue until they were nearly exhausted. Social events were becoming more complex, and recreational activities often failed to provide the needed relaxation and diversion.

Then as now, there was more and more competition and preoccupation with the appearance of being in control. The great stock market crash created anxieties similar to inflation and unemployment. A success image was created. Advertising trained people to want more and more gadgets from the marketplace. To be successful, one had to strive unendingly to fulfill heightened expectations. The barrage of new needs has continued, and we are now expected to buy only designer clothes or the newest electronic instruments.

Dr. Jacobson realized that he, as well as his patients, needed more than just encouragement to relax. Through his long and distinguished career, he developed a systematic program for training people to relax their muscles completely.

Dr. Jacobson studied the effectiveness of his techniques by measuring the amount of electrical activity produced in the muscle fibers. The results suggested that many people report feeling totally relaxed when asked simply to 'sit and relax.' But, Dr. Jacobson discovered that he was not alone. In fact, most of the people had what he called 'residual tension,' of which they are unaware. His later studies demonstrated that people can produce greater relaxation by practicing progressive relaxation than by simply trying to sit and relax.

Over the years, Dr. Jacobson and other scientists have carefully studied and refined progressive relaxation. It now offers a proven, systematic way to control muscle tension. In addition to helping people learn how to relax, the techniques have been used for many disorders, including anxiety, insomnia, headaches, backaches, and hypertension. Physiological research has demonstrated that the procedures produce a profound relaxation. When measured with sensitive electromyographic instruments, major muscle groups can be trained to what is called zero firing threshold. This is total muscle relaxation.

The physical relaxation produced is pleasant and tends to leave the individual with a sense of refreshment. Dr. Jacobson believed that tense muscles had a lot to do with tense minds and that mental relaxation would follow physical relaxation.

Many people use progressive relaxation techniques as a form of recreation. More and more of the techniques are being incorporated into physical fitness programs and exercise classes. Some people find that after vigorous exercise it is helpful to bring their bodies back into a resting state by using these relaxation procedures.

Why Learn Relaxation?

Many people question the need to learn how to relax. Some individuals see muscle tension as a sign of strength. For others, tension equals fitness rather than flabbiness. In the rush of everyday living, however, men and women have forgotten how to live without unnecessary discomfort. Muscle tension is not always a sign of strength but can be a sign that energy is being wasted.

To have various muscles constantly tense, as we wrinkle our

forehead, squint our eyes, tap our fingers, and shift our positions is not a sign of strength. When we nervously make a path to the coffee machine or automatically light up a cigarette, we are often looking for ways to release pent-up tensions.

Learning and practicing relaxation can be a sign of strength in how to be selectively tense when a particular task must be performed. You also learn how to avoid wasting energies needlessly by conserving them for important accomplishments.

A football player may get up slowly and walk back to the huddle, as if he were dead tired. Yet a minute later, the same football player is carrying would-be tacklers with him down the field. He does not run to the huddle and jump up and down waiting for the next play to be called. He saves his energies for those things he truly wants to do.

It is important to know that people who learn to relax do not lose motivation. An executive who complained of neck and shoulder pain came to us but insisted that he was not tense and did not need to become more relaxed. He was a successful man in a large oil company and feared that, if he learned how to relax, he would become less productive.

It was only after several weeks of encouragement and practice that this high-level executive realized that he had been chronically carrying tension in his shoulder and neck muscles throughout the day and during the commute home. He was surprised that he was able to learn to relax these muscles without a decrease in his job performance. Consequently, he felt more energetic and productive. This energy was directed into more productive work and recreational activities.

It is important to remember that when we talk of teaching you to relax, we do not mean we will teach you how to become lazy, bored, or tired. A medical student in one of our classes reported that his father learned progressive relaxation as a bomber pilot during World War II. By using progressive relaxation, the pilots could remain alert and avoid fatigue.

Where to Find Muscle Tension

To relax muscles progressively, you begin by tensing and relaxing the major muscle groups of the body. In this way, you become aware of exactly where your muscles are located. Tensing and relaxing muscles helps you to increase your awareness of your body's muscular response to stress. As one becomes more aware of the location and feeling of muscle tension, the absence of tension becomes clear. In essence, you begin to recognize muscle tension and the difference between being tense and being relaxed.

The muscle groups around the head, face, neck, and shoulders are particularly important areas of stress. A great deal of tension may accumulate in these muscles. Every person is different. Other muscle groups should also be explored, including the arms, hands, chest, back, stomach, hips, legs, and feet.

It is also important to know which muscles seem to stay tense. Take a moment to look in the mirror and think about being angry or anxious. Are your legs in a defensive stance? Is your jaw tight? Do your eyes seem intense? During the next few days, observe how you sit and stand in different places and at different times. Try to find out which of your muscles seem to stay tense.

Testing Your Muscle Relaxation

It is important to know that, after tensing, a muscle will automatically relax more deeply when released. The feeling of relaxation is increased further by experiencing the difference between muscle tension and muscle relaxation.

Relaxation simply means doing nothing with your muscles. One way to test a person's depth of relaxation is to have someone lift or bend a relaxed arm at the elbow. If the arm is resisting or assisting the movement, it is not relaxed. The arm should be as easy to move as any other object of the same weight.

Why Start with Progressive Relaxation?

Progressive relaxation is an excellent starting point for stress management training. It increases general bodily awareness and the recognition of specific muscles where tension is troublesome.

As you may recall, the oil company executive discovered that he had been living with excessive tension in his shoulders and neck. His reaction to this discovery was one of surprise. He had insisted that he did not need relaxation, but progressive relaxation increased his awareness of the difference between tension and relaxation. The realization that his shoulders stayed needlessly tight did not come to him immediately, but progressive relaxation helped him to recognize that muscle tension was mounting before he experienced pain.

Most people feel surprisingly comfortable after their very first session of progressive relaxation. Progressive relaxation techniques may seem simple. The exercises are neither spectacular nor difficult. Do not be fooled! The important parts of this aspect of the stress management program are the systematic exercise sequences, awareness of residual tensions, and the regular practice needed to make this new muscle relaxation a routine way of life.

Differential Relaxation

Another use of progressive relaxation is differential relaxation. Differential relaxation involves relaxing the parts of the body not needed for a certain task, while tensing the necessary muscles that are in use. For example, when driving a car, it is not necessary to tense every muscle in your body. Often people find that their jaws or shoulders are tense while driving.

After practicing with progressive relaxation, you will find it easier to relax the muscles that are not needed to perform a task. At the same time, you learn how to keep only a moderate amount of tension in the needed muscles. This is very helpful in situations such as typing a report, preparing a meal, standing in line, and discussing business on the phone.

Building Relaxation into Everyday Living

It is useful to leave reminders in the office and at home to help you remember to observe your tension and to relax differentially. Small pieces of colored tape may be attached to your watch, the telephone, or rearview mirror. These will help remind you to scan your body for signs of tension every time you look to see what time it is, receive a telephone call, or prepare to change lanes.

Looking at your watch or a clock is often associated with nervousness and excessive tension. Converting 'What time is it?' tension habits to the habit of responding with creative relaxation helps to build a sense of control over your body's tensions.

It may also be useful to put a sign on the bathroom mirror, your desk, or the dashboard of the car. Something like 'Am I relaxed?' or simply 'Relax' will work. Even the letter 'R' can represent a cue to relax. A vacation snapshot in the office can provide a pleasant reminder of relaxation. A concerned wife of one of the authors of this book gave both writers needlepointed paperweights. Each paperweight displays the word 'Relax!'

Relaxation for Headaches

Remember to continue practicing relaxation until it is as automatic as breathing. One of our patients, whom we will call Ms. Thomas, suffered from daily tension headaches at work in the afternoons. Occasionally the pain was so intense that it forced her to leave work early. This only added to the stress she had to face the next day. As a secretary, she already had enough work stressors. Before she was referred by her physician for stress management training, she was unaware of the muscle tension in her neck and shoulders that preceded the onset of her headaches.

When Ms. Thomas began learning progressive relaxation, she discovered that her tension had been increasing over the course of each day. She placed reminders to relax in the typing paper drawer and on the corner of the desk. In addition, she brought a travel alarm clock to work and set it under a pillow to ring quietly each hour. This helped her to remember to check her tension level and practice progressive relaxation. She also began to use her morning and afternoon coffee breaks as additional opportunities for practice.

Over the course of several weeks, Ms. Thomas's headaches decreased in frequency and intensity. As with many of our patients who discover the joy of managing stress, she had more energy for her personal life.

About a month later, she felt cured of her headaches and began skipping her relaxation at work. Her headaches returned. As one would expect, she experienced relief when she once again began to practice regularly.

Creative Cuing

Be creative with relaxation cues and use spare time to practice progressive relaxation. There are many times during the day when most of us have a few seconds to practice. Practice while waiting for an elevator, sitting in an office, holding the telephone, or stopping at a red light. These situations should become cues to scan the body for tension. If you find unnecessary tension, use the time to relax and let go.

You may occasionally need to tense and release certain muscles that are difficult to keep relaxed. Briefly tensing all of the muscles at once and then letting all of them go is helpful. Additional tensing and releasing may be especially helpful when first beginning stress management training.

Daily practice will help you become aware of which muscles are most troublesome. You may want to tense and release these muscles several times throughout the day. After practicing progressive relaxation several times, relaxing even the most difficult muscles should become easy by merely taking a deep breath and silently saying, 'Relax and let go' as the breath slips out. This routine should become automatic.

When you stop for a red light, scan your body for tension, take a deep breath, and say, 'Relax and let go.' Do the same when the phone rings or when any other frequent event occurs. In this way, you can teach yourself to relax your body automatically and quickly.

BEGINNING PROGRESSIVE RELAXATION PRACTICE

Scheduling Formal Relaxation Practice

We recommend practicing progressive relaxation at the same time twice each day for twenty to thirty minutes. Practice may be scheduled in the mornings and afternoons. Try to wait at least an hour after eating to practice relaxation or you may tend to fall asleep. During the work week, use the morning coffee break or lunch hour, and then practice in the afternoon before or after going home. Some individuals prefer to practice after returning home from work and then later in the evening.

Relaxation practice is especially important at work if your job is even mildly stressful. Practicing at least twice a day at work may be necessary if you do not have a quiet place at home. If work is noisy, arrange quiet times at home.

If your home and work settings are not appropriate, find a quiet park, recreational center, or library. But be aware that the harder it is to get to your place of practice, the more difficult it is to maintain regular practice.

Scheduling Brief Relaxation Practice

Many people feel good in the morning but become more and more tense as the day wears on. They may finish work only to find themselves unable to enjoy their leisure time because of headaches, heartburn, fatigue, or other discomfort. The minor but constant problems encountered during the day generate tension and anxiety. This stress may grow as they wonder if there will be more problems and how long they can cope. The stress spirals upward.

Brief relaxation practice throughout the day can help break the dangerous stress spiral. These practice periods may last less than five minutes, but they can bring great benefit by helping you keep tension below critical levels. If you are unable to schedule formal relaxation practice in your working day, at least take brief breaks to relax.

Alternate Schedules for Learning Relaxation

We have found that to learn stress management thoroughly, a person needs to practice relaxation daily. We recommend that you practice twice daily and work with one technique until you have mastered it. This usually takes at least a week. We recognize that some people will be able to schedule only one formal relaxation session per day. If this is the only way you can schedule your relaxation session, be sure to take brief breaks throughout the rest of your day.

An alternative approach to learning stress management involves an initial overview. Some people may prefer to go through each relaxation exercise one time before returning for extensive practice of each technique. When we are training groups of people, we sometimes introduce all the different types of relaxation first and then begin individual practice of each technique.

If you like to read a book rapidly from cover to cover, then by all means do so with this book. You may want to read each chapter, practice each new relaxation exercise once, and then continue reading. When you have finished the book, you can come back to this chapter and begin exercising so that progressive relaxation becomes a part of your life.

Remember your first experience with the alphabet. You may have repeated each letter after someone, one letter after another, but you really learned it by practicing over and over saying 'A, B, C, . . .' until you could also say '. . . X, Y, Z.' This may sound dull, but it does not have to be. Remember the colorful pictures in your alphabet book? Some people use colorful anatomy books or images to increase their understanding of which muscles they are learning to relax. Others find friends to practice with. Learning the alphabet was the first step to reading your favorite books. Progressive relaxation is just the beginning of finding satisfaction through stress management.

Hospital and Other Programs

If you are learning stress management training through a hospital, clinic, or health resort program, you may practice as often as the program recommends to ensure that you gain maximum benefits in the shortest possible time. After you have completed the formal program, you may want to go back to each of the recommended steps of stress management training. In this way, you can increase your ability to apply all of the skills to your daily life.

Keeping Good Progress Records

Each time you practice, record the technique you used and how long you practiced on the Home Practice Chart on the last pages of this book. In addition, before and after each practice session, record your overall pre- and postpractice ratings. A score of 100 means total tension and a score of 0 means complete relaxation. If you have a frequent symptom such as headaches, you want to put marks for each occurrence next to the appropriate day. In a few weeks, you can count the marks and see your progress.

Preparing for Progressive Relaxation Practice

For the most successful beginning, it is best to find a place where all outside noise is reduced to the lowest possible level. Practice the exercises in a quiet room and keep the lights dim. Tell others what you are about to do or put a 'Do not disturb' sign on your door. Take the phone off the receiver. The room temperature should be comfortable. If needed, have a blanket available to cover yourself. The exercises may be practiced while reclining on a sofa, lying on a bed, or sitting in a comfortable chair. We recommend using a lounge chair that reclines.

Lying on one side or with the chest down may strain parts of your body. This is not to say that it is impossible to benefit from relaxation in this or other positions, but it is easier to learn the exercises the first time while reclining on your back. Later, it will be beneficial to practice while sitting up and standing.

Clothing should always be comfortable and loose when practicing relaxation. Belts can be loosened in preparation for the exercises. It is often best to remove ties, jewelry, shoes, and eyeglasses or contact lenses.

Problem Solving: Cramps and Falling Asleep

If the room is very cold and your muscles are tired, do not tense the muscles too tightly or they may develop mild cramps. If a cramp occurs, knead the muscle and stretch it out. The most frequent cramp occurs in the calf muscle. If this occurs, pulling the toes toward your face and kneading the calf muscle will usually relieve the cramp. Using a room with a comfortable temperature and being sure that your muscles are not tired should eliminate cramping.

Never overstrain a muscle when you tense it. Tighten your muscles, but not to the point of quivering. If you have had any physical problems that may be affected by tensing various muscle groups, seek your physician's advice before practicing.

Some individuals have difficulty staying awake and will need to practice in a sitting position. It may be necessary to rest your elbow on the arm of the chair or surface of the bed while holding your hand up. In this position, if you start to fall asleep the hand should drop to the side and wake you up. Others have found it helpful to sit in a chair and hold an unbreakable object in one hand in such a way that the object will fall to the floor when released. When it falls, the sound arouses them.

Remember, the major advantage in learning relaxation comes from being able to relax when you are awake. If you wish to use the exercises to help you fall asleep at night, practice when you go to bed. Studies with insomniacs have shown that their sleep onset time can be decreased an average of about twenty minutes. If you use the exercise to go to sleep, be sure to continue your daily relaxation practice. There is no substitute for regular day-time practice.

One of our patients who suffered from insomnia described his use of progressive relaxation in the following way. He was tensing and releasing each muscle group and adding the words, 'legs relax and sleep, feet relax and sleep, toes relax and sleep.' At this point in his practice, his wife came into the bedroom dressed in a sexy nightgown. The patient smiled and said, 'OK, everybody up!' The joy of stress management is knowing you can raise or lower your stress response, depending on whether you are facing distress or healthy stress. Drugs and external chemicals can't make this important distinction for you.

HOW TO DO PROGRESSIVE RELAXATION

Using Relaxation Tapes

If you are using recorded relaxation exercises, schedule times now and begin listening to the tape of progressive relaxation. Review the relaxation tapes suggested in Appendix III to help select an appropriate practice tape. Remember to list for each practice session your overall relaxation levels on the Home Practice Chart at the end of this book.

Guiding Yourself

If you will be guiding yourself through the relaxation exercises, review the directions below. You may find it helpful to read the directions several times. You may also want to ask someone to read the relaxation instructions slowly to you. If possible, you may want to record these instructions on a tape and then use the tape to practice.

Helpful Hints to Tape and Self-Instruction Users

Begin learning relaxation by lying on a bed or reclining in a comfortable lounge chair. Although you may begin practice by lying down, in time you will want to be able to do these exercises while sitting and even while walking. Practice in a quiet environment and loosen any tight clothing. Be certain that the temperature is pleasant and not distracting. Remember, if you find you have a tendency to fall asleep, rest your elbow on the arm of the chair or next to you on the bed, and balance your hand in the air directly over your elbow. If you start to fall asleep, your arm will drop, and this should arouse you.

The following written exercises recommend a particular sequence of relaxing your body. The sequence begins with your head and ends with your feet. We have found that most people prefer to relax their facial and head areas first. After relaxing the rest of the body, it may be annoying to tense and relax facial muscles. Some individuals, however, prefer to start with their hands or feet and finish with their head. If you find this to be your preference, modify the sequence or return to the head area after completing the progression through the rest of the body.

Some people find certain muscles more difficult to relax than others. For example, relaxing the neck or shoulders frequently requires extra practice. Return to difficult muscle groups and repeat the tension-relaxation contrast for these muscles after progressing through all the other exercises.

We recommend that you read the next chapter the same week you practice progressive relaxation. In it, you will learn how to become deeply relaxed by scanning your body for tension and breathing deeply for relaxation. The time it takes for you to become deeply relaxed will grow briefer as you refine your relaxation skills. Eventually, relaxation will become as automatic as breathing.

OUTLINE FOR PROGRESSIVE RELAXATION

I. BASIC TECHNIQUE
  A. Separately tense your individual muscle groups.
  B. Hold the tension about five seconds.
  C. Release the tension slowly and at the same time, silently say, 'Relax and let go.'
  D. Take a deep breath.
  E. As you breathe slowly out, silently say, 'Relax and let go.'

II. MUSCLE GROUPS AND EXERCISES
  A. Head
    1. Wrinkle your forehead.
    2. Squint your eyes tightly.
    3. Open your mouth wide.
    4. Push your tongue against the roof of your mouth.
    5. Clench your jaw tightly.
  B. Neck
    1. Push your head back into the pillow.
    2. Bring your head forward to touch your chest.

3. Roll your head to your right shoulder.
4. Roll your head to your left shoulder.
C. Shoulders
1. Shrug your shoulders up as if to touch your ears.
2. Shrug your right shoulder up as if to touch your ear.
3. Shrug your left shoulder up as if to touch your ear.
D. Arms and hands.
1. Hold your arms out and make a fist with each hand.
2. One side at a time: Push your hand down into the surface where you are practicing.
3. One side at a time: Make a fist, bend your arm at the elbow, tighten up your arm while holding the fist.
E. Chest and lungs
1. Take a deep breath.
2. Tighten your chest muscles.
F. Arch your back.
G. Stomach
1. Tighten your stomach area.
2. Push your stomach area out.
3. Pull your stomach area in.
H. Hips, legs, and feet
1. Tighten your hips.
2. Push the heels of your feet into the surface where you are practicing.
3. Tighten your leg muscles below the knee.
4. Curl your toes under as if to touch the bottom of your feet.
5. Bring your toes up as if to touch your knees.

WORD-BY-WORD PROGRESSIVE RELAXATION

Preparation

Spend a little time getting as comfortable as you can. While you are finding a good position, you will also want to loosen any tight clothing. Loosen your belt or tie if they are not already loose. If your shoes feel tight, you may wish to take them off. Your legs and arms should be slightly apart.

Slowly open your mouth and move your jaw gently from side to side . . . Now let your mouth close, keeping your teeth slightly apart. As you do, take a deep breath . . . and slowly let the air slip out.

While you tighten one part of your body, try to leave every other part limp and loose. Keep the tensed part of your body tight for a few seconds and then relax and let it go. Then take a deep breath, hold it, and as you breathe out, silently say, 'Relax and let go.' In time, this will be a technique you can use to produce rapid relaxation. Now begin your relaxation practice.

Total Body Tension

First, take a deep breath and tense every muscle in your body. Tense the muscles of your jaws, eyes, arms, hands, chest, back, stomach, legs, and feet. Feel the tension all over your body . . . Hold the tension briefly and then silently say, 'Relax and let go' as you breathe out . . . Let your whole body relax . . . Feel a wave of calm come over you as you stop tensing. Feel the relief.

Gently close your eyes and take another deep breath . . . Study the tension as you hold your breath . . . Slowly breathe out and silently say, 'Relax and let go.' Feel the deepening relaxation. Allow yourself to drift more and more with this relaxation . . . As you continue, you will exercise different parts of your body. Become aware of your body and its tension and relaxation. This will help you to become deeply relaxed on command.

Head and Face

Keeping the rest of your body relaxed, wrinkle up your forehead. Do you feel the tension? Your forehead is very tight. Briefly pause and be aware of it . . . Now, relax and let go. Feel the tension slipping out. Smooth out your forehead and take a deep breath. Hold it. (Briefly pause.) As you breathe out, silently say, 'Relax and let go.'

Squint your eyes tightly as if you are in a dust storm. Keep the rest of your body relaxed. Briefly pause and feel the tension around your eyes . . . Now, relax and let go. Take a deep breath and hold it. (Briefly pause.) Silently say, 'Relax and let go' as you breathe out.

Open your mouth as wide as you can. Feel the tension in your jaw and chin. Briefly hold the tension . . . Now, let your mouth gently close. As you do, silently say, 'Relax and let go.' Take a deep breath. Hold it. (Briefly pause.) As you breathe out say, 'Relax and let go.'

Close your mouth. Push your tongue against the roof of your mouth. Study the tension in your mouth and chin. Briefly hold the tension . . . Relax and let go. Take a deep breath. Hold it. (Briefly pause.) Now, silently say, 'Relax and let go' as you breathe out. When you breathe out, let your tongue rest comfortably in your mouth, and let your lips be slightly apart.

Keep the rest of your body relaxed, but clench your jaw tightly. Feel the tension in your jaw muscles. Briefly hold the tension . . . Now relax and let go, and take a deep breath. Hold it. (Briefly pause.) Silently say, 'Relax and let go' as you breathe out.

Think about the top of your head, your forehead, eyes, jaws, and cheeks. Make sure these muscles are relaxed . . . Have you let go of all the tension? Continue to let the tension slip away and feel the relaxation replace the tension. Feel your face becoming very smooth and soft as all the tension slips away . . . Your eyes are relaxed . . . Your tongue is relaxed . . . Your jaws are loose and limp . . . All of your neck muscles are also very, very relaxed.

All of the muscles of your face and head are relaxing more and more . . . Your head feels as though it could roll from side to side, and your face feels soft and smooth. Allow your face to continue becoming more and more relaxed as you now move to other areas of your body.

Shoulders   Now shrug your shoulders up and try to touch

69

your ears with your shoulders. Feel the tension in the shoulders and neck. Hold the tension . . . Now, relax and let go. As you do, feel your shoulders joining the relaxed parts of your body. Take a deep breath. Hold it. (Briefly pause.) Silently say, 'Relax and let go' as you slowly breathe out.

Notice the difference, how the tension is giving way to relaxation. Shrug your right shoulder up and try to touch your right ear. Feel the tension in your right shoulder and along the right side of your neck. Hold the tension . . . Now, relax and let go. Take a deep breath. Hold it. (Briefly pause.) Silently say, 'Relax and let go' as you slowly breathe out.

Next, shrug your left shoulder up and try to touch your left ear. Feel the tension in your left shoulder and along the left side of your neck. Hold the tension . . . Now, relax and let go. Take a deep breath. Hold it. (Briefly pause.) Silently say, 'Relax and let go' as you slowly breathe out. Feel the relaxation seeping into the shoulders. As you continue, you will become loose, limp, and relaxed as an old rag doll.

Arms and Hands

Stretch your arms out and make a fist with your hands. Feel the tension in your hands and forearms. Hold the tension . . . Now, relax and let go. Take a deep breath. Hold it. (Briefly pause.) Silently say, 'Relax and let go' as you slowly breathe out.

Push your right hand down into the surface it is resting on. Feel the tension in your arm and shoulder. Hold the tension . . . Now, relax and let go. Take a deep breath. Hold it. (Briefly pause.) Silently say, 'Relax and let go' as you slowly breathe out.

Next, push your left hand down into whatever it is resting on. Feel the tension in your arm and shoulder. Hold the tension . . . Now, relax and let go. Take a deep breath. Hold it. (Briefly pause.) Silently say, 'Relax and let go' as you slowly breathe out.

Bend your arms toward your shoulders and double them up as you might to show off your muscles. Feel the tension. Hold the tension . . . Now, relax and let go. Take a deep breath. Hold it. (Briefly pause.) Silently say, 'Relax and let go' as you slowly breathe out.

Chest and Lungs

Move on to the relaxation of your chest. Begin by taking a deep breath that totally fills your lungs. As you hold your breath, notice the tension. Be aware of the tension around your ribs . . . Silently say, 'Relax and let go' as you slowly breathe out. Feel the deepening relaxation as you continue breathing easily, freely, and gently. (Briefly pause).

Take in another deep breath. Hold it and again feel the contrast between tension and relaxation. As you do, tighten your chest muscles. Hold the tension . . . Silently say, 'Relax and let go' as you slowly breathe out. Feel the relief as you breathe out and continue to breathe gently, naturally, and rhythmically. Breathe as smoothly as you can. You will become more and more relaxed with every breath.

Back

Keeping your face, neck, arms, and chest as relaxed as possible, arch your back up (or forward if you are sitting). Arch it as if you had a pillow under the middle and low part of your back. Observe the tension along both sides of your back. Briefly hold that position . . . Now, relax and let go. Take a deep breath. Hold it. (Briefly pause.) Silently say, 'Relax and let go' as you breathe out. Let that relaxation spread deep into your shoulders and down into your back muscles.

Feel the slow relaxation developing and spreading all over. Feel it going deeper and deeper. Allow your entire body to relax. Face and

71

head relaxed . . . Neck relaxed . . . Shoulders relaxed . . . Arms relaxed . . . Chest relaxed . . . Back relaxed . . . All these areas are relaxing more and more, becoming more deeply relaxed than you thought possible.

Stomach

Now, begin the relaxation of the stomach area. Tighten up this area. Briefly hold the tension . . . Relax and let go. Feel the relaxation pour into your stomach area. All the tension is being replaced with relaxation, and you feel the general well-being that comes with relaxation. Take a deep breath. Hold it. (Briefly pause.) Silently say, 'Relax and let go' as you slowly breathe out.

Now, experience a different type of tension in the stomach area. Push your stomach out as far as you can. Briefly hold the tension . . . Now, relax and let go. Take a deep breath. Hold it. (Briefly pause.) Silently say, 'Relax and let go' as you slowly breathe out.

Now, pull your stomach in. Try to pull your stomach in and touch your backbone. Hold it . . . Now, relax and let go. Take a deep breath. Hold it. (Briefly pause.) Silently say, 'Relax and let go' as you breathe out.

You are becoming more and more relaxed. Each time you breathe out, feel the gentle relaxation in your lungs and in your body. As you continue to do these exercises, your chest and stomach area will relax more and more. Check the muscles of your face, neck, shoulders, arms, chest, and stomach. Make sure they are still relaxed. If they are not, then tense and release them again. Whatever part is still less than fully relaxed is starting to relax more and more. Soon you will be able to tell when you have tension in any part of your body. You will learn that you can always relax and let go of the tension you may find in any part of your body.

72

| Hips, Legs, and Feet | *Now, begin the relaxation of your hips and legs. Tighten your hips and legs by pressing down the heels of your feet into the surface they are resting on. Tighten these muscles. Keep the rest of your body as relaxed as you can and press your heels down . . . Now, hold the tension . . . Relax and let go. Feel your legs float up. Take a deep breath. Hold it. (Briefly pause.) Silently say, 'Relax and let go' as you breathe out. Feel the relaxation pouring in. Notice the difference between tension and relaxation. Let the relaxation become deeper and deeper. Enjoy the relaxation.* |

Next, tighten your lower leg muscles. Feel the tension. Briefly hold the tension . . . Now, relax and let go. Take a deep breath. Hold it. (Briefly pause.) Silently say, 'Relax and let go' as you breathe out.

Now, curl your toes downward. Curl them down and try to touch the bottom of your feet with your toes. Hold them and feel the tension . . . Relax and let go. Wiggle your toes gently as you let go of the tension. Let the tension be replaced with relaxation. Take a deep breath. Hold it. (Briefly pause.) Silently say, 'Relax and let go' as you slowly breathe out.

Now, bend your toes back the other way. Bend your toes right up toward your knees. Feel the tension. Try to touch your knees with your toes. Feel the tension. Hold the tension . . . Relax and let go. Feel all the tension slip right out. Take a deep breath. Hold it. (Briefly pause.) Silently say, 'Relax and let go' as you slowly breathe out. Feel the tension leaving your body and the relaxation seeping in.

| Body Review | *You have progressed through all the major muscles of your body. Now, let them become more and more relaxed. Continue to feel yourself becoming more and more relaxed each time you breathe out. Each time you breathe out, think about a muscle* |

*and silently say, 'Relax and let go' ... Face
relax ... Shoulders relax ... Arms relax ...
Hands relax ... Chest relax ... Back relax ...
Stomach relax ... Hips relax ... Legs relax ...
Feet relax ... Your whole body is becoming more
and more relaxed with each breath.*

*Spend a few more minutes relaxing, if you
would like. If, during your day, you find yourself
getting upset about something, remember the
relaxation you have just experienced. Before you
get upset, take a deep breath, hold it, and as you
breathe out, silently say, 'Relax and let go.' With
practice, you will be able to use this technique to
relax whenever you begin to feel the stress of
everyday living.*

PROGRESSIVE RELAXATION SUMMARY

We recommend that you practice your progressive relaxation every
day, twice a day if possible. Be sure to mark your practice on the
Home Practice Chart at the end of this book. We usually recommend
that a person continue to practice progressive relaxation exercises
twice daily for at least a week.

If you are under the guidance of a psychologist or other professional,
follow his or her instructions. If you are overviewing the book first,
practice progressive relaxation once and continue reading the book.

After a few sessions, you will be able to relax unneeded muscles differentially while you perform tasks with needed muscles. For example,
you do not need a tight jaw or clenched fist while writing a memo at
your desk. Be sure to use progressive relaxation whenever you see the
cues that you have set up in your home or office to help you relax.

If you drive to work, you may want to use stopping at a red light as
a cue to scan your body mentally. Whatever your cues, ask yourself
different questions: Is my forehead wrinkled? Are my jaw muscles
tight? Is my stomach knotted up? Then let your breathing become
smooth and rhythmic. Allow the relaxation to replace tension, and a
wave of calm comes over your body. Try to be creative and find more
places where you can practice your new skills.

6 Scanning for Tension and Breathing for Relaxation

The last chapter showed you how to recognize and reduce muscle tension. The instructions for progressive relaxation also taught you how to scan your body for muscle tension, but only in very general terms. Scanning is a very helpful technique. It is worthy of thorough study and daily use. You may want to continue practicing progressive relaxation twice each day as you learn more about scanning.

What is Scanning?

Scanning means to examine or pass over quickly. Most people think of scanning as rapidly looking something over with their eyes. Body scanning uses your inner awareness, rather than your eyes, to examine your body. This kind of scanning involves directing your attention quickly and easily to various parts of your body.

Body scanning is very much like looking in a mirror; but the mirror is the awareness in your mind. You can use this inner awareness to check whether you have collected any unhealthy muscle tension.

Scanning is a skill that you may want to use every day for the rest of your life. Yes, every day for the rest of your life! Fortunately, with time and practice, scanning can easily become a habit as automatic as looking in the mirror. Many of our most successful patients have found scanning a favorite technique. It is quick and can be done everywhere. You need not sit or recline. You can even learn to scan as you are walking through the office or your home.

Your Body's 'Mirror'

We look in the mirror to see if our hair is just right, our makeup needs refreshing, or our tie needs straightening. If everything on the outside looks all right in the mirror, we are usually satisfied; but a mirror cannot tell us if everything on the inside is also all right.

A mirror is a common convenience for checking our appearance. It is also a helpful cue that reminds us to straighten our tie or fix our hair. Unfortunately, there are few such reminders readily available for scanning our muscles, so we have to be creative and come up with some of our own. We suggested several ideas in Chapter 5. Remember the pieces of colored tape that could be placed on your watch and signs that could be arranged in different places?

Situations arise that allow us enough time to scan and look at our body's tension. They can also act as cues. They include driving slowly through a school zone, stopping at a red light, waiting for an elevator, being put 'on hold' when on the telephone, and standing in line. As you can tell, most of these situations involve waiting. Most of us have many short periods daily of such free time. The cues associated with such situations as the elevator or the red light can help us remember to look into our body's 'mirror.'

An ulcer patient who was a sergeant in the service found scanning to be an answer to the army's 'hurry up and wait.' We may chuckle at the army, but think of all the time you have while you wait for people who are late and meetings that do not start on time. Think of the hours you spend each month in your car waiting for your children or in the waiting rooms of doctors or lawyers. Previously trying situations can become opportunities to enjoy calm relaxation.

Cues for Using Your Body's 'Mirror'

Start a list of the cues you have already begun to use and cues you will want to try out during the next few days.

Think about the things you do and see every day that could be effective cues for scanning. The mirror we have been using to describe scanning can also be a cue to look inside. You may wish to put a 'scan' sign on a few of your mirrors.

Commercials on television can become a cue. If you teach school, the buzzer or bell can become one. Let answering the telephone become a cue. With enough practice, you will be able to check your tension and relax during the first two or three rings before you answer the phone. When you hang up you can scan your body again.

Any change in what you are doing can be used as a cue to change your level of tension. Secretaries can scan for muscle tension while the copying machine scans the originals to make copies. Sales clerks can use the cash register as a cue to relax unnecessary tension. Many physicians whom we have trained use the beepers they wear as cues to scan. Bathroom breaks and meals can also be times to make certain we are not uptight.

Scanning and Everyday Living

The more cues you find and use, the more unhealthy tension you will scan away. The object is to use scanning to remain relaxed throughout the day. Try to become aware of small amounts of tension before they build up. Rather than one moment of tension leading to another, many situations can be used to scan for tension and breathe for relaxation.

How to Do Scanning Relaxation

When we look in a mirror, we check our appearance, but we probably look at several aspects of our reflection. We may pay attention to clothes, hair, and other parts of our bodies. The same is true of scanning. As you will see in the exercise that follows, when you scan, you will imagine various parts of your body and check to see if they are tense. Some people imagine a picture of their body, others imagine the muscles as they would be drawn in an anatomy book, and still others imagine parts of a stick figure. One individual found it easier to imagine an x-ray machine scanning her muscles.

Most people scan their bodies by becoming aware of and directing attention to each part of the body that might be tense. At first, it may seem like a long journey through all the muscle groups. With practice, the scan can be made very rapidly. Eventually, when you take one breath, you may be able to scan all the muscles from head to toe and 'relax and let go' as you breathe out.

Just as most people take special note of certain parts of their appearance when they look in a mirror, a good scanner will learn to do the same in his body's 'mirror.' Most people have areas that are tense more often than other areas. Many carry tension in their shoulders, others put it into their wrinkled brow. Still others clench their teeth. Most people begin by identifying these areas. As time goes on, they know where they will find tension before they even start to scan their body.

An Executive Scan

A hard-driving executive who attended one of our groups on stress management found that he always clenched his jaw when driving. He reported that this was almost a habit. He did it whether he was in a hurry getting to work or driving leisurely while on a vacation. Long trips left him exhausted.

After learning how to scan, he began using red lights and stop signs to and from work as short scanning breaks. When driving long distances on the freeway, he used the reactions of other drivers. He also had a sign on his speedometer to remind him to scan his body whenever he looked to see how fast he was going. During the first week, he found that his jaw muscles were less tense and that he could relax quickly.

The executive also began to listen to books on tape in the car. These are recorded novels available from Books on Tape, P.O. 7900, Newport Beach, CA 92660. With continued scanning practice and 'reading' while he drove, the executive reported that he enjoyed driving and looked forward to it as a time to relax.

At a follow-up session six months after completing our group training, he continued to report ease in driving as a result of frequent body scanning. He was surprised how little effort it took to remain relaxed and to enjoy driving.

Experiment and see what works best for you in a variety of settings. When you first start your scanning practice, try not to overlook any opportunities to practice on any area of tension in your body. After frequent practice, looking into your body's mirror can become as effortless as glancing in a mirror to check your appearance. Knowing how relaxed you are can be as comforting and pleasing as knowing your nose is powdered or your tie is straight.

Using Relaxation Tapes

Once progressive relaxation has been learned, scanning is one of the easiest techniques to master without a tape. For this reason, many of the prerecorded tape series do not include a specific scanning tape. But you may wish to use an excellent tape by C. H. Hartmann entitled *Mixed Scanning Relaxation Program*. The first side presents progressive relaxation and stretching exercises, followed by a basic scanning technique.

The Hartmann tape and other taped scanning programs with which we are familiar do not emphasize breathing as we do. We have found that if breathing is paired with scanning, relaxation can become as automatic as breathing. Since we breathe all the time, breathing can become an unbeatable cue for relaxation.

Guiding Yourself

If you will be guiding yourself through the exercises, review the directions below. At first, it may be helpful to have someone read the instructions slowly to you. If possible, you may want to record these instructions on a tape and then use the tape for practice.

Helpful Hints to Tape and Self-Instruction Users

Begin slowly at first. Many people think scanning is an easy technique and gloss over it. This is one of the reasons we decided to spend a full chapter on scanning to help you to understand it.

Another common problem is making the change from progressive relaxation to scanning relaxation. In progressive relaxation you are physically active. Scanning involves steady breathing but uses more of the power of your mind. At first, it may be helpful to touch the parts of your body you are scanning or to look at them as you imagine and explore them in your mind's 'eye.'

You may want to continue your progressive relaxation training. Progressive relaxation can help you get tuned in to where your muscles are and what they feel like. Start practicing with the Word-by-Word Detailed Scanning Relaxation. Find a quiet place, take your time, and enjoy the sensations. You may wish to use scanning relaxation after practicing progressive relaxation to check if all of your muscles responded to the tension-relaxation exercises.

For a couple of days, you may want to use scanning relaxation with the longer detailed instructions. Then you may begin alternating between the brief and long forms of instructions. If things are going well, start using the brief scanning relaxation everywhere you can, whenever you have a free moment.

OUTLINE FOR SCANNING RELAXATION

I. BASIC TECHNIQUE

    A. Breathe in while scanning one area of your body for tension.

    B. As you breathe out, relax that area.

    C. Progress through each area of your body.

II. MUSCLE GROUPS

    A. Face and neck.

    B. Shoulders and arms.

    C. Chest and lungs.

    D. Stomach area.

    E. Hips, legs, and feet.

III. WHEN TO USE SCANNING RELAXATION

    A. Starting or completing a stressful task to help you relax and prepare or relax and unwind.

    B. Standing in line, stopping at a red light, waiting for an elevator, or during any free time.

WORD-BY-WORD DETAILED SCANNING RELAXATION

Preparation

I want you to scan all the parts of your body as I call them out. This is called 'body scanning.' Think about a muscle area and, as you breathe out, feel the tension slipping away. Move progressively through your body. Remember, as you breathe in, scan the muscles for any tension, and, as you breathe out, feel the tension slip away. Let's begin.

Face and
Neck

As you breathe in, scan your face and neck . . . As you breathe out, feel the tension slip away. Face and neck relax. Once again, as you breathe in, attend to your forehead, eyes, jaw, and neck . . . As you breathe out, your relaxation is becoming deeper and deeper.

Shoulders and Arms	*As you breathe in, scan your shoulders and arms . . . As you breathe out, feel the tension slip away. Arms and shoulders relax. Once again, as you breathe in, attend to your shoulders, arms, and hands . . . As you breathe out, your relaxation is becoming deeper and deeper.*
Chest and Lungs	*As you breathe in, scan your chest and lungs . . . As you breathe out, feel the tension slip away. Chest and lungs relax. Once again, as you breathe in, attend to your chest and lungs . . . As you breathe out, your relaxation is becoming deeper and deeper.*
Stomach Area	*As you breathe in, scan your stomach area . . . As you breathe out, feel the tension slip away. Stomach area relax. Once again, as you breathe in, attend to your stomach area . . . As you breathe out, your relaxation is becoming deeper and deeper.*
Hips, legs and Feet	*As you breathe in, scan your hips, legs and feet . . . As you breathe out, feel the tension slip away. Hips, legs and feet relax. Once again, as you breathe in, scan your hips, legs, and feet . . . As you breathe out, your relaxation is becoming deeper and deeper. Now allow your breathing to become smooth and rhythmic.*
Return to Activity	*Let your body continue to relax as you return to your daily activities. Continue to feel calm and at ease . . . If at any time during the day, you begin to feel tense or uptight, scan your body to find the tension and then relax and let go with each breath.*

BRIEF SCANNING RELAXATION

Practice this brief scanning exercise while you are waiting for an elevator or a red light or standing in a line. In the time it takes to breathe in and out three times, you can become aware of any tension and release it.

1. As you breathe in, scan your face, neck, shoulders, and arms.
2. As you breathe out, feel any tension slip away.
3. As you breathe in, scan your chest, lungs, and stomach.
4. As you breathe out, feel any tension slip away.
5. As you breathe in, scan your hips, legs, and feet.
6. As you breathe out, feel any tension slip away.

7 Reaching Deeper Levels of Relaxation

Deep muscle relaxation is a form of progressive relaxation. It makes use of your new skills but does not include the tensing part of the progressive relaxation exercises. Deep muscle relaxation directs suggestions of relaxation to each muscle group in turn. The step-by-step nature of these exercises is similar to progressive relaxation, but now you learn to rely on mental awareness, deep breathing, and calming words or phrases.

Some individuals have learned deep muscle relaxation without first practicing progressive relaxation. The main reason we recommend the tension-relaxation exercises first is that deep muscle relaxation uses only the power of your mind to relax your muscles. This can be more difficult than using a physical exercise to achieve relaxation.

A successful young lawyer, whom we will call John, joined a stop-smoking group conducted by one of the authors. He had tried deep muscle relaxation before but always felt silly trying to tell his body to relax. He had no real idea of what to expect or where to expect it. When the use of relaxation came up in the stop-smoking group, John was disappointed, and he told the group about his previous experiences.

None of his earlier attempts at relaxation had involved the progressive relaxation technique discussed in Chapter 5. John had experienced only frustration in his attempts at deep muscle relaxation, primarily because he started with an advanced relaxation procedure without first learning the basics. He was a little skeptical, but he gave deep muscle relaxation another chance after he learned progressive relaxation. To his surprise, it became a favorite technique for coping with stress after he permanently gave up smoking.

What You Have Achieved

Progressive relaxation instructions helped you to tense and release each of the muscle groups in your body systematically. When you focused on a specific area, such as your forearm, you tensed the muscle tightly and then released it slowly, as you said, 'Relax and let go.' This exercise achieved two goals.

First, by tensing the forearm muscle, you became aware of the location of the muscle and how it felt when it was tense. Learning this helped you to recognize when your muscles were tense, which muscles were tense, and how tense your muscles were. Some people teach themselves early in life to ignore tension and keep striving. They have trouble knowing when they are and are not tense. Progressive relaxation helps reverse this early learning.

The second goal of tension-relaxation exercises was gradually to increase the depth of your relaxation until the word 'relaxation' came to have a clear and very real meaning. Focusing on a muscle and suggesting relaxation may be very frustrating and almost worthless until you know what relaxation feels like. First tensing and then relaxing a muscle builds up momentum so that the muscle relaxation becomes deeper with each release. It is as if tension is gradually being used up. Consequently, through the release of tension, a very deep level of relaxation is reached, and a clear memory trace is laid down in your mind.

With practice, you eventually reach the point at which you can use this memory to focus on a muscle, think about the feelings of releasing tension, and produce deep relaxation. This use of memory is why deep muscle relaxation is also referred to as 'recall relaxation.'

Looking Forward

You can look forward later in your training to relaxing by simply taking a deep breath and silently saying, 'Relax and let go' as you slowly breathe out. At that time, tensing a muscle may be necessary only for muscles that are particularly difficult to relax or for the few situations in which tension becomes extreme. Of course, all of this comes with a great deal of practice. After having practiced progressive relaxation every day, you should be able to bring about some of these feelings of relaxation without first having to tense your muscles.

You may feel that you have not practiced progressive relaxation enough to learn where your tension builds up and what relaxation feels like. If so, you may want to finish reading this chapter but practice more progressive relaxation before trying deep muscle relaxation. Remember that John, the lawyer, found deep muscle relaxation frustrating before he had learned progressive relaxation.

Resist the temptation to rush through this book. You may want to preview future chapters, but you should learn to practice relaxation the way you learned to read. You had to know the alphabet before you could learn to read words, sentences, and paragraphs. You learned to count before you learned to add, subtract, multiply, or divide. You learned to crawl before you walked, walk before you ran, and run before you were able to play sports. The basics of relaxation must also be practiced and learned before advancing to other techniques.

Cultivating Deep Muscle Relaxation

Turn your attention for a moment from this book to your body. Are you comfortable? Is your body supported and resting? Are your back muscles tight? Are your jaw muscles tight? Is there any muscle tension in your stomach area? What about your arms and hands? How are you holding this book?

You just observed how your body was supported, the amount of tension in your body, and the way you were holding this book. Did you move around to become more comfortable, slacken your jaw muscles, or loosen your grip? If you did, you were using mental awareness similar to what we will teach you to use for deep muscle relaxation.

Have you ever noticed your jaw becoming clenched while you were driving in heavy traffic? Do you grip the steering wheel too tightly? Imagine you are in a heated discussion at work, or you are telling children to stop doing something. Do your legs and stomach become tense as you assume a defensive posture?

In all these situations and even while reading this book, it may not be possible or practical to tense and relax your muscles. Of course, you would not want to tense and relax your muscles if it would interfere with an activity or if it would be embarrassing. But you can learn to use deep muscle relaxation for the muscles you are not using without interfering with your activity or calling attention to yourself.

Beyond Releasing Muscle Tension

Becoming aware of tension and releasing it is helpful, but deep muscle relaxation does even more than this. Deep breathing exercises are practiced to be sure your breathing is calm and regular. In addition, deep muscle relaxation helps you to learn cues that quickly produce relaxation on command. After you are able to recall the feelings of relaxation and deepen them, you will add key words and phrases to help you remember and to reinstate these feelings whenever and wherever you want them.

Some people pick up a tennis racket and seem to be a 'natural.' Others need extra practice and discipline. The same is true with relaxation. Some individuals will be able to progress through the exercises quickly. Others will feel a need to continue tensing and releasing certain muscles that are troublesome. Your only competition is tension. Take your time and be patient. Remember, trying too hard and rushing can make you tense. Go at your own pace.

HOW TO DO DEEP MUSCLE RELAXATION

Scheduling and Recording Relaxation Practice

Deep muscle relaxation should be practiced during the same times you previously practiced progressive relaxation. Again, we recommend that you practice twice daily. During the work week, for example, you may wish to practice during the morning coffee break or lunch hour and then again in the afternoon after you arrive home.

Any time you find muscles that have not become completely relaxed after you have finished deep muscle relaxation, tense them and release them by using progressive relaxation. Occasionally, we recommend that a person work on progressive relaxation during one practice session and deep muscle relaxation during the other. This alternation is helpful if a person feels moderately confident about his or her results with progressive relaxation but has some difficulty relaxing certain muscle groups.

After the relaxation sessions, record your practice on the Home Practice Chart at the end of this book. Remember to record the technique used, how long you practiced, and an estimate of how relaxed you became during each session.

Preparing for Deep Muscle Relaxation

Once again, as with progressive relaxation, plan on practicing deep muscle relaxation in a place that is private, quiet, comfortable, and free from distractions. Be sure family, friends, and coworkers will not interrupt you.

At this stage of your training, it is best to practice while sitting rather than lying. Most people practice their relaxation while sitting in a large, comfortable, overstuffed chair. Ideally, this chair should have a high back to support your neck and head. If you practice at work, you may need to move your desk chair next to a wall to gain this support.

If you do not have a good chair to practice in at home, you can practice on a bed. It may be best to pile pillows at the head of the bed and sit up with your feet in front of you and your back, neck, and head supported by the pillows. Experiment if you like. Remember, the goal during practice is not to fall asleep. If you do, you are certainly relaxed, but unless it is bedtime and you are using the relaxation to promote sleep, your goal is to become very relaxed while remaining awake and alert.

Common Problems and Their Solutions

Mary, one of our relaxation patients, had a painful and chronic degenerative nerve disease. She had always been active, hardworking, and conscientious. She kept busy throughout her life and rarely had a spare minute. She liked life this way, and the only thing that was more active than her body was her mind. Mary always thought of new projects to do and always seemed to get a lot of them done. Her friends described her as vivacious and full of life. With the onset of her disease, she found that she had less and less physical energy. Her mind was still active, but it was now out of step with her physical capabilities.

Mary was able to gain moderate success in relieving some of her pain, sleeping better, and relaxing more during activities. But she found deep muscle relaxation very difficult. Her concentration on the relaxation exercises was constantly interrupted by intruding thoughts of wanting to do something active. When she did progressive relaxation, tensing and releasing the muscles kept her active enough to occupy her mind. Deep muscle relaxation did not offer the same advantage, but the following suggestions helped her to benefit fully from deep muscle relaxation.

87

Prescriptions for Intruding Thoughts

If you experience problems with intruding thoughts, you may want to try some of the following techniques. First, be gentle with yourself and do not get angry when you realize you have lost your concentration. Allow your thoughts to leave your mind as quickly as they came, and bring your attention back to the exercises or muscle group you were focusing on.

If your thoughts are persistent, you may want to command yourself very firmly to stop the distracting thoughts and return to the relaxation. At first, it may be necessary to say 'Stop!' out loud. With practice you can say it in a whisper, and finally you can say it silently to yourself. A similar approach is to repeat the silent 'Stop!' or 'No!' several times and then return to the relaxation exercises. These techniques are called 'thought stopping.' They can be used in many situations when you want to control unwanted thoughts.

It is also helpful to make the relaxation very brief. You might set an alarm (a kitchen timer works well) for five minutes to see if you can concentrate that long. If not, then set it for fewer minutes. When you succeed, gradually increase the time until you can do all of the exercises.

Another technique involves attempting to relax just a few groups of muscles without losing your concentration. Decide that you will first try to relax just the face and neck. Congratulate yourself on your success and then move to your arms and hands. In this fashion, go through the other muscles briefly. Try the chest and stomach, the hips and thighs, and then the calves and feet.

If you are unable to complete a small group of muscles, try again, but this time make the group even smaller. For example, relax only your forehead and eyes. When your concentration improves, you may go through larger muscle groups until you can progress throughout the body without stopping.

Assuming a Passive Attitude

An important principle related to concentration and relaxation is assuming a passive attitude. This is a very necessary part of deep muscle relaxation and of many other techniques you will learn in this book. Passive is the opposite of active. In this case, it means to be open to new experiences. An attitude is a mental disposition or way of emotionally approaching things. Assuming a passive attitude is a way of allowing things to happen by adopting a quiet and open mental orientation that will help you to become more receptive to the enjoyment of successful stress management.

Most of us have learned that we do not get anywhere without doing something. In deep muscle relaxation, the doing is the assuming of a receptive attitude. This means allowing things to happen rather than trying to make anything happen. It also means acknowledging unrelated thoughts that come into our minds and letting them slip away as soon as we can. Try to have a passive, receptive attitude whether you listen to taped relaxation or guide yourself through the relaxation techniques.

Meditation

Many people are exploring meditation as a form of stress management. Meditation is often associated with Eastern religions, but it can be practiced with or without a religious emphasis. Herbert Benson, M.D., a Harvard professor specializing in cardiovascular diseases and internal medicine, studied Transcendental Meditation scientifically and wrote about a meditative technique which he called the relaxation response. The relaxation response has been shown to be of significant value in the treatment of hypertension and other psychosomatic illnesses.

The basic elements of the relaxation response and of most meditation techniques include finding a quiet place which is free from distraction; assuming a passive attitude; getting into a comfortable position; and focusing attention on one sensory input such as a word, sound, thought, feeling, or symbol. The repetition of cue words in deep muscle relaxation training can be considered a form of meditation.

If you are interested in meditation, we encourage you to explore different forms such as yoga, Zen, or Transcendental Meditation. For this purpose, we have recommended several books, including Dr. Benson's *Relaxation Response*, in Appendix III. Some of the unique benefits of meditation, in addition to relaxation training, are the self-discipline of learning to concentrate on one thing at a time and the insights that can be gained into our inner world and outer reality. We emphasize cue-controlled forms of relaxation for stress management, however, because people may have trouble setting aside time for daily meditation for the rest of their lives. In addition, our goal is to help you manage stress effectively throughout your day wherever you are, rather than in special places or at special times. Zen, a Buddhist sect, envisions an ideal personality, which we feel is worth striving for, that is capable not only of quiet meditation but also of life-affirming action.

Using Relaxation Tapes or Guiding Yourself

If you are using recorded relaxation exercises or guiding yourself, schedule time now to rate your subjective degree of muscular tension and practice deep muscle relaxation. If you are using relaxation tapes, see the recommended recordings in Appendix III to help select the appropriate tape.

If you will be guiding yourself through the exercises, review the directions below. If possible, tape them or ask someone to read them to you. Before and after you have practiced, be sure to record your relaxation ratings on the Home Practice Charts in the back of the book. You may occasionally want to use the summary at the end of this chapter for quick review.

How to Find Time for Cue-Controlled Relaxation

Cue-controlled scanning and relaxation are very important techniques that you will want to use for the rest of your life. To find time for these 'six-second tranquilizers,' think of all the time you spend waiting. According to one study, the average American spends about forty minutes a day waiting. This adds up to more than two years over a lifetime! Make use of the time you spend waiting in lines, stopping for lights, and standing at the checkout counter. Use the time to recuperate from stress, lower your blood pressure, and enhance your feelings of well-being.

OUTLINE FOR DEEP MUSCLE RELAXATION

I. DEEP BREATHING

    A. Breathe deeply and slowly.

    B. Silently say, 'Relax and let go' each time you breathe out.

II. BODY SCANNING

A. Focus on relaxing each muscle.
B. Feel the tension slip out each time you breathe out.
C. Progress from your forehead and the top of your head to your feet and toes.

III. EXAMINE THE FEELINGS OF RELAXATION

IV. MASSAGING RELAXATION

A. Imagine a gently massaging relaxation flowing through your body.
B. Feel the massaging relaxation move slowly from forehead to toes.
C. Move to another muscle each time you breathe out.

V. CUE WORDS

A. Silently say, 'Peaceful and calm' while continuing to relax.
B. Silently say, 'I am at peace' while continuing to relax.

VI. RETURN TO ACTIVITY

A. Count forward from one to three.

WORD-BY-WORD DEEP MUSCLE RELAXATION

Preparation
Spend a little time getting as comfortable as you can. While you are finding a good position, loosen any tight clothing. Loosen your shirt or blouse at the neck. Loosen your belt. If your shoes feel a little tight, take them off. Allow your eyes to close.

Mentally, you should begin to clear your mind of the business and rushing that may characterize your life. Allow a passive attitude to develop. Try to let the relaxation begin.

Open your mouth for a moment and move your jaw slowly and easily from side to side . . . Now, let your mouth close, keeping your teeth slightly apart. As you do, take a deep breath . . . and slowly let the air slip out.

91

| Breathing | Take another deep breath ... As you breathe out, silently say, 'Relax and let go.' Feel yourself floating down. Now that you are comfortable, let yourself relax even further. The more you can let go, the better it will be. |

Take another deep breath ... As you breathe out, silently say, 'Relax and let go.' Feel yourself floating down. Now that you are comfortable, let yourself relax even further. The more you can let go, the better it will be.

Again, take a deep breath. (Briefly pause.) As you breathe out, silently say, 'Relax and let go.' Let the air slip out easily and automatically. Already you may be feeling a little calmer. Now, just carry on breathing normally.

Study your body and the feelings you are experiencing. (Briefly pause.) As you relax more and more, your breathing becomes slower. You may notice that it is slower now and that you breathe more and more from the bottom of your lungs.

It's too much trouble to move, just too much trouble to move. All tension is leaving you, and you are very comfortable. Notice that you have a feeling of well-being as though your troubles have been set aside and nothing seems to matter.

Body Scanning

Now, as we continue, let's use the natural abilities of your mind and body to experience feelings of deep, deep relaxation. We will do this by going through your body from head to foot and progressively instilling those good feelings of relaxation. Each time you breathe out, you should feel more relaxed.

Keep your eyes gently closed. Relax your jaw muscles. Keep your teeth slightly apart and your face, neck, and shoulders loose and relaxed.

As you think about each part of your body and you allow that part of your body to relax, you will feel all the tension flowing away, and that part of your body will be comfortable, calm, and peaceful. Each time you breathe out, you will become more relaxed and feel the relaxation spreading slowly through your body.

Head and Neck Scanning	*Now, think about the top of your head. Feel the area. As you breathe out, feel the top of your head relax more and more, as it becomes loose and free of wrinkles. Let tensions flow from the top of your head. The top of your head is becoming completely relaxed.*

Think of your forehead. Feel the skin that covers it. Feel your eyes and the muscles that are around them. Feel those muscles relaxing more and more with each breath. Feel your forehead relaxing more and more.

Your eyelids grow heavier and quieter with each breath. Let yourself go as you breathe gently in and out. Let the relaxation spread naturally as the tension flows out each time you exhale. Your forehead, your eyes, and all these muscles are relaxing more and more.

Feel your throat and neck. Feel them relax. As you breathe out, say, 'Relax and let go.' Your throat and neck are loose, quiet, and comfortable.

Shoulders and Arms Scanning	*Feel your shoulders and upper back. Be aware of the skin and muscles of your shoulders and upper back. Effortlessly, allow relaxation to spread into your shoulders and upper back. With each breath you take, each time you breathe out you become more and more relaxed. The muscles are loose and comfortable. Feel quiet in your shoulder muscles.*

Feel your upper arms relaxing. Feel your arms and hands. Your arms, hands, and fingers are feeling very, very relaxed. You may feel warmth or tingling in your arms and hands. Feel your arms, hands, and fingers relaxing. Feel the tension dropping from your arms, hands, and fingers.

Chest and Stomach Scanning	*Now, think about your chest. Feel it. Sense the muscles under the skin around the chest. Be deeply aware of your chest. Feel relaxation*

spreading throughout your chest and stomach area. As you breathe out, feel the calm and relaxation in your chest. As you breathe naturally, feel relaxation and quiet in your chest and in your stomach area. Tension flows from your chest as you breathe out.

You are breathing in and breathing out. More and more you feel calm. Feel your stomach. Be aware of the skin and muscles in this area. Feel these muscles relax. Feel the tension being replaced by pleasant relaxation. As you breathe out, feel relaxation spread to your stomach and lower back.

Hips and Legs Scanning

Now feel your legs, your hips, your calves, and your ankles. Be aware of these parts of your body. Feel the muscles in these areas. Allow them to relax more and more. Let calm flow down to your legs. Feel the tension leaving. Your hips, thighs, calves, and ankles are becoming loose and relaxed.

Feel your feet and your toes. Become deeply aware of your feet and of each toe. Feel how still and relaxed they are. Let all the tension leave your feet and toes.

Body Review Scanning

How does your body feel? Is it tingly? Is it heavy? Does it feel hollow? Does it feel light as if you were floating? How does your body feel?

Become aware of the tiniest feelings and try to describe these feelings to yourself. Now, for about thirty seconds or so, scan around your body for any signs of tension. If you find any tension in any muscle group, let it slip out. Try to let the tension flow out and the relaxation flow in to take its place. (Briefly pause.)

Think about the ocean as you continue to scan your body for tension. Imagine that each wave that rolls in brings with it massaging and gentle relaxation and calmness. As the wave rolls out, it pulls along with it any tension that remains in your body. Scan your body. If you find any tension, let it go.

Massaging
Relaxation

Go through your body once more, and relax even more until a very profound relaxation finds its place everywhere in your body.

Picture the ocean waves rolling in . . . and out with each breath. And with each breath imagine gently massaging relaxation flowing all over your body.

Picture massaging relaxation coming over and flowing around the top of your head. Feel the relaxation flowing into each part of the skin on your head and coming over the forehead and relaxing the eyes. The relaxation is entering parts of your eyelids and making your eyelids feel heavy and your eyes feel at rest, completely relaxed.

Now the relaxation gently massages the rest of your face, and the feelings of relaxation move down to your nose. These massaging feelings of relaxation move over your nose and over your cheekbones and down through your throat and your mouth. These waves of gentle relaxation and massaging energy come one after another over your head and over your eyes. Your eyelids feel very heavy, and it's a very good feeling, a very relaxing feeling.

Let this relaxation move on down the back of your head and enter the very deepest muscles of your shoulders and neck. Feel the relaxation as it seeps into the muscles of your neck, relaxing each part of your neck. And as the muscles of your neck relax, the muscles of your shoulders relax, and the skin on your neck relaxes.

If you feel any tension, move your neck and shoulders a little bit until you feel more comfortable. Allow this relaxation to continue flowing over the shoulders to the upper arms and to the lower arms, coming down and relaxing the very deepest muscles of your arms. This relaxation pours down from your shoulders in waves of gentle massaging, over your skin, into your muscles, even into the flow of blood.

Every part of your body is becoming perfectly balanced, relaxed, and in harmony. It is flowing down over the shoulders into the upper arms, the lower arms, and through the fingers.

And, as this flow comes down from your head and neck, it also enters your back muscles, down through the neck into the back, so that you feel relaxation around each bone of your back and in all of the muscles in your back.

This energy continues through your stomach, into each part of your lungs, so that your breathing becomes low and quiet. You feel that all is well. Let it go down into the stomach and gently massage it, making it feel very heavy and warm.

Now down through the legs, the thighs, into the knees and the calves, and down to the feet and the toes. Feel wave upon wave of this relaxation pouring over your body.

Cue Words

Now, let's try to deepen the relaxation still further by using some cue words. Let's use the words 'peaceful' and 'calm.' As you relax even further, think these words to yourself. Just say to yourself as you relax, 'peaceful' and 'calm,' and then feel the deepening, ever-deepening waves of relaxation, as you feel much more peaceful and calm. Think of these words, these cue words, 'peaceful' and 'calm.' Think very, very clearly about them as you say them over and over to yourself: 'peaceful' and 'calm.'

Let the words echo in the back of your mind. Continue to relax and repeat the words 'peaceful' and 'calm' over and over again. In the back of your mind the words 'peaceful' and 'calm' echo over and over again.

96

Pleasant feelings of quiet have spread throughout your body. Feel your body and feel the calm. Let it relax fully. Feel at peace. Your breathing is regular and calm, calm and regular. Your are now in a deep state of calm and relaxation. It is comfortable. You feel good. You feel refreshed.

'I am at peace.' Say this to yourself. Feel the peace and the tranquillity throughout your body. You will enjoy a good feeling every time you do these exercises, and you will feel more and more relaxed.

Return to
Activity

If, during the rest of the day, or for that matter, if, at any time, you find yourself getting upset about something, remember the relaxation you have just enjoyed. Before you get upset, take a deep breath and, as you breathe out, think the word 'relax.' Just think the word 'relax' as you breathe out. Then for a brief period of time, think of the words 'peaceful' and 'calm,' and let the feelings of relaxation that you are now enjoying come back to you. This will help you to control situations rather than being controlled by them.

Now, count from one to three. When you reach three, open your eyes. You will be relaxed, but you will be alert and refreshed.

One, relaxed, but alert . . .

Two, mentally wide awake . . .

Three, eyes open, alert, and refreshed.

Deep Muscle Relaxation Summary

Practice your deep muscle relaxation every day, twice a day if possible. Be sure to mark the times you plan to practice on your Home Practice Chart or in your appointment book. We usually recommend that a person continue to practice deep muscle relaxation exercises twice daily for at least a week. If you are under the guidance of a psychologist or other professional, follow the professional's instructions. Once again, you will want to put the pre- and post-session ratings on your Home Practice Chart. If you are over-viewing the book first, practice reading through the deep muscle relaxation instructions at least once before going to the next chapter.

After a few sessions of deep muscle relaxation you will be able to relax unneeded muscles differentially while you perform tasks with needed muscles. For example, you do not need a tight jaw or a clenched fist while writing a memo at your desk.

Be sure to use deep muscle relaxation whenever you see the cues that you have set up in your home or office. If you drive to work, you may want to use stopping at a signal light as a cue to scan your body mentally. Then let your breathing become smooth and rhythmic. Allow the relaxation to replace any tension, as a wave of calm comes over your body. Try to be creative and find new places where you can practice your deep muscle relaxation.

8   Countdown to Relaxation

By practicing progressive, scanning, and deep muscle relaxation, you have learned how to relax your muscles and scan your body to release any residual tension. Now you are ready to begin practicing exercises to help you produce deeper levels of relaxation very quickly. One of the major goals of this stress management training program is to show you ways of becoming deeply relaxed at will.

Handling life stress successfully often calls for several abilities. The ability to size up the stressful situation is important. Next is the skill to relax quickly. Finally comes the ability to do calmly what is needed. If you are able to count down from ten to zero and allow yourself to become comfortably relaxed, you have the self-control to deal effectively with many of life's difficult situations.

The idea of counting to increase self-control and regain composure is not new. When you were a child, your mother may have told you to count to ten before yelling at someone who made you angry. Counting often gives a person enough time to decide if what is happening is what the person wants to be happening. The decision may well be to get into an argument; but enough self-control can be gained between ten and zero to decide if the consequences are worth it.

Counting down from ten to zero for relaxation is a similar self-control technique. The brief time needed to count backward can be used to break spiraling anxiety and release growing tension. Counting forward could be used to promote the same response, but most people with whom we have worked prefer counting backward. One reason seems to be that zero is a natural stopping place. Some people say that when they first learned to count from one to ten, they were always asked if they knew what came next. Rarely are you asked what comes after zero.

Another reason given for counting backward is that some people

99

feel that as the numbers decrease, they are reminded that the amount of tension in their body is also decreasing. Others say it is like counting down their age until they are as young and carefree as a sleeping baby. For these and other reasons, counting backward seems to work best. Try the exercises and see if they work for you.

The Troubled World is Shrinking

Mr. Crane, an accountant, was in a stress management program conducted by one of the authors. Mr. Crane had a history of seasonal blood pressure elevations. He worked for a large corporation and experienced many important deadlines, in addition to the usual April 15 deadline most American taxpayers face. After a period of years, his blood pressure remained high even when he was not facing a deadline. He was taking two different medications to control his hypertension.

Mr. Crane developed a very pleasant picture in his mind when he practiced counting backward from ten to zero. As he started counting, he noticed that his breathing became slow and rhythmic. Then he felt a gentle wave of relaxation spread over his body, from his head to his feet. Before he got to the number five, he began to experience a good feeling that he found difficult to describe. He said it was as if 'the troubled world was shrinking.'

Mr. Crane went on to say that, as he counted, he imagined the piles of books on which he was currently working becoming smaller and smaller. Along with this image, he had the feeling that he no longer needed to worry about the work. He discovered that worry did not make him work faster and that he could be relaxed and still work effectively.

In fact, Mr. Crane was as productive as ever, but he now felt better and less uptight. Throughout the day, Mr. Crane would take brief thirty-second breaks without leaving his desk. He would count backward from ten to zero, imagine his worries shrinking in importance, and then return to his work refreshed and relaxed. Eventually, his blood pressure began to decline and his doctor no longer had to prescribe one of his medications.

Elevators, Escalators, and Stairs

Mr. Crane had a pleasant image of his troubled world and shrinking work. Not everyone will want to imagine his or her world or work when counting down from ten to zero. Many people like to use the brief seconds to imagine being somewhere very pleasant.

We often suggest that people try imagining a slowly descending elevator or escalator. As they count backward, the elevator or escalator slowly moves down. Some people imagine the floor numbers lighting up on the elevator panel as they count down. You can also imagine yourself walking slowly down sturdy stairs. Many people prefer going at their own pace down the stairs. They seem to gain a sense of control by slowly guiding their legs and feet.

No matter which image is used, when zero is reached, the image of arriving in a pleasant place should be triggered by the opening of the elevator door, the end of the escalator, or the bottom of the stairs.

Most people are very creative with the pleasant scene they imagine when they reach zero. Many are surprised at what pops into their mind's eye. One person saw herself riding a horse in slow motion through the surf. The summer sun was warm and sparkled on the beach. Another saw himself relaxing on a king-sized bed that was covered with satin sheets and pillows. The morning sun filtered through his bedroom window, which opened onto a flower garden. You may be surprised at what you find when you take the elevator in your mind to a pleasant place.

Deep Breathing and Counting Down

A favorite technique for one of the authors is simply to focus on breathing in and out while counting backward from ten to zero. Each time he breathes out, he silently says the next number. Instead of focusing on visual images, he concentrates on the breath rolling in . . . and rolling out. He imagines the sound as it rolls out, carrying with it all the noise and troubles of the day. With practice, this technique has become so effective that a very deep relaxation can be produced by counting backward just from three to zero.

Count up to Relaxed Alertness

Diving into a pool of crystal-clear water is refreshing for many people. The cool, pleasant water relaxes and refreshes at the same time. When you are becoming fatigued, counting down to relaxation can have a similar refreshing effect. Spend a few seconds becoming totally relaxed. Do not think about worries or work. These breaks can be important for anyone experiencing a stressful day.

After the brief relaxation, you can return to a state of relaxed alertness by bringing your attention back to yourself and counting forward from zero to three. This time, silently count the next number as you breathe in rather than when you breathe out. Let the breaths become deeper and stronger as you approach the number three. With each number, feel the energy and vitality flow into your lungs. When you reach the number three, open your eyes and feel alert and eager to resume your activities. Your mind will be fully alert, but your body will be calm and relaxed.

Ways to Use Countdown Relaxation

Use a countdown to relaxation any time you need a brief break from work or activities. It can be combined with scanning relaxation. First, scan to see if any muscles are tense, feel these muscles relax more and more with each breath, then deepen the relaxation by counting down from ten to zero. After practicing, you may find that you can return to a very relaxed state of counting down from three to zero.

It should be evident, after practicing this and the other muscle-relaxation techniques, that relaxation is not wasteful inactivity. On the contrary, relaxation is a purposeful and active state that you control. You take the breaks you need from your work and replace excess stress and tension with relaxation. You conserve energy so you can draw from your reserves. Be creative in finding times and ways to cultivate the habit of relaxing.

Common Problems and Their Solutions

The difficulty most frequently reported with countdown relaxation is failing to become totally relaxed after counting to zero. This problem can be avoided by taking several precautions. First, remember that countdown is a deepening technique. By this, we mean it should be used to deepen the relaxation, after you have already become some-what relaxed. If you briefly practiced progressive, deep muscle, and scanning relaxation without becoming deeply relaxed, counting down from ten to zero probably will not have a great effect. But if you have practiced the other techniques until you experienced deep relaxation, you are ready to start using the countdown procedure.

A second way of avoiding disappointment with the countdown

102

technique is to make it part of your regular practice sessions. You may want to complete your sessions of progressive or deep muscle relaxation practice by counting down from ten to zero. This should help you develop your ability to use the procedure at other times to become deeply relaxed.

Do not be concerned if, when you first practice countdown relaxation, you feel relaxed but not as relaxed as when you have experienced the more detailed progressive or deep muscle relaxation. Continue to practice during brief breaks in the day to see if you are able to become more and more relaxed in less and less time. Building brief relaxation breaks into your day is just as important as the longer relaxation practice you have already scheduled.

How to Do Countdown Relaxation

Countdown relaxation is a simple and short technique. We are not aware of any relaxation tapes that focus exclusively on this procedure. The Charlesworth and Peiffer progressive relaxation and deep muscle relaxation tapes use countdown relaxation procedures to deepen relaxation, but the exercise is only a small part of each tape.

We emphasize learning countdown relaxation to use during thirty-second breaks throughout the day. When the technique is used in this fashion, tapes are not needed. You may wish to make some countdown signs that read '10-9-8-7-6-5-4-3-2-1-0' or '3-2-1-0' and add them to your relaxation reminders. On elevators, use the descending lights to remind yourself to use countdown relaxation.

The best way to start is to read over the outline and word-by-word instructions that follow, then attempt the procedure on your own. We have included two different word-by-word guides for countdown relaxation. One describes only the countdown procedure. The other uses imagery to accompany the countdown procedure. Read both techniques and select the one you prefer.

If you have difficulties with countdown relaxation, record and listen to your own relaxation tape using the instructions or listen to the Charlesworth and Peiffer progressive relaxation or deep muscle relaxation tape. Remember, too, to practice countdown relaxation at the end of your practice sessions with progressive or deep muscle relaxation.

OUTLINE FOR COUNTDOWN RELAXATION

I. BASIC TECHNIQUE

A. Count down from ten to zero while becoming progressively more relaxed.

B. Silently say each number as you breathe *out* and feel tension flowing out with each breath.

C. After you reach zero, briefly experience the relaxation.

II. COUNTUP

A. Count from one to three to return to an alert but relaxed state.

B. Silently say each number as you breathe *in* and feel mental alertness returning while you remain calm and relaxed.

III. IMAGERY ADDITIONS

A. Imagine yourself moving slowly down a stairway or on a gently moving elevator or escalator.

B. When you reach the number zero and the bottom of the stairs, elevator, or escalator, see yourself getting off in a pleasant and relaxing place.

C. When you start to count forward from one to three, imagine yourself returning to the place where you are practicing the exercises, but imagine that everything around you is relaxed and calm.

WORD-BY-WORD COUNTDOWN RELAXATION

Counting Down

Count backward from ten to zero. Silently say each number as you breathe out. As you count, you will relax more deeply and go deeper and deeper into a state of profound relaxation. When you reach zero, you will be completely relaxed.

Ten, deeper and deeper . . . Nine, relaxing more deeply . . . Eight, relaxing deeper and deeper . . . Seven, serene and calm . . . Six, I feel more and more relaxed . . . Five, deeper and deeper . . . Four, becoming as limp as a rag doll . . . Three, profoundly relaxing . . . Two, deeper and deeper . . . One, very, very relaxed . . . Zero, profound relaxation . . .

Now drift still deeper with each breath. Deeper and deeper. Feel that deep relaxation all over and continue relaxing. Now, relaxing deeper and deeper, you should feel an emotional calm . . . tranquil and serene feelings . . . feelings of safe security . . . and a calm peace.

Try to get a quiet inner confidence, a good feeling about yourself with the relaxation. Study once more the feelings that come with relaxation. Let your muscles switch off; feel good about everything. Calm and secure feelings make you more and more tranquil and peaceful.

Return to
Activity

Now, count from one to three; silently say each number as you take a deep breath. When you reach three, open you eyes. You will be relaxed and alert. When you open your eyes, you will find yourself back in the place where you started your relaxation. The environment will seem slower and more calm, however, and you will be more relaxed and peaceful.

One, relaxed, but more alert . . .

Two, mentally wide awake . . .

Three, eyes open, alert and refreshed.

WORD-BY-WORD COUNTDOWN RELAXATION WITH STAIRWAY IMAGERY

Stairway
Imagination

Use your imagination now. In your mind's eye, imagine that you are standing at the top of a large, winding staircase. See the steps in front of you. See the handrail.

You are all alone standing in front of the staircase. It's your private staircase, and you know it well. You feel comfortable being there. Count backward from ten to zero. Silently say each number as you breathe out. As you count, imagine you are stepping down the stairway, very slowly.

Imagine yourself walking slowly down the

staircase. You move yourself down the steps deeper and deeper. With each count you will relax more deeply as you go deeper and deeper into a state of profound relaxation. When you reach zero, imagine you have reached the bottom of the staircase. You then find you are in a place of perfect calm.

Counting Down

Ten, and you take your first step ... Nine, relaxing more deeply ... Eight, deeper and deeper relaxation ... Seven, gently walking down the stairs ... Six, feel more and more relaxed ... Five, deeper and deeper ... Four, serene and calm ... Three, very relaxed ... Two, deeper and deeper ... One, very, very profoundly relaxed ... Zero, gently step off the bottom step into a perfectly relaxed and calm peace.

Now, drift still deeper with each breath. Deeper and deeper. Feel that deeper relaxation all over and continue relaxing. Now, relaxing deeper and deeper, you should feel an emotional calm ... tranquil and serene feelings ... feelings of safe security ... and a calm peace.

Try to get a quiet inner confidence, a good feeling about yourself with the relaxation. Study once more the feelings that come with relaxation. Let your muscles switch off; feel good about everything. Calm and secure feelings make you more and more tranquil and peaceful.

Return to
Activity

Now, count from one to three. Silently say each number as you take a deep breath. When you reach three, open your eyes. You will be relaxed and alert. When you open your eyes, you will find yourself back in the place where you started your relaxation. The environment will seem slower and more calm, however, and you will be more relaxed and peaceful.

One, relaxed, but more alert ...
Two, mentally wide awake ...
Three, eyes open, alert and refreshed.

9 Autogenic Phrases and Images: How to Relax from the Inside

'Autogenic' means self-regulation or self-generation. This relaxation technique was developed by Johannes Schultz, M.D., and Wolfgang Luthe, M.D. It uses and builds on the passive, receptive attitude you learned in deep muscle relaxation training. The power of the trained mind to influence the body in a healthy fashion is the cornerstone of this technique.

Autogenic training is thought to help balance the body's self-regulating systems of the 'homeostatic' mechanism. Just as a thermostat regulates temperature inside a room, the homeostatic mechanism regulates what goes on inside of our bodies.

Our internal, self-regulating systems automatically help to control heart rate, blood circulation, breathing, and many other functions we need to survive. If we lacked such an automatically regulated system, we would have to spend our time consciously commanding our heart muscles to pump and our diaphragms to pull air into our lungs.

These functions are also a part of the fight-or-flight system we described earlier. The sympathetic nervous system can automatically increase arousal to help us prepare for confronting or retreating from a potential danger. This reaction is adaptive when the threat requires such action; but for modern man, most threats are psychological or philosophical. For these threats, it is not adaptive to increase heart rate and breathing, nor to constrict peripheral blood vessels to help redirect blood flow to vital organs.

Reprogramming Inner Calm

Autogenic training helps you control stress by training the autonomic nervous system to be more relaxed when you are not faced with a real need to fight or run. This technique follows in a natural progression after you have learned to control tension in your major muscle groups.

It would be difficult to learn autogenic training before learning to produce a general state of relaxation in your muscles because autonomic nervous system responses are more difficult to recognize.

Autogenic relaxation is accomplished by passively paying attention to verbal cues for relaxation. It can be thought of as helping to reprogram the subconscious mind to create a state of internal calm. In contrast to progressive and deep muscle relaxation, autogenic training involves no direct muscle relaxation exercises. Instead, the body is conditioned to respond to particular verbal cues that generally reduce physical arousal and tension. Autogenic training emphasizes smooth and rhythmic breathing, regular and calm heart beating, and pleasant warmth with relaxing heaviness throughout the extremities of the body.

Passive Concentration and the Receptive Mode

You will need to assume a passive, receptive attitude even more than you did in deep muscle relaxation training. In autogenic training this is called 'passive concentration.' In some ways being passive and concentrating seem to be contradictory; and this is one of the reasons that Drs. Schultz and Luthe's work was a breakthrough in modern science. An example may explain the technique of passive concentration better than a definition can.

Recall an occasion when your eyes began to fill with tears or you began to cry. You may remember a relationship breaking up or a loved one dying and the sadness you experienced thinking of the person you were losing. You may also associate crying with dirt or onion juice in your eyes. For a few seconds, close your eyes and imagine a personal memory or any of the above examples. If you take the time to recall the experience vividly, you will notice that when you open your eyes they are wetter than before you closed them.

Now, if you do the same thing but actively tell yourself that you must cry, and try to force yourself to cry, you will probably find that you are unsuccessful. Crying is an automatic function. Without practice, most of us cannot do it on command. We all probably know someone who has practiced this automatic response and seems to be able to produce 'crocodile tears' at will. This person may have learned to focus on sad events and thoughts and conditioned the tear ducts to flood the eyes.

Autogenic training involves conditioning positive and relaxing responses. The originators of the process, Drs. Schultz and Luthe, maintain that by concentrating passively, a person can lapse into an unstructured, free-floating state of mind, which is relaxing in itself. The key is to focus on a relaxing phrase or image that will help to 'mediate' or passively cue the automatic response you desire.

Focusing on the words, 'My breathing is smooth and rhythmic,' or an image of gentle waves rolling in and rolling out can trigger a relaxed respiration rate. But although the process of focusing must be deliberate, it does not involve the usual rules for human achievement. If you were to focus on 'I want my breathing to be smooth and rhythmic,' or 'I am going to make my breathing smooth and rhythmic, or else!' you probably would not be successful.

Learning to accomplish something worthwhile by learning not to work actively at it is unusual for most people. Passive concentration skills and autogenic training require careful practice; but if you have been successful learning progressive and deep muscle relaxation, this technique will seem much easier.

Biofeedback – The Machines Say You Can

At first, many of the people we train do not believe that they can control 'automatic' functions. Biofeedback machines, however, show them that they can produce changes. The instruments also show them the amount of change they have produced.

The word 'biofeedback' can be divided into three parts to make it more understandable. 'Bio' refers to living organisms or tissues. 'Feed' means to give or, in this case, display. 'Back' refers to the direction in which this information is provided. Thus biofeedback is simply a term for the modern technology of measuring a person's internal (bio) response and giving the person immediate knowledge (feedback) about that response.

An early form of biofeedback was taking your own pulse for a minute. Now, machines can tell you second by second exactly how many beats per minute occur and whether the beats are increasing or decreasing.

It is known that one of the common automatic responses that accompanies relaxation is vasodilation or widening of the arteries in the arms, hands, legs, and feet. A pleasant, warm, and heavy sensation occurs as the blood flow increases into these areas. With a biofeedback machine, the temperature of the hands or feet can be measured while this internal relaxation takes place.

Blood Circulation, Temperature, and Biofeedback

Autogenic exercises help train the arteries and circulatory system to remain in a more relaxed state. A way of thinking about this form of internal tension is to consider that all the blood vessels are made out of muscle – a special form of muscle. Thus blood vessels can tighten up (constrict) or relax and widen (dilate). If the balance between this action is 'disregulated,' a person may experience physical stress responses.

Let's consider some of the disorders that can be influenced by the disregulation of this balance. If the peripheral vascular system is constricted, for example, there is less space for the blood to flow, and a person's blood pressure may increase. Constantly cold feet or hands may also reflect constriction and poor circulation. In addition, migraine headaches are thought to be caused by overdilation of the arteries of the brain after a period of constriction.

The use of autogenic training and temperature biofeedback has been helpful in regulating blood flow. This method has even been successful when vasoconstriction was complicated by blocked arteries. One of the authors worked for six months teaching a patient with severe arterial blockage how to increase blood flow to his legs and arms. The patient, whom we will call Allan J., was afflicted with what is known as Buerger's disease. Allan's arteries were so extensively blocked and his circulation so poor that both of his legs had been amputated below the knees. Lack of circulation to the fingers contributed to constant pain and frequent infections.

At the time, biofeedback was a relatively new treatment, and there were still many skeptics. We may have been the first to attempt to use biofeedback with Buerger's disease. Allan was willing to try anything.

When Allan began autogenic training and biofeedback the temperature at the tips of his fingers was below 70°F – lower than the surrounding room temperature. As the training progressed, he would come into the session with an average finger temperature of 85°F and could increase it to as high as 94°F while receiving the temperature feedback.

Although autogenic training and biofeedback could not remove the blockage from his arteries, it did appear to help increase the blood flow, probably by dilating the smaller accessory arteries that were not blocked. As you can imagine, when biofeedback helped to keep Allan from further surgery, he almost became the hospital's biofeedback salesman.

Exactly how autogenic training works is not completely known. The technique works for many people, and we now know that the heavy and warm feeling of relaxation in the arms, hands, legs, and feet is a real phenomenon. Not only have temperature changes been reported, but Dr. Luthe's early research showed that the increase in blood to an area also contributed to an increase in weight.

The Little Girl in a Swing Who Calmed an Irregular Heart

Tachycardia is a condition with symptoms of rapid and irregular heartbeats. Mary C. had experienced tachycardia for three years before she was seen by one of the authors. Mary was twenty-one years old and had worked as a secretary for the same company since graduating from high school. She was a good worker, conscientious and very interested in constantly bettering her skills. She aspired to become an executive secretary, took college courses at night, and always received excellent ratings from her supervisors.

Mary complained that when her boss said he needed a letter or report typed immediately, her heart rate would increase and become irregular, and her heart would feel as if it were 'pounding.' She usually was able to finish the work, but over a period of years she became more and more distressed. The tachycardia became more frequent as Mary accepted more responsibility.

Mary began autogenic training after learning to use progressive and deep muscle relaxation. When she practiced autogenic training, she was able to produce a calm and regular heart rate. With encouragement, Mary slowly began practicing in front of a typewriter at home.

Mary discovered that she could increase her heart rate control by imagining a small girl swinging rhythmically under a tree, while the wind gently blew through her blonde hair. She began practicing autogenic training and using this imagery.

Eventually, Mary was able to imagine the little girl swinging while she was typing at work. This helped her to remain calm. Her tachycardia became less and less of a problem as she was able to regulate her heartbeat by imagining the girl swinging to and fro.

When describing her success at work, she also reported that, if she quickly got this image and held it in the back of her mind while she

111

typed, her typing seemed to have a smoother rhythm. She felt that this practice contributed to greater speed and fewer errors.

Self-Regulation and Symbolic Imagery

The use of imagery to help regulate various bodily responses is not new. A symbol is something that stands for or suggests something else. The little girl swinging under the tree stood for, or represented to Mary, the more rhythmic beating of her heart. This sort of symbolic imagery has been used in hypnosis since the time it was discovered, and, more recently, it has been incorporated into both relaxation and biofeedback.

Why does symbolic imagery work? Why does it seem very important in trying to regulate the automatic bodily systems? One theory suggests that different parts of our brain think in different ways. The left side of the brain is very logical and verbal. 'Talking' yourself through a problem or telling yourself to lift a glass of water and drink from it may originate there. The right side of the brain seems to think more in pictures and is less logical.

This phenomenon may explain why people have counted sheep to go to sleep all through the ages. The technique probably survives because verbal counting tends to bore the left side of the brain to sleep, while the picture of the sheep jumping over the fence tends to bore the right side of the brain to sleep. With both sides of the brain occupied, we have a hard time worrying about something that might arouse us and keep us from falling to sleep.

According to a related theory, the right side of the brain may control the autonomic nervous system and our automatic functions. If this theory is correct, it would help us understand why we must both passively concentrate and use images to help regulate blood flow or heart rate. If we actively and logically concentrated, we would engage our left brain. This part of the brain may not be where the control for circulation originates. In addition, the left brain may critically evaluate a suggestion for your heartbeat to become regular and decide, 'I don't have control over my heartbeat. It just happens automatically.'

The autogenic training exercises will introduce you to symbolic imagery and hep you to regulate your respiration and circulation. You may discover, after practicing, that other symbols work for you. Experiment and discover the symbols you use to imagine changes occurring in your body.

One of the authors worked with more than sixty hypertensive individuals and found their symbolic imagery to be highly creative. Some of these people would imagine the complete vascular system and see the vessels relaxing as blood flowed through. One man saw muscles 'tight as rocks' pushing against the vessels and watched the rocks slowly dissolve. A person who worked in gas transmission saw a pipeline system and was able to open up valves and decrease pressure or redirect flow. Others saw the heart connected to a system of flexible hoses. Another person imagined a clear plastic model of the human body and placed a thermometer at the tips of the fingers. She visualized the blood flow increasing to the hands and also watched the temperature rising.

What are your symbols for how your body works? As you practice autogenic training, be creative with the images you use to help your breathing become smooth and rhythmic, your heartbeat calm and regular, and the blood flow to your extremities heavy and warm.

Ways to Use Your New Skills

Many people find they are able to practice autogenic phrases or visualize relaxing scenes briefly throughout their day to promote a calming response. Mary imagined the little girl swinging as she began to type. Several people we know relax their breathing as they go into stressful situations by thinking of the ocean waves rolling in and out. Others allow the image of a slowly ticking metronome to pace their breathing or heart rate.

We recommend that people with high blood pressure check their blood pressure at work. You may bring your own blood pressure cuff and stethoscope or stop by the medical clinic at lunch. This helps you get exact feedback about your blood pressure, and you may decide you need to spend less time eating during your lunch break and use the time to practice autogenic exercises.

Often individuals suffering from migraine headaches prefer autogenic training to other relaxation techniques. Focusing on the continued relaxing warmth of the hands and feet seems to help prevent the onset of headaches. Currently, research is being done to help us better understand how this works.

Certain individuals may experience cold hands or feet and can warm them by imagining the sun shining brightly on them as they work. Discover what responses you need to work with and, after

113

practicing the autogenic exercises, begin incorporating your new skills into your daily activities.

Scheduling and Recording Autogenic Practice

Autogenic training should be practiced during the same times you previously practiced muscle relaxation exercises. Again, we recommend that you use the same times twice daily. During the work week, use the morning coffee break or lunch hour and then practice in the afternoon after arriving home.

Occasionally, we recommend that a person practice a muscle relaxation exercise during one practice session and autogenic training during the other. This alternation is done when a person is relatively confident of his ability to relax his muscles but still has some difficulty maintaining his muscle relaxation levels throughout the day. Some individuals also like to use muscle relaxation exercises or autogenic exercises to help them sleep at night. This should be done in addition to the other scheduled exercise periods.

Record your practice on the Home Practice Chart on the last pages of this book. Remember to record the technique used, how long you practiced, and your relaxation levels.

Preparing for Autogenic Training

Once again, as with muscle relaxation, plan on practicing autogenic training in a place that is private, quiet, comfortable, and free from distractions. Be sure family, friends, and coworkers will not interrupt you.

As before, the first thing to do is to get comfortable. You may wish to practice in the same place that you have been practicing your muscle relaxation exercises. We have already mentioned that it is beneficial to become conditioned to relaxing in a special place. You may already be in a habit of relaxing immediately when you sit in your favorite chair.

Be sure that all of your body is supported so that further relaxation will not cause your arms or legs to fall from the force of gravity. This is sometimes a problem with autogenic training. When the arms begin to feel heavy and warm, they may slip off the sides of the chair if they are not properly positioned.

Your hands should be open, your legs uncrossed, and your clothes loose. Be sure your neck is supported in a high-backed chair or on pillows. If you cannot find something to support your head, you can let your head hang forward or balance it comfortably in an upright position.

Common Problems and Their Solutions

When you first start autogenic training, it is best to allow yourself enough time to experience the changes in respiration, heart rate, and circulation. Often a person can calm breathing and heart rate quickly; but it takes longer to experience heavy and warm relaxation in the arms, hands, legs, and feet. If you have a brief period of time to practice, concentrate only on your breathing and heart rate.

Let us say, for example, that you are able to relax your whole body in five minutes during your morning coffee break. When you first start autogenic training, you will probably find it difficult to produce heavy and warm feelings in such a short time.

It will be better if you schedule adequate time when you come home than to discourage yourself by not producing the feelings at work. You may decide, however, to calm just your breathing or heart rate during a brief period at work. After you are able to produce relaxing heaviness and warmth at home, you may also want to begin briefer practice at work.

Some people find it hard to assume a truly passive attitude. Even when they are repeating the autogenic phrases, other thoughts come to mind. Combining the autogenic phrases with images will usually help. If thoughts still intrude, do not dwell on them or criticize yourself for having them – just gently bring your mind back to the phrases and images.

OUTLINE FOR AUTOGENIC PHRASES
AND IMAGES

I. DEEP BREATHING EXERCISES

    A. Imagine ocean waves rolling in . . . and out.
    B. Silently say, 'Breathing, smooth and rhythmic.'

II. HEARTBEAT REGULATION EXERCISES

    A. Imagine slow ocean waves.
    B. Silently say, 'My heartbeat is calm and regular.'

III. BLOOD FLOW

    A. Right arm and hand
        1. Silently say, 'My right arm and hand are heavy and warm.'
        2. Imagine the warm sun.
    B. Left arm and hand
        1. Silently say 'My left arm and hand are heavy and warm.'
        2. Imagine the warm sun.
    C. Legs and feet
        1. Silently say, 'My legs and feet are heavy and warm.'
        2. Imagine the warmth flowing down from the arms and hands.

IV. SUMMING-UP PHRASE – 'I am calm'

V. RETURN TO ACTIVITY

    A. Count forward from one to three.

WORD-BY-WORD AUTOGENIC PHRASES AND IMAGES

Preparation

First, get into a comfortable position. While you are finding a good position, you will also want to loosen any tight clothing. Become as comfortable as possible.

Let your mouth drop open for a moment and move your jaw gently from side to side. Now, close your mouth slowly, keeping your teeth slightly apart. Take a deep breath . . . Breathe in so that the air flows into your lungs and feels as though it's filling up your stomach area. Now, breathe out slowly . . . Feel yourself floating down.

Breathing – Smooth and Rhythmic

Focus your attention completely and fully on your breathing. Imagine your breathing is as automatic as the ocean waves, rolling in . . . and out . . . in . . . and out . . . Silently say to yourself, 'Breathing, smooth and rhythmic . . .' 'Breathing, smooth and rhythmic . . .' 'My breathing is effortless and calm . . .' 'Breathing, smooth and rhythmic . . .' 'My breathing is effortless and calm . . .' 'Breathing smooth and rhythmic . . .'

As you breathe, imagine relaxation flowing over your body, one wave after another. Feel the waves of relaxation moving through your chest and shoulders. Down into your arms. Through your back muscles. Down into your hips and legs.

With each wave of relaxation, try to feel the heaviness and warmth in your arms and your legs. Now, I want you to think, still in a passive way, about wave after wave of relaxation. Concentrate on the relaxation moving upward from your lungs in waves, up and across your face and scalp.

Tranquillity and
Heart Rate
Calming

Your mind is becoming more passive and tranquil, and you have a placid, relaxed awareness of the feelings of relaxation throughout your body. All of the tensions and worries will slip away from you as you feel waves of relaxation flooding over you. There is a growing feeling of warmth and heaviness in your arms and legs and a passive awareness of your state of relaxation.

Remember how you imagined the waves rolling in and out to help you breathe effortlessly. Try to feel that again as you now imagine your heart beating. Silently say to yourself, 'My heartbeat is calm and regular . . .' 'My heartbeat is calm and regular . . .' 'My heartbeat is calm and regular . . .' 'I feel very quiet, and my heartbeat is calm and regular . . .' 'My whole body is deeply relaxed, and my heartbeat is calm and regular . . .' 'My heartbeat is calm and regular.'

Right Arm and
Hand – Heavy
and Warm

These feelings of relaxation, passivity, and peace will now become more and more profound as you concentrate on just your right hand and arm.

117

Focus all your attention on your right hand and your right arm. In fact, just to make sure you have made mental contact with your right arm and hand, lightly touch these areas with your left hand.

While you gently stroke your right hand and arm, say to yourself, 'My right arm and hand are heavy and warm; warmth is flowing into my arm and down into my hand . . .' 'My right arm and hand are heavy and warm; warmth is flowing into my arm and down into my hand . . .' Let your left arm return to a resting position, if you have not already done so.

Continue silently to repeat to yourself, 'My arm and hand are heavy and warm . . .' 'Warmth is flowing into my right arm, down into my right hand, and it feels pleasantly warm.' Remember, you do not want to try to force any of these things to happen, just allow them to happen. They will occur naturally and gently as you passively continue to focus on your right arm and hand and the feelings of heaviness and warmth. 'My right arm is heavy and warm . . .' 'Warmth is flowing into my right arm and down into my right hand.'

At this time, carefully study the feelings in your arm and hand and attend to the feelings of heaviness and warmth. You may use any thoughts you care to in order to imagine your right arm and hand becoming warm. You can imagine that they are in warm water or that the warm sun is beating down on them. Continue repeating to yourself: 'My right arm and hand are heavy and warm; warmth is flowing into my right arm, and it feels pleasantly warm.'

Left Arm and Hand – Heavy and Warm

Now, I would like you to turn your attention to your left hand, wrist, and arm. Concentrate on this area of your body and focus all your attention there. If you need to, gently touch it as you

118

silently repeat: 'My left arm is heavy and warm; warmth is flowing into my arm and down into my hand.' 'My left arm and hand are heavy and warm.' 'Warmth is flowing down my arm and into my hand.' 'My left arm and hand feel pleasantly warm.'

The feelings of warmth may be deepened by imaging the sun shining on your left hand and arm. Continue saying these words while focusing on your left arm and hand: 'My left arm and hand are heavy and warm.' 'Warmth is flowing down my left arm and into my wrist and hand.' 'Warmth is flowing down my left arm and into my wrist and hand.'

Become fully aware of the feelings in your left arm and hand, and be sure to keep out all other thoughts as you continue to focus on heaviness and warmth in your left arm and hand. If other thoughts come into your mind, you will find it possible to let them go as quickly as they came. You are passively concentrating on heaviness and warmth. Simply let these things happen; allow these feelings of heaviness and warmth to happen to you. Continue silently to repeat to yourself: 'My left arm and hand are heavy and warm; warmth is flowing into my left arm and down into my left hand.'

Can you feel the relaxation? Does your arm feel as if you would need help to lift it? Maybe the warmth reminds you of the summer sun. However you describe it is fine, as long as it is pleasant for you. Just continue to feel the heaviness and warmth, and feel the relaxation.

Both Arms and Hands – Heavy and Warm

Now, I want you to focus on both of your arms and hands at the same time, as you say to yourself: 'My arms and hands are heavy and warm, warmth is flowing into my arms and down into my hands.' 'Both my right and my left arm are heavy and warm.' 'My arms and hands

119

are heavy and warm.' 'Warmth is flowing into my arms and gently down into my wrists, hands, and fingertips, and they feel very pleasant.'

Very good. You are relaxing all over as your arms become very heavy and warm. As the warmth flows into your hands, you will feel your whole body relaxing. You are letting everything go, all cares and worries are far, far away. This is your time to think only of pleasant relaxation and the feelings it brings. It is better for you if you think of nothing but the way your body feels. Let all other thoughts leave your mind.

Once again, focusing on both of your arms, think to yourself: 'My arms are heavy and warm.' 'Warmth is flowing into my hands.' Continue passively to concentrate on your arms being heavy and warm. Be sure you gently push out any other thoughts. In our modern society, the mind is often not used to being quiet and relaxed, and it tends to wander. If you find this happening, do not become upset or disappointed. Just bring your mind back to the thought: 'My arms are heavy and warm; warmth is flowing into my hands.'

Take some time now while you keep your arms very heavy and warm, and check around your body to see if there is tension in any muscle. Check all around. Is your jaw loose and slack, and are your eyelids gently closed? Be sure the muscles in your face are relaxed.

You are becoming very relaxed, and you feel loose and limp – just like an old rag doll. And you really are that relaxed, as you continue to practice autogenic relaxation.

Legs and Feet – Heavy and Warm

Now, I want you to focus on your legs. If you need to, make contact with your legs by touching them and becoming more aware of them. Notice where they are touching the surface on which they are resting. Notice that pleasant heaviness and

*warmth is spreading down from your arms to
your legs. Let it happen.*

*Passively allow the warmth to spread as you
silently say to yourself: 'My legs are becoming
heavy and warm, warmth is flowing into my
feet.' 'My legs are warm and heavy.' 'My feet are
warm and heavy.'*

*'My legs are heavy and warm, and warmth is
pleasantly flowing into my legs and down into my
feet – all the way to the very tips of my toes.' 'My
legs and feet are heavy and warm.' 'Heavy and
warm, very pleasantly warm.'*

*Very good. Now I want you to focus on all your
limbs, arms and legs together. Become very aware
of your arms and your legs. Repeat silently to
yourself: 'My arms and legs are heavy and warm,
warm and heavy.' 'My feet and hands are heavy
and warm, warm and heavy.'*

*'Warm and pleasant feelings are sinking into
every part of my arms, hands, legs, and feet.' 'My
arms and legs are very limp.' 'The muscles in my
arms and legs are letting go, and I am becoming
more and more relaxed.'*

**All the
Limbs – Heavy
and Warm**

*Take a deep breath . . . Breathe in so that the
air flows into your lungs and feels as though it is
flowing way down into your stomach area.
Breathe very deeply down into your stomach area
and, as you breathe out, say to yourself, 'I am
calm.'*

'I Am Calm'

*These are very important words that I want you
to use only when you are relaxed, very deeply
relaxed. These will be summing-up words, which
you will say when you feel deeply relaxed. 'I am
calm . . .' Take a deep breath and say, 'I am
calm . . .'*

*Eventually you will be able to relax yourself by
simply thinking the words, 'I am calm.' When
the day is going badly or you are caught in a*

121

*traffic jam, you will be able to control your stress
by saying, 'I am calm.' You will remember the
feelings of deep relaxation that you are feeling
now.*

*Whenever things make you nervous, whether it
is meeting new people, asking your boss for a
raise, or talking to large groups, you will find you
can relax yourself by simply thinking the words,
'I am calm.' But at first, be sure to say it only
when you are deeply relaxed. After practicing,
you can begin to use it in everyday life.*

Return to
Activity

*Now as we complete this autogenic relaxation
practice, take a deep breath and slowly let it out.
Now, I want you to see yourself lying in the room
where you started these exercises. Imagine yourself back where you were when you started these
exercises, safe, secure, and pleasantly relaxed.
You will enjoy a good feeling every time you do
these exercises, and you will feel more and more
relaxed.*

*Now, count from one to three. Silently say
each number as you take a deep breath. When you
reach three, open your eyes. You will be relaxed
and alert. When you open your eyes, you will find
yourself back in the place where you started your
relaxation. The environment will seem slower
and calmer, and you will be more relaxed and
peaceful.*

*One, relaxed, but more alert . . . Two, men-
tally wide awake . . . Three, eyes open, alert
and refreshed.*

*(If you plan to return immediately to a physi-
cal activity, follow these suggestions. Yawn and
stretch as you do in the morning. Also, if you are
going to do manual activities, shake your hands
briskly.)*

10 Imagery Training: The Windows of Your Mind

'It's All Inside Your Head,' She Said to Me

Our thoughts, images, and other mental activities can be harmful when they are upsetting to us. What does 'upsetting' mean? You could say that you are pushing 'up' the 'setting' of your arousal. This adds to stress.

Most of us have struggled with unwanted thoughts only to find ourselves upset. Maybe something at work is extremely pressing, or perhaps a personal problem is troubling us. Thoughts about the problems keep spinning in our minds, almost as if they were being rolled around in a clothes dryer. One idea leads to another, and soon we find ourselves totally worked up and in a frazzle. We keep rehashing the problem without finding a solution. We may find that we are unable to pay attention to anything else during the day, or we become so aroused that we cannot sleep at night.

I Think, Therefore I Am

When introducing progressive relaxation, deep muscle relaxation, and autogenic relaxation, we made the point that these relaxation techniques work because it is almost impossible to be physically relaxed and tense at the same time. You simply cannot do both simultaneously – at least not very well! Relaxing your mind is based on the same principle. You cannot be thinking relaxed, peaceful, and calming thoughts while your mind is racing wildly up and down the stairways of your life.

Picture Yourself on a Boat on a River

You have read how to relax muscles that are under your voluntary control and how to calm systems of your body that are usually

123

regulated automatically, such as heart rate and blood flow. You are now about to learn how to produce relaxing images and thoughts. These images and thoughts can be used to block out intruding and upsetting ideas. You can learn how to do this with imagery training. The goals of imagery training are to reduce and control mental anxiety.

Anxiety usually involves both physical and mental parts, but at times one of these may be stronger than the other. For example, one may be physically tired and yet be unable to sleep because of upsetting thoughts. This is mental anxiety.

By using pleasant visual images, we can control upsetting thoughts and enjoy a deep state of physical relaxation. Learning to control your thoughts takes knowing what you need to think about, practicing those thoughts, and then using them when you want to relax.

Once you have developed your ability to create pleasant mental images, you will be able to begin to visualize yourself being successful and meeting the goals to which you aspire. There are additional ways of learning to control and enjoy what you think and feel. Some of the additional ways will be presented in later chapters.

Imagery, Music, and Your Mind

Mental imagery is a little like a daydream. You may want to start by trying to visualize, in your mind's eye, a pleasant scene you have seen many times. Try to reexperience the scene in every way you can.

The technique should use both sight and sound. We could use the term audiovisual imagery to describe the procedure.

Many people listen to music to calm themselves. It is hard to be calm, to whistle a tune and think anxious thoughts at the same time.

The music on visual imagery tapes helps you produce a state of calm. When you practice visual imagery without using a prerecorded imagery tape, we invite you to add your favorite music. You may also want to use pleasant environmental sounds, such as gentle ocean waves rolling in . . . and out. Appendix I lists different musical and environmental selections that you may find helpful.

Imagery and the Five Senses

As you learn imagery, you will also want to add your other senses: taste, touch, and smell. Maybe mental imagery really means sensory imagery.

When you practice the imagery exercises, try to include all five of your senses. Make believe you can *'see* the lush green of a tropical rain forest' with your eyes, *'hear* the sound of the birds at sunrise' with your ears, *'smell* the scent of the many multicolored flowers' with your nose, *'taste* the salt from the sea breeze' with your tongue, and *'feel* the soft grass' beneath your feet.

Common Problems with Imagery Training:
Intruding Thoughts ·

Be patient with yourself as you begin to learn mental relaxation. Complete concentration, even on pleasant images, requires a great deal of practice. Do not get upset if unwanted thoughts come to your mind. This happens even to the most practiced masters of other mental techniques like yoga and meditation.

Being forewarned is being forearmed. Knowing that unwanted thoughts may come to your mind will help you treat these thoughts calmly. Tell yourself that the thoughts will soon pass if you do not pay attention to them and if you return to your pleasant image. Do not fight them. Let them gently pass. This is where the practice comes in. If you get upset about all these thoughts racing by, you will be increasing your stress rather than decreasing it. Allow the thoughts to leave your mind as easily as they came into your mind. Simply refocus on the imagery once again. Every time you find yourself distracted, gently refocus on the imagery.

If you continue to have difficulty with intruding thoughts, you may want to begin using the thought-stopping technique that was mentioned briefly in the deep muscle relaxation chapter. Now, after saying 'Stop!' quickly refocus on the imagery you were trying to visualize. This two-step technique can be used whenever you find yourself preoccupied and unable to shake a thought and return to the task at hand.

Helpful Hints to Tape and Self-Instruction Users

Make your images your own. Only you can experience and know what images are relaxing to you. Also, only you can know what images and scenes are upsetting and should not be used. Work on having at least one personally relaxing scene that you use for relaxation.

Practice letting your personally relaxing image come rapidly into your mind. Take a deep breath and imagine breathing in the clean air from your special image. As you breathe out, feel the relaxation spread over your body and allow yourself to be in that comfortable place for a brief moment. When you return to whatever you were doing, bring with you the feelings of relaxation from your personally relaxing scene.

Using Relaxation Tapes

If you are using recorded relaxation exercises, schedule times now and begin listening to the tape on visual imagery. Before and after each practice session, remember to list your overall relaxation levels on the Home Practice Chart on the last pages of this book.

Guiding Yourself

If you will be guiding yourself through the relaxation exercise, review the directions below. You may find it helpful to read the directions several times. You may also want to ask someone to read the visual imagery instructions to you. If possible, you may want to record these instructions on a tape, and then use the tape to practice. In either case, the instructions should be read slowly and calmly.

More Helpful Hints

Continue using progressive, deep muscle, and autogenic relaxation whenever you can. Be sure to keep checking and decreasing your muscle tension and autonomic arousal by using the cues and signs you have made for yourself. These methods will not only help you enjoy the health benefits of the relaxation response but will also increase your receptivity to the wondrous world around you.

OUTLINE FOR IMAGERY TRAINING

I. BASIC TECHNIQUE
   A. Form a clear image of a pleasant scene.
   B. Try to include images from other senses such as
      1. Smell – 'smell the scent of flowers.'

2. Touch – 'feel the grass beneath your feet.'
3. Sound – 'hear the birds singing in the trees.'
4. Taste – 'taste the salt air on your lips.'

II. SUGGESTED IMAGES

   A. Tropical island
1. You are on a mountaintop.
2. Below is a tropical rain forest.
3. The morning rains are ending.
4. In the distance is a white, sandy beach and palm trees.
   B. Cloud
1. A cloud gently floats down.
2. It surrounds your body and supports you completely.
3. You are in the cloud and gently float off in a gentle breeze.
   C. Valley
1. The cloud floats down to a green valley.
2. Water laps against the shore of a small lake.
3. You get into a small boat and begin to float gently.
4. You move into a stream and drift until the boat washes up against a shore.
   D. Willow tree
1. You recline next to a willow tree.
2. You begin to sleep and dream of other images:
     a. Sunny beach
     b. Field of wildflowers
     c. Cool forest
     d. Log cabin
     e. Clear stream
     f. Sloping hill

III. RETURN TO ACTIVITY BY COUNTING FORWARD FROM ONE TO THREE

WORD-BY-WORD IMAGERY TRAINING

Preparation   *Spend a little time getting as comfortable as you can. Move around if necessary as you get into a very comfortable position.*

Breathing	*Close your eyes and take a deep breath ... Breathe out very slowly and easily. Take a second deep breath ... Slowly breathe out. As you do, feel yourself floating down. Concentrate on your breathing ... Allow your breathing to become smooth and rhythmic.*
Island Imagery	*Picture yourself on a mountaintop, above a tropical rain forest on a small island. The morning rains have finished, and the wind is carrying the clouds away. The sky is clear and blue, with the warm tropical sun shining down.*
	You can see below you the bright green trees in the rain forest. The raindrops on the leaves are reflecting the bright morning sun. Artistically scattered within the dense greenery are bright, colorful flowers: reds, yellows, and blues.
	In the far distance you can see a line of coconut palms all along the sugar-white, sandy beach. Beyond that, as far as you can see, is crystal-clear, brilliantly blue water.
Cloud Imagery	*The sky is completely clear, except for one small, fluffy cloud that drifts alone in the gentle breeze until it is directly over you. Slowly this little cloud begins to sink down upon you ... It is a very pleasant, delightful feeling. As the small, fluffy cloud moves down across your face, you feel the cool, moist touch of it on your forehead and on your cheeks. As it moves down your body, all tension slowly slips away, and you find yourself letting go completely.*
	The soft cloud moves across your shoulders, your chest and upper back, and across your arms as it gently brings with it a feeling of complete relaxation. It sinks down around your waist, your lower back, your hips, and your legs; and it moves down around you, bringing a deep feeling of relaxation. Then the little cloud sinks underneath you, and you are now floating on it. The

128

cloud holds you up perfectly and safely. It is a pleasant feeling.

You are now lying back in relaxation on the soft cloud. The warm tropical sun is shining. Your body is warm from the sun but still with the soft moist touch of coolness on your forehead and face. You are feeling very pleasant. You are held up comfortably and securely.

The little cloud begins to drift downwind, and from your safe position on the cloud, you can see the world go by below you. There is a gentle, pleasant, rocking motion as you drift along. All your cares and concerns are left behind you. The cloud is magic and can take you any place you want to go, as it silently floats along.

Valley Imagery

In the far distance, you see a delightful green valley. The valley is between some gently sloping mountains. This is a place where you can be completely at peace and totally happy. Gradually, the fluffy cloud takes you drifting down, through the sky, to this beautiful place.

As you move into this valley, the cloud gently comes to the ground and stops. You get off the soft cloud in this beautiful place, and you are completely at peace and alone.

Take some time to look around at the fresh, green valley. You are next to a lake. Listen to the birds. Feel the sun shining on you. The scent of spring is in the air.

Lake Imagery

The water is just barely lapping along the shore of the lake. You see a small boat tied there. You enter the boat and find some blankets in the bottom. Now, lying on the soft blankets, gently untie the boat. You are floating in the quiet, shallow lake. The boat is rocking gently from the motion of the water, as it drifts on and on. The boat drifts gently on and on, rocking and massaging.

As the boat carries you along, the lake lazily

flows into a stream. Feel the warm sunlight once again. There is a soft breeze as you continue to drift. You feel relaxed, peaceful, and calm. The gentle rocking motion massages you with feelings of peace. All is well. Your state of relaxation will become more and more profound as the boat gently tosses to and fro.

You drift deeper and deeper into your feelings of relaxation. As you continue to drift, become aware of the sounds of nature: the soft breeze, the lapping water, and the birds and animals on the shore. Smell the grass and flowers as the breeze brings you their pleasant scents. You are lazily drifting deeper and deeper into a profound feeling of peace and pleasantness until very slowly and gently, the small boat washes up against the shore. You remain in a very complete and total state of relaxation.

Willow Tree Imagery

Get out of the boat and take the soft blanket with you. Walk up the slightly sloping bank to a huge willow tree that hangs out over the water. You feel drowsy. The gentle, rocking motion of the boat has made you very, very drowsy.

The old willow tree has thick, soft grass around the base, and you find a perfect spot to spread your blanket for a comfortable bed. There are some roots above the ground, and you rest your head, as you snuggle into a restful position. The temperature is perfect, not too cool and not too hot. Everything is restful and peaceful.

Dream Scenes

Imagine you fall asleep under the willow tree and begin to dream. Practice a few more scenes in your imagination as you dream. This will help you know that you can go to any relaxing place you wish to by using the power of visual imagery.

Beach Imagery

Now, see yourself walking along a warm, sunny beach at the edge of crystal-clear blue water. Hear the roar of the waves. *Feel the clean sand under your feet. Smell the clean salt air. (Pause.)*

Field of Flowers Imagery

From there, move to a picture of yourself sitting in a field of wildflowers on a spring day. The temperature is just right. The air smells fresh with wildflowers, and the sounds of birds and animals are very soothing. (Pause.)

Forest Imagery

Then move to a view of yourself walking through a forest. You are under the cool shade of the tall trees, and the sunlight moves through the trees to the ground. See the ferns and small plants. Smell the clean freshness. Feel the gentle breeze blowing through the trees. Hear the birds, very high in the trees.

Stream Imagery

See yourself standing beside a clear stream as it rushes across the rocks with a pleasant gurgle. Feel the coolness and moistness of the spray on your forehead and cheeks as the stream splashes off the rocks, as you bend down to get a drink of the crystal-clear water.

Sloping Hill Imagery

Then see yourself moving down a long, gently sloping hill in the country, with the soft feel of the wind in your hair and on your face. As you move slowly through the green grass, you are happy, smiling, very comfortable, and deeply relaxed.

Using Imagery

You can use the power of your imagination to create a feeling of relaxation whenever you want. If during the rest of your day, or for that matter at any time, you find yourself getting upset about something, remember the feelings of relaxation you have just enjoyed. Before you get upset, take a deep breath; and, as you breathe out, see yourself in whatever place you find relaxing. For a little while, let yourself enjoy all the calm feelings you have with your peaceful imagery. This will allow you to control situations rather than being controlled by them.

Return to
Activity

Now, count from one to three. As you take a deep breath, silently say each number. When you reach three, open your eyes. You will be relaxed and alert. When you open your eyes, you will find yourself back in the place where you started your imagery exercises. The world around you will seem slower and more calm, and you will be more relaxed and peaceful.

One, relaxed, but more alert . . . Two, mentally wide awake . . . Three, eyes open, alert and refreshed.

Part Three

Overcoming Your
Special
Stressors

11 Stress in the Here and Now

Recognizing Your Own Stress Response

Knowing how to recognize your own stress response is similar to knowing when your car sounds 'funny' or when the engine is 'pinging.' If you drive your car every day, you may be able to tell when something is in need of repair by the way it feels or sounds. If you have repaired the car yourself, you may even know what is wrong. In general, the more knowledge you have about automobiles, the more likely you will be to notice the changes and know if a repair is needed.

The more we study our bodies and how they respond to stress, the more we will be able to prevent major stress problems. If we have been driving ourselves beyond reasonable limits, we may have the same trouble our car would have if we always drove it all day at eighty miles an hour. We may not notice the little things that are going wrong that may lead to major problems. Likewise, if we get used to a strange sound or racing motor, it may be hard to hear, even when we listen for it.

If you have learned to ignore your personal stress response, try studying your body's response during an exciting part of a movie or television show. This is like taking a drive to listen to your car.

In a stress management group for hypertensive executives, one of the authors learned that many participants had increased blood pressure during TV programs. Several executives began to monitor their blood pressures during the half time of football games on television. Their blood pressures were significantly higher than before the game. The executives then began using half times for their Sunday afternoon practice sessions. Realizing that stressful situations at work and home were having similar effects, they started monitoring their blood pressure levels and analyzing the stressors in their lives. They

135

began using coffee breaks and lunch hours to assess their stress levels and to practice relaxation.

Your body's response to an exciting show will help teach you what happens to your body when you are uptight. Much of the pleasure associated with watching a show is your emotional involvement as the actors realistically portray the drama. If you take time to notice, you may find your heart pounding during a chase scene or your stomach full of butterflies during a horror picture.

The Habit of Being Uptight

Being uptight in the real world can produce discomfort and feelings of terror even greater than when viewing a horror film. Think of common, everyday stressors such as traffic jams, deadlines, problems at work, or quarrels at home. This is not an easy world in which to relax.

In an unusually stressful situation, you may notice your emergency response as your heart beats faster, muscles tense, and blood pressure soars. But all too often, our stress is slowly and steadily grinding away at us. Many people stop listening to their stress warnings and may not realize how tense they have been until their daily headache starts pounding.

An active executive may have 250 blood pressure peaks during each day, until eventually his blood pressure stays up permanently. The habit of being uptight is something we cultivate, but relaxation can also be cultivated.

Another Habit: Quiet Confidence

Imagine your heart slowing down, your breathing becoming smooth and rhythmic, and all tension slowly slipping away. Now, imagine someone rushing in to ask for an important decision. You slowly breathe in and slowly breathe out. As you do, your body relaxes and your mind clears of distractions; you make the decision calmly. This moment of relaxation is often seen by others as a sign of quiet confidence. Imagine how good it must feel to have cultivated such a habit.

One of the first steps to making this form of relaxation a habit is to recognize the habit of being uptight. Each of us responds to different stressors, and stressors vary in the amount of response they trigger. For example, a student may experience a great deal of stress when taking an examination in a subject he finds difficult or uninteresting. Before, during, and after the test he may experience constant worry.

The same student may respond in a totally different fashion to a test in his favorite subject. He may still experience stress in preparing for this test, but it will be less intense. He may go through the same activities to prepare for each test, but the emotional and mental stress will be different.

In modern life, stress from emotional frustration is more likely to produce disease than is physical stress. One famous cardiovascular surgeon works eighteen to twenty hours a day. He is often on his feet and usually takes the stairs instead of the elevator to be sure he gets exercise. Although his schedule is hectic and demanding, he seldom becomes ill or experiences the effects of chronic stress. Why? Because he is not experiencing distress from a job he finds frustrating. He is doing work he enjoys and finds meaningful.

In our complex world, we may realistically find that not everything about our lives and jobs is as rewarding as we would like. Sometimes jobs are frustrating. Retirement is sometimes boring. Work may be good if you achieve something meaningful by doing it. It may wear you out if you never seem to get anything done or if what you get done is not important to you. Marriage and family life are also frustrating and stressful at times. By learning how you currently respond to the stress in your everyday living, you will be able to learn how to respond differently in the future. First, we must learn to recognize the stressors in our lives.

Charting Your Stress

Make a chart or a list of your current stressors. You may find Chapter 3 helpful in listing the stressors you are currently experiencing. Try to become more and more aware of your stressors. As you do, your list should grow.

To quantify how much current stress you experience, label it from 0 to 10 SUD (Subjective Unit of Distress), with 0 being no stress and 10 being the maximum you could imagine. Also, consider whether relaxation and controlling your body's stress response would be helpful. You may not find stressors such as noise or pregnancy distressful. List such stressors to help you understand all areas of stress in your life. Other stressors you face may benefit from relaxation by helping you feel calm, in control, or in less pain.

In the next chapter, we will use the list of your current stressors to practice stress management techniques for each of the major stressors in your life. Update your list frequently by adding, removing, or changing stressors.

12 Image Rehearsal: Tapping Your Brain's Success Circuits

You have now learned progressive and deep muscle relaxation to relax muscles over which you have voluntary control. You have also learned autogenic training to help you relax and regulate those parts of your body that are usually not under your voluntary control. In addition, you know how to relax by using visual images of pleasant scenes. Now you are ready to apply these skills in new ways to deal with some of the major stressors in your life.

Choosing a Target Stressor

Most of us have some areas of our lives that are particularly stressful. In the last chapter, you began to list your personal stressors. We would like you to go back to this list and group them into a few difficult situations. These will be called your target stressors. Choose one of these to work on.

Some people choose talking in front of a group or with a person of the opposite sex. Many people select a work stressor. If you have a phobia, such as a fear of heights, air travel, crowds, or closed spaces, you may choose this as your target stressor. If you are reducing your weight, you may want to focus on your eating behavior in difficult situations. If you are stopping smoking, you may want to work on scenes where the urge to smoke is strong. It is often stressful to resist urges when you are modifying harmful habits.

All of us have our own particular stressors. Pick one that is not the most difficult for you but still gives you a good deal of trouble. Use the SUDs (Subjective Units of Distress) rating to decide on the stressor's level of difficulty. It is best to pick a mild to moderate stressor so as to increase the likelihood of success before you tackle your most upsetting stressors. But you should pick one that is important enough to you to make your efforts seem worthwhile and keep your level of motivation high.

Research and clinical work have shown that if we imagine stressors while feeling calm and relaxed, we can gain control and mastery over them. In this way, the techniques of relaxation that you have learned can be transferred to any situation you find upsetting. But first, we need to build a twenty-step stress ladder.

A stress ladder is a list that goes from the smallest or lowest stressor to the largest or highest stressor. In this case, we want you to take small steps to deal with one of these stressors. If you have a good deal of trouble with examinations, for example, you may have picked examinations as your mild-to-moderate stressor. You probably find certain parts of taking an examination less upsetting than others. Studying for an exam that is three months away is not as upsetting as studying the night before or sitting down to take the actual examination.

Before you build your stress ladder, turn to pages 141–2 and study the ladder constructed by a student with test anxiety. Notice that the closer he got to the exam time, the more stress he experienced and the higher he placed the stressor on his ladder. Notice also that each step is clear and specific.

Building a useful stress ladder is not as easy as it looks. Therapists spend a good deal of time with patients tailor-making the ladders. There are 'prefabricated' ladders for some stressors, but the best ones reflect the person's real-life experiences and individuality. What is very stressful for one test-anxious person may be only mildly stressful for another. Another important aspect of a good ladder is that the steps between rungs are very small and about the same distance apart.

To help you organize your ladder into small, equal steps, use 3 × 5 filing cards or cut paper into small strips. Start by writing down one step of a stressor on each card or slip. Write as many as you can up to about twenty. Think of a two- or three-word code for each card and write it on the top of the card. Then take these cards and arrange them from the least to the most stressful.

AN EXAMPLE OF A TWENTY-STEP STRESS LADDER FOR TEST ANXIETY

Code Words for Stressor	Full Description of Stressor
1. *Teacher announces final* :	Teacher announces final exam in three months
2. *Buying text books* :	Buying books for the course and thinking about the exam
3. *Studying month before* :	Studying when the final exam is one month away
4. *Talking month before* :	Talking with friends about the exam one month before.
5. *Studying week before* :	Studying when the final exam is one week away
6. *Talking week before* :	Talking with friends about the exam one week before
7. *Studying day before* :	Studying when the final exam is the next day
8. *Talking day before* :	Talking with friends about the exam the next day
9. *Studying night before* :	Studying the night before the final exam
10. *Lying in bed night before* :	Lying in bed the night before the final exam
11. *Talking hour before* :	Talking with friends about the exam one hour before

Code Words for Stressor	Full Description of Stressor
12. Walking to building	Walking to the building where I will take the exam
13. Entering building	Entering the building where I will take the exam
14. Entering classroom	Entering the classroom where I will take the exam
15. Finding a seat	Finding a seat where I will take the exam
16. Watching teacher hand out	Watching the teacher hand out the exam
17. Reading directions	Reading the directions on the examination
18. 1st question not understood	Not understanding the first question on the exam
19. Forgetting and guessing	Not remembering and having to guess on the exam
20. Rushing to finish	Rushing to finish the exam when others have left early

Using Relaxation Tapes

If you are using recorded relaxation exercises, schedule times now and listen to a tape on image rehearsal or stress management. The tape will help you use four steps on the stress ladder you just created to desensitize yourself to four mildly stressful situations.

You can also use a tape recorder to tape and later present sounds associated with the steps of your stress ladder. For example, one flight-phobic executive asked his wife to take a flight and tape the sounds of the airplane on the runway and in the air, as well as the voices of the ticket clerk and the pilot over the intercoms. He then played the four-step relaxation tape on one recorder and turned it off to listen to these air travel sounds on the second recorder when the instructions were given to visualize those steps of his stress ladder.

Guiding Yourself

If you will be guiding yourself through these exercises, review the directions below. You may find it helpful to read the directions several times. You may also want to ask someone to read the image rehearsal instructions to you. Be sure the person reads the instructions slowly and calmly. If possible, you may want to record those instructions on a tape and then use the tape to practice. Set aside about fifteen to thirty minutes for each practice session.

Helpful Hints for Tape and Self-Instruction Users

During the next week, practice once or twice a day on your four-step stress ladder. Be sure to get a firm footing and become fully relaxed on the first four steps of your ladder before you use a new four-step ladder. One way of doing this is to make sure your home practice ratings of relaxation and image clarity are as good or better than the ratings you made of your responses to the earlier tapes. This should take only one or two practice sessions.

Sometimes the first step of a stress ladder is too anxiety-provoking. If this is the case, you may find it helpful to lower the stress of the whole ladder. The test-anxious student whose original ladder appeared above did this by using the ladder for an easy subject before applying it to his most difficult subject. Another way of dealing with the problem of getting started is to add easier steps before the original first step. Practice these before trying the original first step again.

Occasionally, people get stuck on one step of a ladder and can't go up to the next one without a lot of anxiety. The problem may be the distance between the two steps, and the solution is to add more steps between the step you are on and the next one.

When you have succeeded in desensitizing yourself to the first four steps, you can replace them with additional stressful situations from your twenty-step stress ladder. Continue doing this once or twice a day during the next week until you have climbed all the way up the stress ladder for the stressor you have been working on. When you finish one stress ladder, choose another, more challenging stressor. Build another stress ladder for the stressor you choose. You can continue this process until you have conquered your most difficult stressors.

It is often helpful to practice with a friend. You can help each other build your stress ladders and guide one another using the word-by-word instructions that follow.

Mental Simulation and Rehearsal

Most athletes use imagery to rehearse winning performances in their sport. In fact, a study involving college students demonstrated that image rehearsal can be almost as effective as real practice. A number of students were tested for accuracy in basketball shooting and divided into three groups. One group was told to come back in twenty days but not to practice. Another group was asked to practice shooting baskets twenty minutes per day. The last group was asked to rehearse in their minds shooting the baskets for twenty minutes per day. They were told to watch the ball go through the hoop and hear the swish of the net. After twenty days, the group that did nothing was retested and showed no improvement. When the image-rehearsal group was retested, the improvement was about the same (23 percent) as for the group that had actually practiced (24 percent)! This is a good example of how rehearsing success helps people become winners. You will not find successful athletes rehearsing failures. In fact, if they do not play well, they often will immediately rehearse doing better the next time.

You may also want to use your imagination to rehearse acting in a skillful and relaxed manner in the face of your life challenges. You will not only become less anxious, but you will build up your confidence and your ability to handle the situation. The winners in life practice and rehearse every situation that they find difficult. Make it your goal to experience your stressors in a calm fashion.

To strengthen your stress management skills, you may also wish to practice stress reduction while watching a movie or a show on television. When you are in the middle of a tense scene, use your training to relax. You may be surprised at how calm you can become after a while. This is very good practice for the stress reduction you will want to use in your everyday life.

'Taking It to the Streets'

Once you have desensitized yourself to a stressor in your imagination, it is time to try out your new skill. The most common mistake people make in applying what they have learned is to try their most difficult stressor first. Practice relaxing and being calm first with your easier situations. Go slowly up the ladders in order of their difficulty. Get a good firm footing on one step before moving up to the next. If the going gets rough and your anxiety is too great, alternate between imagination and real-life practice or add more steps to your ladders. With practice, you will be surprised how easily you handle your stressors, and your self-confidence will grow.

WORD-BY-WORD LADDER CLIMBING AND SCENE REHEARSING

Getting Comfortable	*Let's begin by getting totally relaxed all over. Spend a little time getting as comfortable as you can. Move around, if necessary, as you get into a comfortable position. Become as completely relaxed as possible.*
Focusing on Breathing	*Focus your attention fully on your breathing. Imagine your breathing is as automatic as the ocean waves, rolling in . . . and out . . . in . . . and out. Silently say to yourself, 'Breathing, smooth and rhythmic.' 'Breathing, smooth and rhythmic.' Become aware of the air flowing in and out of your lungs.*
Relaxation	*As you breathe, imagine air moving through your body in massaging waves of relaxation. Feel the waves of relaxation moving through your chest and shoulders, down into your arms, through your back muscles, down into your hips and legs. With each wave of relaxation, feel the growing heaviness and warmth in your arms and legs.*
Ten to Zero	*Now, I am going to count down from ten to zero. Each time I move from a higher number to a*

*lower number, you will feel more relaxed, even
more relaxed than you feel right now. When I
reach the number zero, you will feel profoundly
relaxed. Ten . . . more and more relaxed. Nine
. . . 'I am calm.' Eight . . . relaxing deeper and
deeper. Seven . . . calm and peaceful. Six . . .
peaceful and calm. Five . . . heavy, warm, and
comfortable. Four . . . more and more relaxed.
Three . . . feeling very quiet. Two . . . muscles
like jelly. One . . . deeper and deeper. Zero . . .
profound relaxation.*

Limp Rag Doll

*You are becoming as relaxed and limp as an old
rag doll, and you really are that relaxed. See
yourself in your imagination, lying back, warm,
comfortable, calm, peaceful, and relaxed, totally
relaxed, as limp and loose as a rag doll.*

In a Meadow

*You might want to imagine that you are lying in
a beautiful meadow. You may know of a place
such as this; if so, imagine you are there. If you
don't know such a place, use your imagination to
create it: a beautiful meadow with the temperature just right, not too hot, and not too cool. Try
to see yourself there in the meadow. You are perfectly comfortable on a bed of very soft, green
grass. Feel a beautiful and warm sense of relaxation all around your body. You have nothing to be
worried about. Just let go and feel the relaxation.*

*Continue to stay in a peaceful, safe, imaginary
meadow, and try to keep the feelings of peace and
calm as we now imagine some scenes that may be
slightly stressful (anxiety-producing or anger-
provoking). Try to see the scenes as clearly as you
can, but know in your mind that* if, at any time,
the scene makes you uncomfortable, you can
immediately return to the pleasant image of
yourself lying peacefully in your meadow.

Success Rehearsal

See yourself very much in control, confident, and

146

the master of the scene. See yourself very success-
fully meeting the problems head-on, with confi-
dence and control. Now begin.

Scene One   *Look at the first scene. See yourself in control.*
               Master the scene. Pause thirty seconds and
               visualize the scene in your mind.

Return to the *Now, leave that scene behind and return to your*
Meadow and   *peaceful meadow. Think to yourself: 'Face relax.*
Relaxation   *Neck relax. Shoulders relax. Arms relax. Chest*
               relax. Stomach relax. Hips, legs, and feet relax.'
               Remember the relaxation you have felt before and
               let it flow back into your body. You are safe and
               comfortable, deeply relaxed.

'I Am Peaceful *Say to yourself, 'I am peaceful and calm.' 'I am*
and Calm'   *calm and peaceful.' Once again begin to imagine*
               the same scene. (You can go on to another scene if
               the last scene did not trigger a lot of stress or
               tension.) Picture yourself in total command of the
               situation.

Scene Two   *Pause thirty seconds and visualize the scene in*
               your mind.

Back to the   *Now, in your mind return to the meadow. See*
Meadow   *yourself there, very comfortable, very much at*
               peace. Say to yourself, 'I am calm,' each time you
               breathe out. 'I am calm.' 'I am calm.' You are
               alert and awake but fully at ease. Now, pay
               attention to your body and use the natural
               abilities of your mind to relax. Focus on feelings
               of deep, deep relaxation. You feel good. You feel
               refreshed. 'I am at peace.' Say this to yourself. 'I
               am at peace.' Feel the peace and calm throughout
               your body.

Scene Three   *Now, once again, imagine the scene you are work-*
               ing on. Begin seeing it now, and try to make it as

147

clear as possible. This is your time to be master of that scene. You are in control. Pause thirty seconds and visualize the scene in your mind.

Return to the Meadow

Leave that scene now, and return to the image of yourself lying comfortably in the pleasant meadow. The temperature is just right, and you feel very deeply relaxed. Concentrate on waves of relaxation moving through your body. Waves of relaxation flood into every part of your body, as you are lying in your meadow.

If you find any tension, any tension at all, let that part of your body relax. Try to remain mentally alert, and don't let yourself get tired or fall asleep because you need to see the scenes as clearly as possible.

Scene Four

Try another scene, scene four, if you are ready. See it clearly and stay in control of it. Pause thirty seconds and visualize the scene in your mind.

Return to the Meadow

Now, in your mind, return to the meadow and relax.

More Scenes

(You may wish to go through more scenes. If not, then complete the following exercises.) Your practice is over for today, but spend a few more minutes being as relaxed as possible. As you practice thinking of stressful life areas (anxiety or anger scenes) and seeing yourself in command and relaxed, you will continue to gain more and more control. Soon you will be able to face real-life situations with greater confidence. You will control these situations, rather than allowing them to control you. You will have the power to imagine yourself in your relaxing place. You will be able to do this quickly and easily, getting control of yourself and then facing life's challenges.

Awakening Safely   *Now, see yourself safe and secure, exactly where you started these exercises. Remove yourself from the meadow. Count forward from one to five. Open your eyes on five. One, still profoundly relaxed. Two, very relaxed. Three, relaxed, but more alert. Four, eyes open. Five, wide awake. Before getting up, stretch your muscles. Take a deep breath, and you will feel confident, alert, and refreshed.*

Part Four

*Attacking Your Stressful
Behaviors,
Thoughts,
and Attitudes*

13   Life-Change Management

Most of the stressors we have been learning to recognize and manage are day-to-day, week-to-week stressors. These might be called the stressors of the prevailing winds – the stressors that prevail in our daily lives.

In Chapter 3, we asked you to consider some stressors under a category called 'change stressors.' Just like weather conditions, change stressors are more intense and variable than the prevailing winds. They can range from bad weather to scorching sunlight to tropical storms.

It is said that about the only thing that we can count on in life, besides death and taxes, is change. For better or for worse, nothing ever stands still. Modern life presents us with more change than ever before. Alvin Toffler wrote a popular book about the acceleration in the rate of change called *Future Shock*. We change everything rapidly: where we live and work, our friends, and even our spouses.

Change of any sort can be scary or exciting, and it usually triggers our stress response. Some people make a change in lifestyle to reduce stress, but it backfires. During his first interview, one of our patients described why he had moved to the Southwest. He had gone to a counselor in Florida, who had listened to his problems and suggested that his anxiety might be the result of difficulties in his marriage, his job, or his friendships, so he had filed for divorce, gotten fired, and moved to Texas! His decisions may have shown poor judgment, but many of us make other decisions that in advertently add up to just as much stress.

In this chapter you will have the chance to chart the changes in your life. In the last part of this chapter, you will learn ways to manage these life changes better.

From the Laboratory

Dr. Thomas Holmes and Dr. Richard Rahe, at the University of Washington School of Medicine, have made major breakthroughs in our understanding of the effects of life changes on health and disease. Convinced by their own experiences as physicians, and following up on the earlier work of Dr. Adolf Meyer at Johns Hopkins and Dr. Harold Wolff at Cornell University, Drs. Holmes and Rahe set out to measure the life changes that seem to precede illnesses.

From case histories of five thousand patients, they gathered a long list of life events that seemed to precede major illnesses. They then asked about four hundred people to compare the amount, intensity, and length of time they needed to adjust to each life event on the list. The people were asked to assume that marriage had a certain numerical value, use it as a standard of comparison, and assign a numerical value to each of the other life events on the list.

Scientists began using this scaling system to understand and predict susceptibility to illness. Thousands of individuals reported the number of times they had experienced the events. Holmes, Rahe, and others multiplied the number of times an event was experienced by the readjustment value given to the event and summed these products to find a life-change score for each person. Those who had a high life-change score were much more likely to contract an illness following the events. The illnesses ranged widely, from accidents to alcoholism, from cancer to psychiatric disorders, and from flu to the common cold.

Charting the Winds of Change

Carefully follow the directions on the Social Readjustment Rating Scale. Take your time and try to include any event that is similar to the one given in the scale. Sometimes a friend or a family member can help you. They may also want to take the test. When you are finished, total up your life-change units for the past year.

When to Increase Your Health Insurance Coverage

The studies that Drs. Holmes, Rahe, and other scientists have conducted provide us with a way of looking at our life changes. In general, a score of 150 to 300 is considered moderate, while a score above 300 is considered high. High scores have been correlated with susceptibility to illness and accidents in large group studies. High life-change scores have even been associated with injury among college football players. But if you scored above 300, it does not mean you are going to get sick or have an accident.

People seem to respond on an individual basis depending upon how much hassle each life event creates for a particular person. For example, people who have clear and meaningful goals or tend to be stimulus-seekers seem to be able to withstand more change. A high score for someone in distress, however, means that it might be wise for that person to increase health insurance or to learn how to manage life change more effectively. Regardless of your score, you may find the following techniques helpful.

How to Manage Life-Change Stressors

The first step that Dr. Holmes suggests is that we all become familiar with the life events and become aware of the amount of change they require. This can be done by discussing the number of points given to each life event with a friend. You could also simply review your life and think about the changes that you have experienced.

To familiarize yourself with the values, see if you agree or disagree with the ratings that were given by hundreds of people. Obviously, some events are easier for you to adjust to than they would be for other people. Likewise, some events are more difficult for you to cope with than they would be for other people. The points given are averages, but, in general, they apply to all of us.

Don't be fooled by the tendency to view positive changes such as marital reconciliation (45 points) or gaining a new family member (39 points) as free of stress. These also take a great deal of adaptive energy. Even outstanding personal achievement takes a toll of 28 points.

Dr. Holmes suggests putting the scale where you and your family can see it frequently. We often suggest to our patients that they reassess their current life changes at the end of every month, when they pay the bills and reassess their financial changes. It is helpful to keep the rating scale with the folder where you place the bills. This will help to remind you to take a good look at your current life conditions every month.

THE SOCIAL READJUSTMENT RATING SCALE*

Directions: Read each Life Event and indicate in the space provided the number of times you have experienced the event in the last year. Multiply the number of times you experienced the event by the points next to it and total up the products.

Life Event	Stress Value		Number of times you experienced the event last year		Your total life change scores
1) Death of spouse	100	X		=	
2) Divorce	73	X		=	
3) Marital separation from mate	65	X		=	
4) Detention in jail or other institution	63	X		=	
5) Death of a close family member	63	X		=	
6) Major personal injury or illness	53	X		=	
7) Marriage	50	X	1	=	50
8) Being fired from work	47	X		=	
9) Marital reconciliation with mate	45	X		=	
10) Retirement from work	45	X		=	
11) Major change in the health or behavior of a family member	44	X		=	
12) Pregnancy	40	X		=	
13) Sexual difficulties	39	X		=	
14) Gaining a new family member (e.g. through birth, adoption, oldster moving in, etc.)	39	X	3	=	117
15) Major business readjustment (e.g. merger, reorganization, bankruptcy, etc.)	39	X		=	
16) Major change in financial state (e.g. a lot worse off or a lot better off than usual)	38	X		=	
17) Death of a close friend	37	X		=	
18) Changing to a different line of work	36	X	1	=	36
19) Major change in the number of arguments with spouse (e.g. either a lot more or a lot less than usual regarding childbearing, personal habits, etc.)	35	X		=	
20) Taking on a mortgage greater than $10,000 (e.g. purchasing a home, business, etc.)	31	X	1	=	31
21) Foreclosure on a mortgage or loan	30	X	1	=	30

22) Major change in responsibilities at work
(e.g. promotion, demotion, lateral transfer)............. 29 X _____ = _____

23) Son or daughter leaving home (e.g. marriage,
attending college, etc.)........................... 29 X _____ = _____

24) Inlaw troubles....................................... 29 X _____ = _____

25) Outstanding personal achievement .... 28 X _____ = _____

26) Wife beginning or ceasing work outside the home....... 26 X _____ = _____

27) Beginning or ceasing formal schooling................. 26 X _____ = _____

28) Major change in living conditions (e.g. building
a new home, remodeling, deterioration of home
or neighborhood)................................... 25 X __1__ = __25__

29) Revision of personal habits (e.g. dress,
manners, associations, etc.)....................... 24 X __1__ = __24__

30) Troubles with the boss.............................. 23 X _____ = _____

31) Major change in working hours or conditions .... 20 X _____ = _____

32) Change in residence .... 20 X __1__ = __20__

33) Changing to a new school .... 20 X _____ = _____

34) Major change in usual type and/or amount of recreation..... 19 X _____ = _____

35) Major change in church activities (e.g. a lot
more or a lot less than usual) .... 19 X _____ = _____

36) Major change in social activities (e.g. clubs,
dancing, movies, visiting, etc.)...................... 18 X _____ = _____

37) Taking on a mortgage or loan less than $10,000
(e.g. purchasing a car, TV, freezer, etc.) .... 17 X _____ = _____

38) Major change in sleeping habits (e.g. a lot more
or a lot less sleep, or change in part of day when asleep)..... 16 X _____ = _____

39) Major change in number of family get-togethers
(e.g. a lot more or a lot less than usual)............... 15 X _____ = _____

40) Major change in eating habits (e.g. a lot more
or a lot less food intake, or very different
meal hours or surroundings)......................... 15 X _____ = _____

41) Vacation .... 13 X _____ = _____

42) Christmas .... 12 X __1__ = __12__

43) Minor violations of the law (e.g. traffic tickets,
jaywalking, disturbing the peace, etc.) .... 11 X _____ = _____

GRAND TOTAL .... __347__

Anticipating Life Changes

Dr. Holmes also suggests anticipating life changes, planning for them in advance, and pacing yourself. Just as weather conditions change on a seasonal basis, many life changes can be predicted. Christmas and many vacations are seasonal. In addition, some events follow the seasons of life. For example, retirement from work, children leaving home to get married or attend college, and beginning or ending formal schooling are all stressful changes.

Still other life events can be planned well in advance, so that we don't have to face too many life changes in too short a time. For example, we can choose the date for our marriage, we can apply for new work now or later, and we can delay buying a home or moving. If some of the things we have less control over occur, such as being fired from work, we can put off making the changes over which we do have control. It is similar to taking our temperature. If we are living life at a near feverish pace, recording our change score can remind us to cool off and put the freeze on big changes.

Other changes in our society can be anticipated by reading or hearing the predictions of scientists who use the trends and events in our current situation to project future developments. An excellent cassette program, entitled *Encounters with the Future*, by Marvin Cetron, Ph.D., and Peter O'Toole is listed in Appendix III.

Seasons of Life

Two books have recently appeared that shed light on the predictable crises that people go through in life. Daniel Levinson, Ph.D., wrote *Seasons of a Man's Life*, and Gail Sheehy wrote *Passages*. Both of these books deal with the different predictable crises we are faced with as we go from birth to death.

An important part of your stress management training is to realize that some life crises are predictable. The evolution of our lives is not determined by chance alone. We all go through a series of stable periods alternating with transitional periods. During stable periods, we make certain crucial choices and seek to attain particular goals and values. During transitional periods, we work toward terminating previous patterns and begin to work toward initiating new patterns. Realizing that certain patterns of living occur in a predictable fashion gives us the opportunity to cope with these life changes in a more adaptive and healthy fashion.

Early Adulthood

One of the first major transition periods that adults go through begins at the end of adolescence. This transition may start around the age of seventeen and last until around the age of twenty-two. During this transition, we begin to modify existing relationships with important individuals, groups, and institutions. We make a preliminary step into the adult world. We begin to explore the possibilities of the adult world and to imagine ourselves as a participant in it.

Transition periods do not affect everyone equally. Many individuals will remain in a student/learning capacity throughout the chronological years of seventeen to twenty-two, which may postpone the transition crises of early adulthood.

Entering the Adult World

Typically, an individual will begin to enter the adult world between the ages of twenty-two and twenty-eight. There is a shift from a position of being a child in a family to the position of being a novice adult. Choices are made regarding occupation, relationships, values, and lifestyles.

During the transition into the adult world, a person tends to explore the possibilities of adult living but also avoids making strong commitments. At the same time, and almost paradoxically, a person begins to create a stable life structure. A person tries to avoid making strong commitments and attempts to view all the alternatives but also tries to settle down and become more responsible. This is a time of many crises as one attempts to balance out the conflict between stability and exploration.

During this crisis period, some individuals may capriciously change jobs, relationships, and places of residence. Others find that they make a strong commitment in one sector of life, such as work, but do not make that commitment to other sectors, such as their personal life. Still other individuals will not suffer a great deal from crises during this period and may postpone exploring and questioning their values and goals.

As individuals begin to approach their late twenties, they may begin to question the commitments they have previously made. They may also begin to question whether they want to keep life forever the way they have established it.

Turning Thirty

Around the age of thirty, a major transition period occurs. During this transition period, a person becomes more serious, more restrictive, and more 'for real.' People feel a strong need to move forward and to produce the elements that they may feel are missing from their lives. There is a feeling that perhaps too soon it will be too late. During this period, some people will build upon the past without making fundamental changes, while for others this will be a stressful crisis.

During the transition period around age thirty, marital problems and divorce peak. It is often a time for changes in occupation or for settling down after a period of transient jobs. During the early thirties, many people enter psychotherapy as they experience the strong emotions that often accompany crises.

Settling or Settling Down?

After going through this period of transition, a person reaches a settling-down point that may last from the age of about thirty-two until the ages of thirty-nine or forty. During this period, the major tasks include establishing a place in society and 'making it' in a vocation. Great efforts are made to build a better life and to attain certain goals.

Toward the end of the thirties, a dilemma is reached when an individual wants to be more independent and more true to his or her own wishes. The dilemma is that the person at this stage also wants to continue to retain the respect and reward that he or she has built in the world.

Midlife Transition

The midlife transition, which occurs next, may last roughly from the ages of forty to forty-five. At this time, people may begin to question what they have done with their lives. They try to discover their real values. They look back on their earlier dreams and ask themselves if they still want those dreams.

According to one study of individuals going through the midlife transition, approximately 80 percent of the people experience very severe struggles within themselves and with the external world. The struggles involve questioning virtually every aspect of the life they have created. The person may, at this time, test a variety of new choices out of a need to explore as well as out of confusion.

It is important to realize as you learn how to manage stress that these life changes and crises are very normal parts of development. A transition is often a crisis. But a crisis involves both danger and opportunity. The danger is of losing some security, but the opportunity is of discovering new and untapped inner resources.

People during their midlife crisis often recognize that certain long-held assumptions and beliefs about themselves and the world are not true. They will have gone through a period of seeking to accomplish various goals and fulfill various dreams. But they may find that the dreams they have sought are not the true goals that they want to pursue in life.

Albert Ellis once said that experience is the only thing that we are guaranteed in life. If we set up other ultimate goals, we can find ourselves racing toward them only to be dissatisfied when we reach them. We must also recognize the precariousness and uncertainty of life. It can be taken from us and our loved ones at any time. Perhaps the best goal to strive for in life is to experience fully the richness of living.

This paradox may explain the words of a song that read, 'It is so hard to find, one rich man in a thousand with a satisfied mind.' As we seek to race toward various goals and needs that have been artificially created and may be somewhat illusory, we may find that we grow stressed because we have set up something other than the experiencing of life as an ultimate goal. For example, we may race toward getting certain designer blue jeans only to find out that a new designer is in favor this month. What needs are we trying to fill with designer jeans?

We personally believe it is necessary to think seriously about our goals and the importance we place on achieving them. We hope that the time management chapter will help you establish your true goals. The knowledge of predictable life crises and the identification of valuable goals can help you through the changing seasons of your life.

Boredom

Earlier, we spoke about the stress of boredom. This is also a change stressor because the lack of change often brings on boredom. When we are not excited about what we are doing, we often become depressed, irritated, and uptight. Variety is the spice of life, and without it our senses become dull or we become jumpy. It is during times of boredom that we may wish to consider making some of the changes we can control on the Social Readjustment Rating Scale.

If your score on the Social Readjustment Rating Scale is below 50, it might be a healthy decision to take action to increase your change score. A low score does not mean you are a boring person or that you are necessarily under a lot of stress. But if you have a low score and you feel stressed, you could be experiencing boredom.

You may consider changes such as finding a more rewarding job, changing the number of arguments with a spouse (preferably decreasing them), altering your responsibilities at work, changing your living conditions, revising your personal habits, or changing the type or amount of recreation, church activities, or social activities.

Working Hard at Staying Well

Another way of managing a high level of change stress is to work harder at staying well. You do this by applying the skills that you will learn from this book and slowly adopting healthier living habits. The time to be sure to apply the knowledge in the chapter on nutrition, for example, is when you are experiencing the greatest amount of stress from the prevailing winds or the tropical storms.

Another healthy habit is to get the proper amount of sleep so that you are well rested to face the stress that change can bring. You should also be careful not to neglect your body. During times of change, you need to maintain good hygiene and exercise.

You certainly would not want to change your living habits radically because you would be adding stress. After all, a revision of personal habits adds 24 points, a major change in sleeping habits adds 16 points, a major change in eating habits adds 15 points, and so on. Nevertheless, it is possible to increase your healthy living habits slowly during times of major social readjustment.

A Widow, Mrs. Jones

One of our patients experienced a great deal of social readjustment during a series of life events, and the rating scale was used to help her make a decision regarding still another change she was considering. Mrs. Jones, a thirty-nine-year-old mother of three, lived in a modest home with her husband, who was a salesman. During the previous year, her husband had contracted cancer and died.

Shortly after his death, Mrs. Jones had suffered from severe bronchitis and was hospitalized. She sought stress management and biofeedback training on the advice of a friend whose husband had also died of a chronic disease.

Many issues were discussed during the treatment, particularly her relationship with her husband and his death. In the midst of treatment, Mrs. Jones began discussing her plans for building a new home near a friend who had become ill. She asked the therapist's advice.

To help Mrs. Jones make her decision, the therapist had her complete the Social Readjustment Rating Scale. He suspected that her recent illness might have been partially a result of the tremendous stress she and her family had experienced over the past year.

Mrs. Jones accumulated the following points before her hospitalization. Her husband had contracted cancer, a major change in the health and/or behavior of a family member (44 points). The particular form of cancer prevented their engaging in any sexual behavior. This was considered a sexual difficulty and added 39 points.

Her husband's illness had brought about two major changes in financial status (38 times 2 equals 76 points). When he got cancer, his income dropped considerably, and when he died his insurance once again made a major change in the family's financial picture. The husband's illness brought with it a major change in the number of arguments (35 points) because Mrs. Jones felt that she should not cause him any additional problems and, in some ways, began withdrawing from him.

The illness also brought about difficulties with in-laws (29 points) because Mrs. Jones felt they were insensitive and unwilling to help when she needed it. Other life changes included major changes in usual type and/or amount of recreation (19 points), major change in church activity (19 points), and major change in social activity (18 points). The care which her husband required imposed limitations on the family's ability to leave the home for activities. The medication had to be given at night, and this brought about a change in her sleeping habits (16 points). The family experienced a sad Christmas (12 points), but experienced Christmas nonetheless.

Mrs. Jones's life-change points totaled 407 before she contracted bronchitis. Experiencing over 300 life-change units during a year is considered high.

After hospitalization, Mrs. Jones's life-change units increased by 53 points as a result of illness, bringing her total to 460 points. The therapist helped Mrs. Jones understand how the accumulation of stress during the last year may have predisposed her to illness.

Mrs. Jones added up the increase in change points that building a new home would bring. It was a change in living conditions (25 points), a change in residence (20 points), and a change in church, as well as social activities (37 points). This would only add to her already high life-change total and day-to-day hassles. Mrs. Jones decided against the move.

A Volunteer, Mrs. Jackson

Another person, who was taking stress management training as part of preparation for volunteer work with patients, counted up her points on the rating scale and had a total of 25. Mrs. Jackson had experienced a vacation and Christmas during the last year but had not had any other life changes.

Mrs. Jackson's score is an example of possible understimulation. If Mrs. Jackson was not entering volunteer work and had come for stress management help, the authors might have asked her to consider seeking additional stimulation and making changes in her life to prevent boredom. Joining the volunteer group would add 26 points to her total because she would be beginning or seeking work outside the home. Her sense of excitement and interest in the new project was evident.

An Executive, Mr. Cummings

Another student of stress management who came to us as part of a program for executives in a major industry was surprised to find that he had accumulated a great many potentially stressful life events. Mr. Cummings said that nothing could be better in his life.

During the last year he had married (53 points) the girl of his dreams, who had shortly thereafter become pregnant (40 points). He had decided to get married because he had gotten a raise at work (38 points) and a promotion (29 points). His promotion had come as a result of his selling more real estate than any other man in the office (28 points). In addition, his change in status at the office had allowed him to buy the new home they dreamed of (31 points), and he had even more time away from work (20 points) to spend time enjoying his new son (39 points). Mr. Cummings saw little of his old friends at the bowling alley or the pub (18 points), but he enjoyed his honeymoon (13 points) and the family atmosphere of Christmas that year (12 points).

You can tell from this man's recent experiences that he had accumulated a great deal of change stress. In fact, Mr. Cummings's total was over 300 points, which suggested that he probably should slow down and make fewer major life changes during the next year

164

and be sure he got enough good food, sleep, and rest so as to protect himself from the increased probability of illness. Becoming aware of life-change stress helped this man to anticipate life changes and plan for them in advance.

Are You Sitting on a Two-Legged Stool?

Most of us are striving for a happy and meaningful life. Balance is needed to achieve and maintain such a life. Balance means that you avoid building your life around one person or one thing, no matter how wonderful it may seem. If you do, no matter who or what it is, losing it could be devastating.

Sigmund Freud considered work, play, and love to be three major parts of life. Other psychotherapists have called these by other names, but most agree that they are important building blocks for a balanced life. If we ignore any one of them, we ask too much of the other two. It is like sitting on a stool with only two legs – you may find yourself on the floor.

If you review the Social Readjustment Rating Scale you will notice that a majority of the life events involve loved ones. Some have called this our interpersonal life and community. When things go wrong at work or we are unable to play because of illness, we experience a great deal of stress. Without a supportive network of friends and family, we have no one with whom to share our troubles. Likewise, when things go our way, we have no one with whom to enjoy the pleasure. Loneliness is a major form of stress.

If, on the other hand, we do not know how to enjoy life and to maintain outside interests in hobbies, sports, and the arts, we lose our ability to play, and we may put too much emphasis on work and love. This may lead to work that is draining and a love from which we ask too much. Likewise, if we go through life ignoring the need for contributing to our community through work, even if we were so fortunate as to have an independent income, the balance would be upset. Without an investment in work or volunteer activities, we would place a burden on our loved ones and our recreation.

What if you are not interested in one or two of these factors? If so, it may be worthwhile to review your life situation and to pay particular attention to the factors you are ignoring to see if there is a conflict that needs your attention. Most people have very strong needs for work, play, and love. Try to recognize and fulfill your needs in each of these areas.

165

14 The Help Your Heart Report Card: When Is a 'B' Better Than an 'A'?

Coronary Heart Disease

Heart disease is the major cause of death in the United States. This has not always been the case in America, and it is not true of many other countries in the world. In the United States, the rate of death from heart disease has increased dramatically since the turn of this century. A large percentage of these deaths occur between the ages of thirty-five and fifty and are classified as premature deaths. Unless causes and cures can be found, the World Health Organization predicts that coronary heart disease may well become the greatest epidemic mankind has ever faced.

Coronary heart disease results from damage to the arteries that supply blood to the heart muscles. The damage to the coronary arteries is called atherosclerosis. The heart is a muscle, and without oxygen and nutrients from the blood it cannot survive. Angina pectoris involves brief periodic attacks of chest pain caused by insufficient delivery of blood to the heart. A heart attack occurs if the lack of oxygen is extended and part of the heart muscle actually dies. This is called a myocardial infarction.

Physical Risk Factors

Research suggests that many factors increase the risk of coronary heart disease. Men who are aging and have high levels of cholesterol in their blood, high blood pressure, diabetes, a family history of heart disease, and unusual heartbeat rhythms are at higher risk than other people. People who smoke, become obese, or fail to get sufficient exercise are also at risk. But physical risk factors cannot be found in nearly half of all new cases of coronary heart disease.

Psychological Risk Factors

As early as 1892, physicians were aware of the distinct personality traits of coronary patients. In the late 1950s, Drs. Meyer Friedman and Ray Rosenman led the field of cardiology into a study of what they later called Type A behavior, a coronary-prone behavior pattern. Originally, these doctors were investigating the role of dietary cholesterol in heart disease. In the midst of reviewing the contradictory evidence for this risk factor, they found themselves listening to the then-president of the San Francisco Junior League.

The evidence was not contradictory for this outspoken woman. 'I told you right from the first,' she said, 'that you would find that we are eating exactly as our husbands do. If you really want to know what is giving our husbands heart attacks, I'll tell you.' When the doctors asked, she said, 'It's stress, the stress they receive in their work, that's what's doing it.'

Drs. Friedman and Rosenman investigated the relationship between stress and coronary heart disease as had other scientists; but they discovered a particular pattern of behavior with which they could explain a great deal of what was happening to men in the U.S. In the book *Type A Behavior and Your Heart*, Drs. Friedman and Rosenman introduced to the public the differences between Type A and Type B behavior.

From Theory to Fact

The strongest evidence for the importance of Type A behavior came from a well-controlled study known as the Western Collaborative Group Study. In 1961, Drs. Friedman and Rosenman examined through interviews three thousand healthy middle-aged men for certain behavior patterns. The men were also medically examined for coronary heart disease. About half of these men were classified as Type A.

Eight and one-half years later, the Type A men had twice the coronary heart disease as the men who were originally judged as Type B. Other researchers have documented greater blockage of the coronary arteries among Type A individuals than Type B individuals. Of course, not all Type A men suffer coronary heart disease. But who wants to gamble when we have only one life? This seems to be one of the few situations in which a grade of 'B' is better than a grade of 'A'! Complete the form on page 169 to find out your grade.

What Your Total A/B Score Means

If your total score was 160–200, and especially if you are over forty and smoke, you may have a high risk of developing cardiac illness.

If your total score was 135–159, you are in the direction of being prone to cardiac disease. You should pay careful attention to the advice given to Type A's.

If your total score was 100–134, you are a mixture of A and B patterns. Beware of any potential for slipping into A behavior.

If your total score was less than 100, your behavior is generally relaxed and you express few of the reactions associated with cardiac disease. You probably have a Type B pattern.

Your score should give you some idea of where you stand in the discussion of Type A behavior. Even Type B persons occasionally slip into Type A behavior. It is important to remember that any of these patterns can change over time.

Type A Behaviors

Friedman and Rosenman described Type A behavior as 'an action-emotion complex that can be observed in any person who is *aggressively* involved in a chronic, incessant struggle to achieve more and more in less and less time, and, if required to do so, against the opposing efforts of other things or persons.' It appears that the mechanism involved is related to what we have called the stress response.

In the course of struggling against time and other people, the fight-or-flight response is triggered repeatedly and chronically. As a result of the abnormal discharges of adrenalin and cortisol, most Type A people have an increase in the cholesterol and fat in their bloodstream, have a more difficult time getting the cholesterol out of their bloodstream, and have an increase in clotting within the arteries.

Friedman and Rosenman include the following behaviors in their description of the Type A, coronary-prone individual. Type A individuals always move, walk, eat, and talk rapidly. They tend to emphasize words in their speech like a machine gun. They tend to hurry to the end of their sentences. Type A individuals are impatient with the rate that things happen. They tend to interrupt others and finish the sentences of people who are speaking slowly. They find it difficult to wait for others to do things they might be able to do faster. They hurry themselves in every activity they can.

THE A/B LIFE-STYLE QUESTIONNAIRE

Directions: As you can see, each scale below is composed of a pair of adjectives or phrases. Each pair represents two kinds of contrasting behavior. Choose the number that most closely represents the type of person you are and put it under the column labeled YOUR SCORE. Add your scores to get your total score.

RATING SCALE

			YOUR SCORE
1. Work regular hours	0 1 2 3 4 5 6 7 8 9 10	Bring work home or work late	_____
2. Wait calmly	0 1 2 3 4 5 6 7 8 9 10	Wait impatiently	_____
3. Seldom judge in terms of numbers (How many, how much)	0 1 2 3 4 5 6 7 8 9 10	Place value in terms of numbers	_____
4. Not competitive	0 1 2 3 4 5 6 7 8 9 10	Very competitive	_____
5. Feel limited responsibility	0 1 2 3 4 5 6 7 8 9 10	Always feel responsible	_____
6. Unhurried about appointments	0 1 2 3 4 5 6 7 8 9 10	Frequently hurried for appointments	_____
7. Never in a hurry	0 1 2 3 4 5 6 7 8 9 10	Always in a hurry	_____
8. Many interests	0 1 2 3 4 5 6 7 8 9 10	Work is main interest	_____
9. Try to satisfy self	0 1 2 3 4 5 6 7 8 9 10	Want to be recognized by others	_____
10. Not very precise	0 1 2 3 4 5 6 7 8 9 10	Careful about detail	_____
11. Can leave things temporarily unfinished	0 1 2 3 4 5 6 7 8 9 10	Must get things finished	_____
12. Satisfied with job	0 1 2 3 4 5 6 7 8 9 10	Striving on the job	_____
13. Listen well	0 1 2 3 4 5 6 7 8 9 10	Finish sentences for others	_____
14. Easygoing	0 1 2 3 4 5 6 7 8 9 10	Hard driving	_____
15. Do things slowly	0 1 2 3 4 5 6 7 8 9 10	Do things quickly	_____
16. Do one thing at a time	0 1 2 3 4 5 6 7 8 9 10	Think about what to do next	_____
17. Rarely angry	0 1 2 3 4 5 6 7 8 9 10	Easily angered	_____
18. Slow speech	0 1 2 3 4 5 6 7 8 9 10	Forceful speech	_____
19. Express feelings easily	0 1 2 3 4 5 6 7 8 9 10	Bottle up feelings	_____
20. Rarely set deadlines	0 1 2 3 4 5 6 7 8 9 10	Often set deadlines	_____

YOUR TOTAL A/B SCORE _____

©1982 Edward A. Charlesworth, Ph.D. and Ronald G. Nathan, Ph.D.

Type A individuals try to do two or more things at one time. They may think about business difficulties while they are driving to work or playing a game. They may try to eat and read at the same time. When others are saying something that does not relate to what they want to talk about, they always struggle to bring the conversation back to their interest. They have a difficult time relaxing or doing nothing, even if they are on a vacation. They are often so preoccupied that they do not appreciate things around them that are not related to their main goals.

They are more interested in getting things done than in getting enjoyment from doing them. They try to schedule more and more in less and less time. They often find themselves having scheduled more than can be accomplished and having allowed little time for unexpected interruptions or emergencies.

The Type A personality is extremely competitive, and these people try to achieve more than others. Their goals are more money, more possessions, more friends, more activities, more, more, more. They tend to judge themselves by the number of successes they have rather than the quality of their successes. In addition, they look upon their successes as the result of their ability to get things done faster than others rather than as a result of their abilities. They often exhibit gestures that suggest constant struggle, such as grinding their teeth or clenching their fists.

In summary, Type A individuals are hard-driving, competitive, impatient, and aggressive. They tend to be achievement-striving and hostile. Another way to put it is to say that the Type A's slogan is 'we try harder.'

In the scientific community, increasing emphasis is being placed on the relationship between hostility and heart disease. One follow-up study of 255 physicians conducted about twenty-five years after they took a hostility test in medical school showed that those with scores above the midpoint on the scale had nearly five times as much coronary heart disease than those below the midpoint. The overall mortality for those with high scores was 6.4 times greater than for those with scores at or below the midpoint.

Type B Behaviors

Type B individuals, on the other hand, are free of all the habits described above. They seldom feel any sense of time urgency or impatience. Type B individuals are not preoccupied with their achievements or accomplishments and seldom become angry or irritable. They tend to enjoy their recreation, finding it fun and relaxing. They are free of guilt about relaxing, and they work calmly and smoothly.

Take a Second Look at Yourself

It is important to realize that these are descriptions of extremes. Nevertheless, remember that half of the three thousand healthy men whom Drs. Friedman and Rosenman studied were identified as Type A. If you were familiar with the Type A behavior pattern before you took the exercise, another way to grade yourself is to imagine which group your wife, husband, children, or friends would put you in if they had to choose between one or the other.

If you find that you are a Type A individual, you will want to decrease your risk for coronary heart disease by taking a good look at your lifestyle and making some of the changes we are about to suggest. If you are a Type B, read over these suggestions, use the ones that seem to apply to you, and continue your healthy behavior.

But I'm Healthy

If you have had no signs or symptoms of heart disease, you may wonder why you should try to change. According to Friedman and Rosenman, the Type A's are often the hardest to convince. In 1978, the U.S. National Heart, Lung, and Blood Institute reviewed the evidence and determined that Type A behavior was a risk factor for coronary heart disease of the same magnitude as serum cholesterol.

A statistic that is often helpful in deciding to change is that during 1973 alone, two hundred thousand Americans died suddenly of heart disease without any previous symptoms. This is why heart disease and, in particular, hypertension, are called the silent killers. Another reason to decide to change is to become more efficient and more effective through setting priorities and using other stress management skills. Still another reason, perhaps one of the most important, is to improve the quality of your life.

More Recreation?

Trying to change Type A behavior does not just mean taking more time for recreation. Gary Schwartz, a noted Yale University psychologist, pointed this out by recounting his observation of three fishermen. It was a beautiful spring day, with a blue sky and a calm lake. While sipping cold drinks, two of the fishermen were enjoying the scenery and their companionship. They hardly ever checked their fishing hooks to see if the bait was taken. They were drifting along quietly in a rowboat.

The third fisherman was alone in a boat with a high-powered motor. He had five different rods, all rigged up with lines, positioned off both sides of the boat. This third fisherman ran frantically back and forth checking the hooks to see if the bait was off and yelling wildly downstream, 'Did you catch anything?' He moved his boat with determination from spot to spot.

The first two fishermen are Type B and the third Type A. They were all fishing and might all have been taking their doctor's advice. But, the very different effects on their bodies should be clear.

You might wonder if Type A's can change. The experience of hundreds suggests that they can. The gains are substantial, and the losses they feared seldom occur. You too can change!

Now That I Know That I'm a Type A, How Can I Become a Type B without Losing the Things I Want?

Part of the answer to this question is to decide whether what you are doing will bring you the things you want. Most Type A individuals are achievement-oriented and committed to vocational activities. It is not clear from some of the research conducted subsequent to the work of Drs. Friedman and Rosenman whether achievement-oriented activity is a critical element in Type A behavior. It is our opinion that many of the behaviors which Friedman and Rosenman described can be engaged in without triggering the stress response.

You may wonder whether people who earn a great deal of money in high-status jobs are particularly likely to be Type A individuals. Many are, but many successful people have succeeded without struggling against time. There are Type A's and Type B's at every rung of our society's ladders. Impatience may not lead to success, and success is often found in spite of impatience!

When we try to do things too fast, we invite error and tend to adopt a rigid approach to what needs to be done. Repetitive thinking and acting tend to impede progress. When we are rushed, we are less likely to find creative and effective solutions to our problems. Thus it is not only possible but more likely that we will succeed if we adopt some Type B behaviors. Type A's learn from what they are taught and later from what they experience that Type A behavior is inefficient and that they can be more successful than ever before after they start using stress management skills to achieve what they want.

What Do You Want?

Most Type A individuals have desires that can be quantified. They want to acquire more objects or more money or to increase their production. The artist may want to produce more paintings in less time, the carpenter more homes, the researcher more publications, the broker more sales, the physician more cures, and so forth.

These quantitative accumulations may lead to outward success, but a preoccupation with them can create an inner void. When we die, all that is left is the way we have lived our lives. As the saying goes, 'you can't take it with you.' Set aside some time to examine your goals and your abilities.

Much of the Type A's behavior is an attempt to store up accomplishments to overcome a general sense of insecurity and to control what is often not controllable. We need to take time to know who we are and where we are going. One way of doing this is to imagine yourself five, ten, and twenty years from now. Set aside time and use visual imagery to look back at the goals you are striving for and the ways you are going about achieving them. It is helpful to remember that life is not a destination but a road to be enjoyed.

Although some research has not supported the importance of an achievement orientation, two parts of the Type A behavior pattern have been confirmed over and over. These are time urgency and aggressive competitiveness. Although it would not hurt to decrease the other behaviors described above, we will concentrate on these two.

Time Urgency: Setting Priorities and Slowing Down

One of the best ways to decrease your sense of time urgency is to manage your time better and work more efficiently. We will spend a chapter on this later; but some of the suggestions that follow may be particularly helpful to the person with Type A behavior.

Using a Calendar Instead of a Stopwatch

Most Type A's try to do too much in too little time. They find themselves fighting time. It is as though they are using a stopwatch every minute of their day. One of the best ways to throw away an invisible stopwatch is to substitute a calendar as a time line to success. Think in terms of years and months rather than minutes and seconds. For most people this also involves setting weekly priorities that are realistic and that will take them efficiently from where they are to where they want to be. Read the time management chapter to help establish your priorities.

Slowing Down

Be sure to schedule time every day for the unexpected. Remember Murphy's law. If something can go wrong, it will. By leaving yourself extra time for each task, you will be able to relax and enjoy the work. Schedule some time during the day between activities for relaxation. Avoid procrastination. It can lead to a rush just before the end of the day or a deadline.

When you start to feel impatient with someone or a task, use your impatience as a cue to relax. Type A individuals tend to interrupt conversations. When you feel the urge, or find yourself interrupting, use that impulse as a signal to scan your body for tension and relax. Try not to assume that others are as impatient as you are. If you are late for a meeting, accept this human fallibility and avoid catastrophic thoughts about what the other person will do or say.

At the office, have someone screen your visitors and telephone calls. If you allow everyone to reach you at any time and even when you have someone in your office, you will probably try to hurry the caller or the person that you are with. This struggle will trigger the stress response. If your calls are not screened, try to screen them yourself. Indicate that you are in conference and will call back. This strategy is particularly important for home-makers. You have to show that you have enough belief in your right to decide what you will do to express your wishes to the caller.

Try to clear your desk of reminders of things to do. Make a list of 'To Do's for Today' and leave it inside a drawer or write it in an appointment book so you can concentrate on the task at hand and have a sense of security.

We all have a limited amount of time in life. In the words of Kenneth Grooms, 'There is more to life than increasing its speed.' Rather than hurrying everything, try to choose the activities you will do and the people you will talk to. If someone is chewing off your ear, assert your right to end the conversation politely. Be firm and clear. You may want to read the chapters on assertiveness training to help you keep conversations from getting out of hand. When a telephone call is dragging out and you have things to do, tell the other person and, if necessary, hang up.

Part of the Uncontrollable Is Controllable

A number of researchers have determined that the most stressful situations, and those that are most likely to elicit or trigger Type A behavior, are those that are uncontrollable. Whenever you feel you cannot influence or change a situation, look carefully at your options and your goals. Assertiveness can often help you regain the control you will need so that the situation will not trigger your Type A behavior. In situations that cannot be controlled, remind yourself that, even though you cannot always control the world, you can control your body's response to the world.

When you find yourself rushing to get something done, ask yourself, Has anything ever failed because it was done too well, too slowly? If you sense that you are trying too hard to get closure on something by finishing it, it may help to remember that only a corpse is completely finished! Perhaps this is part of the reason why we use the term 'deadline.'

In many jobs, the worker is the one who decides when the work is done. Too many Type A's never make that decision. If you always choose to work late, time will never make the decision that your work is done until it's too late. Practice deciding when your work for the day is finished.

These changes are not easy to make, and you will need to remind yourself. 'Hurry up' sickness is a chronic illness. Be patient, even about making these changes. Leave yourself messages to slow down. When you do slow down, reward yourself. If you put a project aside at the end of a day rather than pushing yourself to complete it, congratulate yourself. Keep a record of these successes. You could be adding days and years to your life.

175

Aggressive Competition or Calm Confidence

People with Type A behaviors tend to be hostile and competitive. Read the chapter on anger management, and when you start to get angry, remember to use that feeling as a cue to relax and strive for calm confidence. Use your thinking and your self-talk to work on the false perceptions you may have of threats, demands, and challenges. When you start to get angry because someone is not doing something quickly enough, check your beliefs. You may be thinking something like, If I don't get this person to do this in time for the deadline, I will lose my job and look like a fool. Plan time for the unexpected and remember, if at first you don't succeed, you're running about average.

Apply skills from the assertiveness chapters when you feel irritated or hostile. Be aware that some people may try to trigger your aggressive response. Try to avoid those who trigger your hostility, particularly other Type A individuals. If you get into an argument, ask yourself if winning the argument will really bring you what you want.

Developing Your Type B Behaviors

In the coming weeks, try to set aside time to expand your interests and your friendships. Take your lunch breaks if you usually work through them. Find people to share new experiences with. Try to find Type B individuals and increase the time you spend with these people. They will help you appreciate the things you may have left behind in your rush toward accumulating numbers and accomplishments. Rather than rushing past things on your way through life, become more receptive to the world around you.

Try to delegate work. If you think no one else can do your job, imagine what would happen if you died. Most companies would find a substitute. If you own your company, think of delegation as life insurance for your family.

Friedman and Rosenman point out the importance of rituals and traditions as ways of enjoying our lives and bringing new meaning to them. If you have moved away from traditions and have become preoccupied with work, you may find it enjoyable to create new family traditions or revive old ones.

One of the few things we are guaranteed in our travel through life is experience. Try to expand and enrich your experiences through hobbies, reading, the humanities, and nature. You cannot compete for these experiences because you are the only one who can have and enjoy them. If we move through life trying to get more done in less time, the days will pass all too quickly. We may end up having sold our right to experience and having received very little in return.

To begin enjoying new experiences, you may need to give yourself permission to use time for them. You may find yourself saying, 'Tomorrow I'll let myself enjoy that.' Remember, life is fragile and tomorrow may not be yours to count on. There is an old saying that can be applied to changing Type A to Type B behavior: if not now, when?

Social Insecurity

A recent study of heart disease patients showed that it was possible to differentiate between those with more and less serious coronary atherosclerosis. The differentiation could be made not only by Type A behavior patterns but also by measures of social insecurity. Over 90 percent of the patients with both characteristics had severe atherosclerosis.

Social insecurity was indicated by patients reporting bashfulness, low self-confidence, sensitivity to criticism, difficulty being able to talk in groups, difficulty trusting people, and self-consciousness. They also tended to answer 'no' when asked if they were good mixers or enjoyed many different kinds of play and recreation.

This study suggests that Type A behavior individuals who are also socially insecure may have a greater incidence of heart disease. Perhaps their striving for success and their striving to increase their attractiveness to others via accomplishments was a compensation for a lack of social security. Thus those who are socially insecure may tend to spend more of their time pursuing success impatiently and aggressively. If you are socially insecure, you may spend more time at work, and your hard-driving characteristics may be rewarded, but you may never have time to enjoy the social rewards for which you are striving.

Think about your own social insecurity. If you find yourself anxious at parties and with other people, use the techniques in Chapter 12 to desensitize yourself. If you are less fearful of others, you will find it easier to spend more time engaged in Type B behaviors and enjoying the company of others.

15   Taking the Stress Out of What You Tell Yourself

If Names Will Never Hurt You, What Causes Bad Feelings?

Are you ready to learn something about emotions that surprises many people? Feelings and emotions we experience are *not* caused by the events that precede them. For example, if someone calls us a name or if we lose money in the stock market, we might say that this made us angry or brought us disappointment. Our reasoning may seem to be true, but it is faulty.

The same events can cause very different feelings in different people. If you wanted to make someone angry at you and that person called you a name, you might be pleased. If you needed a stock market loss as a deduction for your income tax, such a loss might make you feel good. Feelings are not caused by events. If they were, everyone would have the same feelings after any given event. Another example may help clarify these ideas.

One Event, Many Feelings

One of the authors was teaching an introductory course in psychology. About a week after the mid-term examination, he gave a lecture on emotions. The author arrived with a stack of exams and told the class that the mid-term grades could not be used because widespread cheating had been brought to his attention. He explained that he was giving the test again.

You can imagine what people felt. Think of yourself in this situation. What would you feel? Anxiety? Anger? Confusion? Most people felt these negative feelings. It might surprise you to learn that some people were very happy, some doubted the teacher, some felt guilty, and others claimed not to feel anything. Different people had very different reactions to the same event. It was clear that the event did not cause all these different feelings. If the author's wife had been sitting in the audience, she might have had another feeling. She might have feared for the life of the teacher! How could the same event cause so many different feelings?

The ABC's of Emotions

Albert Ellis, Ph. D., a renowned psychologist, developed a theory to explain the relationship between events and feelings. He reasoned that the true causes of feelings are not the events but the beliefs we have about these events. Dr. Ellis proposed a simple model to help us better understand emotions. Here are the ABC's of emotions:

'A's' are the *a*ctivating events. In the situation described above, the teacher's announcement was the activating event.

'B's' are the *b*eliefs. In this case, these were what each student believed about what the teacher said.

'C's' are emotional *c*onsequences. In the example, these were all the different feelings that the students were having.

Most of the students who felt anger or anxiety had done well on the first exam and were afraid they would do poorly on the second exam. Most of those who were pleased had failed the exam and were happy to get a second chance. Others might have been pleased if they thought there had been widespread cheating and the cheaters were about to get their due. Most of those who claimed that they did not feel any strong emotions did not believe the author's announcement. The author's wife might have believed that someone would throw something at her husband!

This way of understanding our feelings is not new. As Ellis points out, the famous stoic Epictetus wrote, 'Men are disturbed not by things, but by the views which they take of them.' William Shakespeare rephrased this concept in *Hamlet*: 'There's nothing either good or bad but thinking makes it so.' Finally, Abraham Lincoln said people are about as happy as they make up their minds to be.

The Boss and Your Beliefs

Take another example. If your boss calls you into his office, his intent may be to compliment your work. But before you go into his office, you wonder why he wants to see you. You may decide that he wants you to work late again, and you are irritated because you feel you are already doing too much work. By the time you get into his office, you may be angry in anticipation that he will ask more of you. In this example, 'A' is the boss calling you into his office, 'B' is the belief that he wants you to do more work, and 'C' is the anger you feel boiling up inside of you.

You may have prejudiced your feelings, actions, and physiological reactions with your belief about the purpose for your being called into the boss's office. If you knew that the boss was going to compliment you, the activating event (A) would have been the same (boss calling you into his office), but your belief system (B) would have been different. In turn, the emotional consequence (C) would also have been different – perhaps pleasure or even excitement.

Marriage and Your Beliefs

Each partner in a marriage interprets the actions of the other person in terms of certain expectations or beliefs. These beliefs come from early experiences in our original families and the cultural norms of our society. The probability of misinterpretation is great. For example, when a husband does housework (A), his wife can see this as an appropriate contribution (B) or an indirect criticism (B) and thus feel gratitude (C) or anger (C). Another example would be when a wife is preparing for a test and asks her husband to prepare the supper and take care of the children for the evening (A). The husband could feel anger (C) because he thinks a woman's place is in the home (B). Alternatively, the husband could feel pride (C) because he knows that her attending school is bringing them one step closer to their mutual goals (B). The potential for misinterpretations and unhealthy beliefs about a marital partner are some of the reasons why mind-reading can be so dangerous and communications so important to strong relationships.

If beliefs cause the feelings we experience, we should be able to change our feelings or emotions by changing our beliefs. False and irrational beliefs may cause harmful, self-defeating, and unnecessary feelings. To change irrational beliefs, it is necessary to examine our beliefs and dispute them.

Can't Stand-itis, Awfulizing, Musterbation, and Other Stressful Habits: Anger

Four irrational statements can be related to feelings of anger. These are the beliefs that may cause you to feel the stress response in many situations for which it is inappropriate. Do you think one or more of the following irrational thoughts when you are angry?

1. '*I can't stand* your treating me in such an unreasonable and unjust manner.' These are the 'can't stand it' beliefs that many of us suffer from. 'I can't stand-itis' is the pain that comes from 'can't standing' something.
2. '*How awful* for you to have treated me so unfairly.' This can be called awfulizing. How often do you find yourself exploding an event out of proportion and making it 'awful' instead of just unpleasant?
3. 'You *should not, must not* behave that way toward me.' This is sometimes called 'musterbation' and often leads to the stress response and to anger.
4. 'Because you have acted in that manner toward me, I find you a terrible person who deserves nothing good in life, and you should be punished for treating me so.' This is sometimes called undeservingness and damnation thinking.

All these statements tend to exaggerate our view of situations and upset us.

Can't Stand-itis, Awfulizing, Musterbation, and Other Stressful Habits: Anxiety

If you have difficulty with public speaking, you may find yourself using four similar statements that are related to feelings of anxiety.

1. '*I couldn't stand* my poor methods of coping with this situation.' You stood it or you wouldn't be able to upset yourself about it.
2. 'How *awful* if I can't manage things.' This is another form of awfulizing. It may be unfortunate if you can't manage something, but it is not awful.
3. 'If I can't cope as well as I *must* cope, I am an *inferior person*, and I deserve what I get for not handling the situation.' Perhaps you will have another chance. Why should you be punished for

181

trying? Are you an inferior person or do you simply lack skills in a particular area?

4. 'I *should have* the ability to deal with the situation better.' Who says you should? Do you have enough training to do it better? Where is it written that you should?

As you can see, anxiety statements can exaggerate the situation. Such statements tend to equate an evaluation of your actions with an evaluation of your whole being. Beware of labels: 'I'm dumb,' 'I'm ugly,' 'I'm hopeless,' and others. These are irrational and unhealthy beliefs. Such thinking is sometimes called 'negative inner chatter' or 'negative nonsense,' and it is best avoided or replaced with healthier statements. The only way you can evaluate yourself or another person is to evaluate all of his or her actions over an entire lifetime. Few of us have the time to do so or the desire to take the responsibility!

Finding the Enemy Beliefs

How can we attack and dispute these irrational beliefs so we can remain calm and avoid the anger or anxiety that can trigger the stress response? First, we much discover our main irrational beliefs. We can do this by looking for the 'shoulds,' 'musts,' and 'have to's' in what we say and think. We can listen for words like 'awful,' 'terrible,' and 'impossible.' Finally, we can listen for words like 'I can't stand that.'

Common Problems: Finding the Sharks under the Fins

Sometimes irrational beliefs are difficult to find. We may think them so quickly that they are almost automatic. In this case, one has to trace his or her thinking step-by-step, backward and forward, to figure out where the irrational beliefs are lurking.

Helpful Hints

Another way of uncovering the self-defeating beliefs from which you may suffer is to go through a list of beliefs which Albert Ellis and his colleague, Robert Harper, introduce in their book, *A Guide to Rational Living*. Most irrational ideas concern either ourselves and our self-worth or the people and events around us. For this reason, we have divided the list into beliefs that seem to be primarily about ourselves and those that are primarily about other people and other things. As

182

you go through these lists, check off those that seem to be causing you pain and problems in living, so you can return to them later.

Self-Directed Irrational Beliefs

The first five beliefs have to do with yourself:

1. I need everyone's love and approval for just about everything I do.
2. I should be able to do everything well.
3. If something bad happens, I should worry about it.
4. It is easier to avoid difficult things than to try them and risk failure.
5. I will enjoy life more if I avoid responsibilities and take what I can get now.

Other-Directed Irrational Beliefs

Five other irrational beliefs, which Ellis and Harper describe at length, are equally important to recognize. These are beliefs we may have about the way things or other people 'should' be.

1. Some people are bad and should be punished.
2. When things aren't going well in my life, it is terrible.
3. If things go wrong, I'm going to feel bad and there's very little I can do about those feelings.
4. What has happened to me and what I have done in the past determine the way I feel and what will happen to me now and in the future.
5. People and things should be different, and perfect solutions should be found for everything.

Categorize Some Common Irrational Beliefs

To help you begin to identify irrational beliefs and categorize them as coming from thoughts about ourselves or about other people, read the following statements and underline only those that are about yourself. The thoughts you do not underline are about other people or events outside yourself.

The world is unjust. My parents should not boss me around. It would be awful if I wasn't popular. I deserve to be punished the rest

183

of my life. People should not get divorced. Because I work hard people should love me. If I ask her and she refuses, it's going to be awful. Because I have suffered, people should be kind to me. If I fail, I am worthless. My parents should love me and approve of what I do. If he doesn't like me, I am worthless and valueless. If I can't find a solution, I must be dumb or stupid. You just can't trust anyone. I was born a loser.

Unhealthy Beliefs about Work

Another way to review these ten commonly held unhealthy beliefs is to consider the following problems that a secretary can get into if she holds these beliefs about her job.

One of the authors treated a secretary, whom we will call Mrs. Williams. Mrs. Williams was referred by her gastroenterologist for a nervous stomach. She worked for two executives who were very demanding, yet they seldom spoke to her except to point out corrections she needed to make.

Mrs. Williams began to worry that she was incompetent and that she might lose her job. She began to type faster, making more mistakes, and to avoid difficult tasks for fear of failing. At the same time, she was angry at her bosses for not being different, and she felt they should be called on the carpet by their superior. Life seemed terrible. Mrs. Williams knew she would feel bad every day she continued working.

It became clear in our interviews that Mrs. Williams's central irrational belief was that without approval for her work, she 'would just die.' By slowly disputing this and other beliefs, she was able to accept the conditions at the office until she could apply for a transfer. For example, she came to realize that, although gaining the approval of everyone she worked for would be very nice indeed, it was an unrealistic expectation and that she was more likely to get the approval of her friends and family than of her bosses.

Mrs. Williams also saw that trying to be a faster typist and avoiding difficult tasks were making the problem worse. She began to reason that it would be great if her bosses were reprimanded, but they were, in fact, getting the work done satisfactorily. It was unlikely that they would be reprimanded or change their ways. Then, through the assertiveness skills that she was learning in therapy she learned how to express her feelings and her needs. She also realized that, no matter

184

what happened at work, part of her life might be unpleasant, but life itself was not terrible.

As a result, her stomach was upset less of the time. At follow-up, she stated that she had decided to get a new job. She also said that she was pleased because she could take the ups and downs better now because her happiness was less dependent on what happened in the office.

Role-Related Irrational Beliefs

Each of us has a variety of roles in life that can hook us into suffering the emotional consequences of irrational beliefs. One good example is the super mom who may believe that she has to be all things to all the people in her family and at her job. Take some time to look at your roles and the irrational beliefs you may have about them.

Attacking Your Irrational Beliefs

The next step is to debate your irrational beliefs actively and vigorously. Ask, What makes it awful (or 'terrible' or 'horrible')? *Why* can't I stand it? Why *must* they never do that? and Where is it written that they must not do that or that I must do that? Finally, ask, Why should I judge the whole person or myself on the basis of one or even several acts? You will have to attack your irrational beliefs vigorously and repeatedly to get the full benefit of thinking and feeling better.

Exposing Your Inner Enemies: ABC Charts

To help you detect and dispute your irrational beliefs create a chart like the one overleaf. First, identify the stressful emotions you are experiencing. Write those on the line next to emotional consequences. Then, fill in the activating event that seems to trigger your stress response under 'A' for *a*ctivating event.

Now, go back and try to figure out the beliefs you hold and fill those in under 'B' for *b*eliefs. You may find it helpful to check the lists of beliefs just presented. Do this for most of the anger-arousing or anxiety-producing events that you encounter. Then begin to dispute the irrational beliefs by using the questions that we just reviewed. Finally, identify the new, healthier feelings that come with better thinking.

AN EXAMPLE OF A RATIONAL-EMOTIIVE A TO E CHART

AN EXAMPLE OF A RATIONAL-EMOTIVE A TO E CHART

A. Activating Event (Example): *Boss pointing out my errors*

B. Irrational Belief (Example): *I must be totally incompetent and I am sure I will lose my job*

C. Emotional or Stressful Consequence (Example): *anxiety, terror*

D. Dispute Your Irrational Belief (Example): *It would be nice if I did not make any mistakes, but I am not totally incompetent, just human*

E. New, Less Stressful Emotion (Example): *Some appropriate concern motivated to get the work finished*

xxxxxxxxxxxxxxxxxxxxxxxxxxxxxxxxxxxxxxxxxxxxxxxxxxxxxxxxxxxxxxxxxxxxxxxx

Common Problems, Uncommon Sense

Below are some anger and anxiety-management principles which you may find helpful in applying what you have been learning. Some people can easily see themselves in each of the principles. Other people are more involved with one or another or a few of them. Circle or underline the ones that might be of help to you.

Uncommon Sense for Self-Doubt

For many people, becoming angry is related to doubting themselves, being unsure, or feeling threatened by someone. It is important to remember that you are a fallible human being but nonetheless a worthy person with many good qualities. To be fallible means to be able to make mistakes. None of us were born goof-proof! We are sure you realize that you are bound to make mistakes; but many of us have the irrational belief that we should be perfect.

In addition, be sure that you understand you have worth for other reasons than your accomplishments or your appearance. These will fade in time, but you are worthwhile for your natural ability to experience life and to share it with others.

Powerful Words to Wash Away Worries

It is said that overwork never killed anyone, but overworry can. When you are thinking a lot about something and it is distressing you, ask yourself, Am I planning or am I worrying? If you are worrying, stop and plan. If it is the wrong time or place to plan, do something else, perhaps a relaxation technique.

Alternatively, ask yourself, What's the worst thing that could happen? Follow the events out to the very end, and you may find the worst is not so bad and may have a silver lining. Some people who are dissatisfied with their jobs have done this and found their way to another job – a better one!

If you dwell on world events or those you cannot control, remember the words of Ralph Waldo Emerson, 'Can anybody remember when times were not hard and money was not scarce?' It is also helpful to consider Mark Twain's witty remark, 'I am an old man and have known a great many troubles – but most of them never happened.'

Two Rules for Stress Management

Robert Eliot, a cardiologist at the University of Nebraska, combined this cognitive approach with the relaxation response in the following way, 'Rule No. 1 is, don't sweat the small stuff. Rule No. 2 is, it's all small stuff. And if you can't fight and you can't flee, flow.'

Uncommon Sense for Anger

Sometimes we get angry because we take an unpleasant situation personally when there is no need to. When someone is directly offensive to you, you can control and contain your anger by refusing to be distracted from whatever you are doing. This is called being task-oriented. Stay focused and stick to what must be done in the situation to get the outcome you want. When you take insults personally, you get distracted from your tasks and caught up in unnecessary feelings. Recognize that the other person may be deliberately provoking you. By realizing what the other person is doing, you may find it easier to stay task-oriented.

Sometimes we get angry or anxious simply because that has always been our reaction to a certain situation. As you learn alternate ways of reacting to provocations or demanding situations, you will be less inclined to react with anger or anxiety. Try to catch yourself if you are saying self-defeating and irrational things like 'I was born that way,' and 'You can't teach an old dog new tricks.' These are irrational, self-defeating beliefs.

One of the most important ways you can control your anger is to recognize the signs of arousal or the stress response as soon as they occur. As you become more and more sharply attuned to the signs of tension and upset inside of you, you will achieve greater ability to short-circuit the anger process and turn it off before it gets too strong. Intense anger can make you agitated and impulsive. As you learn to relax more easily, and quickly dispute your irrational beliefs, your ability to regulate anger will improve.

Anger as a Useful Signal

Your anger can serve a very useful function. It can alert you that you are becoming upset and that effective action is called for. Knowing that you can short-circuit your anger or anxiety, you will be less agitated and impulsive. When we are agitated or impulsive, we can make more mistakes, which leads to still more anxiety and anger. Stay task-oriented and instruct yourself to relax and dispute your irrational beliefs.

Sometimes we get angry because situations seem to be getting out of hand and we want to take charge. Sometimes we become concerned that things will not go the way we want them to, so we get angry trying to control them. We can learn ways of managing our anger and gaining better control of situations. Dispute your belief that you 'have to' get angry to change something. One of the best ways of taking charge of the situation is to remain calm when most people expect you, or even want you, to be upset.

Sometimes we get annoyed, upset, and angry because we have spent more time being conscious of our failures than of our successes. We sometimes forget or dismiss the good things that we do, and yet we never let ourselves forget our mistakes and shortcomings.

Now that you are learning to recognize and dispute irrational beliefs, be careful not to berate yourself when you have irrational beliefs and when you forget to dispute them. Remember, it's irrational to think you'll learn these skills overnight or become perfect. Beware of the belief that you should be able to relax and stay calm in all situations.

Try to remember to congratulate yourself whenever you accomplish something, particularly if you have been able to relax or manage your anger. Let yourself feel good about all of these successes. Enjoy each step in your journey toward your goals.

16 The Movies of Your Mind: Anxiety

In the last chapter, we described how our thinking affects our feelings. You learned how irrational beliefs can lead to self-defeating feelings and unhealthy stress. In this chapter, we will replace irrational thinking with positive talking.

Many psychologists have proposed that what we think is best understood as self-talk. These psychologists have helped us understand that what we silently say to ourselves about the events we experience influences us in many profound ways. What we say to ourselves changes what we see and hear around us, what we feel within us, and what we remember when we look back on our experiences. In this chapter, we will concentrate on the ways in which the things you say to yourself can help you to prepare for and overcome anxiety. First, let's examine how we can create anxiety by what we say.

What We Say Often Influences What We See, Hear, Feel, and Remember

When we go to a haunted house at a carnival, what we say to ourselves can influence what we will see, hear, feel, and remember about the experience. If we tell ourselves that we are alone in a spooky house, we will see it as threatening and scary. When things loom or leer at us, we will tell ourselves that we are in danger. Likewise, if we tell ourselves that the sounds that are played in the haunted house are real, we are likely to feel chills running up and down our spines.

On the other hand, if we constantly tell ourselves that all of the things in the haunted house are fake and try to figure out how they were made to look real, we will probably not see ghosts or goblins but bed sheets and paint. Likewise, we will hear sheets of metal being fluttered up and down, rather than thunder from lightning. If we say that the frightening sights and sounds are caused by special effects, we probably will enjoy the experience and not feel anxious. We will remember it as an interesting and fun show, rather than a frightening experience.

An example of a frightening situation is preparing to interview for a job. If we are looking through the newspaper for a job advertisement and constantly say to ourselves that there is nothing there for us, we may be overlooking certain sections or jobs that are listed because self-talk is affecting the way we see what is in front of us. Should we finally make an appointment, and walk in saying to ourselves that we do not have any skills and no one wants us, we may hear the interviewer's remarks somewhat differently than the way he says them.

If we are critical of our skills, we may not hear the interviewer's encouragement to see an associate who might be of help in finding a job. We may hear questions as attempts to find out what we cannot do, rather than what we can do. When we start to think this way, we are likely to feel inadequate and anxious. If upon returning home from such an interview, we say to ourselves that we will never get a job, we are likely to remember only the negative parts of the interview and not the positive ones.

All of these experiences are likely to give us what some of our patients have called the 'screaming meemees.' It is clear from these examples and from what we have learned about irrational beliefs in the last chapter that negative thinking and self-talking can upset us and interfere with what we are doing.

Whistling a Happy Tune

One way people deal with the anxiety of their self-talk is to whistle a happy tune. Any distraction can help break the connection between our negative talk and the 'screaming meemees.' Some people chew gum, smoke a cigarette, tap their fingers on a desk, or shuffle their feet on the floor. Most of these activities can lower our anxiety, but they can be annoying, and there are other, more exciting options.

The Power of Positive Talking

The power of positive talking is very similar to the power of positive thinking that has been popularized by Norman Vincent Peale. In this chapter, we will provide you with things to tell yourself that have been

190

shown to improve performance and decrease the 'screaming meemees.' The goal is to cope with anxious feelings so that you can concentrate on what you are doing and remain in a relaxed state of mind and body.

To manage a stressful situation, we need to take steps at four major time periods. These phases can overlap, but usually they follow one another.

We need (1) to prepare for the stressful situation, (2) to cope with feelings as they start to build, (3) to cope with feelings as they start to overwhelm us, and finally (4) to cope when the feelings have passed. Each step is important in helping you to enjoy coping. By breaking a potentially frightening experience into four parts and learning ways of coping with each, we can make the experience interesting and challenging, rather than overwhelming and unbearable.

One of the problems with positive talking occurs when we get stuck and don't know what to say to ourselves. Some of us have this problem in the early phases and others in the later phases of frightening or anxiety-evoking situations. This chapter will help you with each phase by providing clear, positive things to tell yourself each step of the way.

The Talkies

Some of our patients have found it helpful to think of their anxiety-provoking events as part of a scary movie. In an earlier chapter, you learned how to use imagery for relaxing and rehearsing. Up until now, these have been silent movies. It is time to turn them into talkies.

In this chapter, you will concentrate on the horror movies of your life. In the next chapter, you will deal with the situations in which anger can get out of hand. So, when you are finished with the horror movies, you can turn to the war movies.

Waiting in Line for a Ticket to a Horror Movie

Preparing for a stressful situation that evokes anxiety is the first phase in maintaining a relaxed state of mind and body. We need to rehearse what we plan to do, and we need to replace negative thinking with positive thinking. Imagine this rehearsal as what you say while waiting in line for a ticket to the horror movie.

If you are scheduled to give a speech in front of a business group in half an hour, what you say to yourself will affect what you will do and feel. Some of the ways of reducing anxiety while you wait for your turn to speak can be memorized or written on a piece of paper to review.

One of the most important things to say is to ask yourself, What is it that I have to do? This question helps you to focus on the task at hand rather than all of your fears about doing it. You can tell yourself to think about what you will have to say so that you will have less time to upset yourself with thoughts of failure. You may review the outline of what you plan to say and even jot down a few notes about issues to address. Do not, however, make major changes in your presentation.

You have learned several ways of reducing your stress response, and you could say, 'This may be difficult, but I know some ways to deal with it.' You may want to tell yourself, 'Time for a few deep breaths and relaxation. I feel more comfortable, relaxed, and at ease. I know this material very well and I have worked hard at preparing it.' You can also say, 'No putting myself down: I'll just think about what I need to do.' If you start to worry, you can tell yourself, 'Stop worrying, I *can* do it.'

Concentrate on your past successes rather than your past failures. Thinking about your successes will lead to calming self-confidence. You may say that you have never succeeded. This is highly unlikely and usually comes from an irrational belief that what we do is either all good or all bad. In reality, almost everything we do involves some successful actions. Concentrate on these, and you will decrease your anxiety while you build your self-confidence.

When we are waiting to do something that has caused us anxiety in the past, we can work ourselves into a frenzy before it even starts. If, for example, we tell ourselves that we will never be able to give a speech or that people will laugh at us, we may lose sleep the night before and fail to prepare adequately for our talk. One actor repeats two phrases to manage his anxiety before every performance. He says, 'I'm well prepared, and I know what I'm doing,' By saying the positive statements we have just reviewed, you can help keep yourself calm and prepare for the event while you wait for it.

The things you tell yourself are often self-fulfilling prophecies. Let's strive to make the prophecies those of calmness and coping rather than of gloom and doom.

192

As the Plot Thickens

The next part to learn for coping with anxiety is what to say when the feelings start to build. In a film, this is the section created to build tension in the audience. Many of us hope that we will not feel any anxiety, and then we become even more anxious when we begin to feel scared. We start to tell ourselves that because we are feeling a little anxious, we will be overwhelmed before we know it. These pessimistic ideas only increase our anxiety. They are also self-fulfilling prophecies.

Many people are anxious when they know they will meet new people at a party. They may cope well on the way to the party but become very anxious as they walk toward a group of new people. This is when 'the plot thickens,' and we need to know what to say to ourselves to cope with it.

You can tell yourself that the anxiety is a good reminder to begin using the relaxation skills you have mastered. You might say, 'My muscles are starting to feel a little tight. Time to relax. Time to slow down.' As the anxiety builds, you may want to say, 'I *can* meet this challenge.' As you are walking across the floor, each step seems longer than the next, and you don't know what you are going to do when you finally reach the new people. You can say, 'One step at a time; I can handle the situation.'

Of course, you also need to have a plan for approaching any situation. Much fun is made of standard or 'pat' greetings, but they can help open conversations. You may overcome the anxiety that prevents you from entering a conversation but still lack the social skills to carry on a conversation. The classic book *How to Win Friends and Influence People* by Dale Carnegie is a good guide for learning some of these skills.

As your anxiety rises, you can say, 'I'll just think about what I have to do.' This phrase is a reminder that it is best to concentrate on the task at hand. You may wish to observe the people you are meeting, notice what they are wearing and what they are doing, so that you can ask appropriate questions and express interest in them. Next you might say, 'Relax; I'm in control. I'll take a slow, deep breath.' These positive statements should help you cope better and enjoy meeting people.

On the Edge of Your Seat

Being in the middle of an event and concerned that your anxiety might overwhelm you is similar to sitting on the edge of your seat during a scary movie. Knowing what to say to yourself can make a big difference. Some of us expect ourselves to be super cool and do the impossible. When our feelings start to overwhelm us, we are tempted to give up, escape the situation, or try to avoid the next task.

An example is a student who is in the middle of an examination and begins to sweat, shake, and feel dizzy. Giving up, escaping, or avoiding will not help to pass the exam. One of the best things the student can say is, 'I'm not surprised I'm anxious. That's okay. I can handle it.'

In many situations, such as examinations, it is possible to take a break and say to yourself, 'I'll label my fear from 0 to 10. Five is motivating, but I'll pause and relax if it reaches 8.' In addition, a person can say, 'When fear comes, I'll just pause,' or 'It's okay to be anxious. I *can* handle it.' The student may need to remind himself, 'I won't try to eliminate the feeling totally: I'll just keep it manageable.' Finally, the student may find it helpful to say, 'I'll pay attention to the present: I'll answer one question at a time. I'll take a deep breath between questions.'

All of these positive statements can help you when your feelings start to overwhelm you. You can see that they turn irrational beliefs around by helping us to accept our fallibility and to keep us task-oriented.

Studies of anxiety have shown that there are facilitative and debilitative levels of anxiety. A student taking an examination needs to have enough anxiety so his attention does not wander and he is motivated to read the questions and answer them. Too little anxiety would be self-defeating and would be almost as debilitating as when the student is so anxious he cannot concentrate.

Somewhere in the middle between too little and too much is just the right amount of anxiety. This applies not only to examinations but to most activities in life. Many people find trying to do new activities scary. It is good to remember that some of this anxiety will help us to concentrate and to learn. In addition, in many areas of sports the anxiety can help us excel. The positive thinking and talking we have just reviewed help us to keep our anxiety in the right ball park for all of life's games.

A Sigh of Relief

One of the most important phases of anxiety and anxiety management is the final phase, after the event has been concluded and the curtain goes down. We need to know how to optimize coping when it's all over and the feelings have passed.

This is a unique opportunity for positive talk. It helps us to put things in perspective and to reward ourselves for our accomplishments. When we get a reward for something we have done, we are more likely to do it again. If we reward ourselves for positive talking, we are more likely to use the skill again in similar situations.

Take the example of a couple cleaning up after entertaining friends for the first time in a new neighborhood. Some of the guests may have had a good time, and others may not have. It is helpful to put the situation into perspective by saying, 'We didn't do everything that we wanted to do for our guests, but that's okay. We tried, and that is what really counts,' or 'We can only do so much and then it's up to them to enjoy themselves.' The couple might also say, 'That wasn't really as hard as we thought.'

To help themselves continue to use their stress management skills, the couple might say, 'We are doing better at this! We are making progress!' They might spend some time reviewing how they felt and what they did about those feelings. Finally, they might say, 'We can be pleased with our progress.'

Common Problems: But It's Too Scary to Think

Sometimes we are so scared that we cannot think positively. This is why it is important to memorize the coping statements for each phase of the event. If we are anxious, it is more difficult to remember. That is why we must master and overlearn the phrases so they will be available quickly when we are anxious.

Some people find that the phrases we have suggested are not right for their own problems. In this case, we suggest that you write down personal coping phrases. Be sure to include some phrases that will prepare you for the event, some to remind you to relax as the feelings begin to build, some to help you cope when the feelings become stronger, and some to keep perspective after the event and encourage yourself in the future.

Learning Your Lines

It is very important that you put the techniques you have been reading about into practice. To do so, you will need to memorize the phrases and practice them systematically.

Helpful Hints

Many people think they are too busy to memorize these phrases. Try to use periods during the day when you are waiting for a bus or checking out in a supermarket or have other free times. These are good times to relax and review your new self-talk. Keep these phrases on a slip of paper in your wallet or pocketbook for review during your free time. A good time to learn these statements is just before you go to sleep, and for this reason, we recommend that you leave the list on your night stand.

When you practice, remember to avoid negative thinking. Negative thinking will only lead to avoidance or additional distress. Stay on guard against statements like 'I always lose control when I get into arguments' or 'I just can't cope with that, and I know I will get upset.'

If you find that you are unable to remember the words in real life, figure out what times you have the most difficulty remembering them. Then go over the statements for these times again. Go slowly, and use your skill of visual imagery, so that when you begin working on these techniques in real life, you will recall the statements and be able to cope more successfully. Make your 'talkies' as clear and provoking as you can. It is helpful to exaggerate the anxiety-provoking events to test your skill. Continue doing this and you will find yourself better and better able to cope with your feelings in stressful situations.

Do not try to learn all the statements or visualize all the scenes at one time. It may be useful to review all of them in the beginning, but choose a few to memorize or work on each day. This is a little like taking a series of injections for an inoculation against a disease. In fact, these techniques are sometimes called stress inoculation.

You may want to use a movie or a television show to practice these statements. Most shows have a beginning, a middle, a climax, and an ending. To practice, prepare for the excitement, lower your arousal as feelings start to build, cope when feelings start to overwhelm, and, finally, reward yourself when the show is nearly over. You may get caught off guard, but that is not bad preparation for the way stress sometimes catches us napping in real life.

You may find it easier to start practicing with reruns of your favorite adventure shows. Of course, you will not want to practice these skills all the time because part of the fun of watching a show is the excitement we experience. This is also true of life!

The Positive Self-Talk of Winners

Dennis Waitley, in his book *The Psychology of Winning*, emphasizes that we are motivated by our current dominant thought. We move in the direction of what we are thinking of most. Positive self-talk should focus on solutions and goals. It is much more effective to focus on what we want to achieve than to move away from our fears. If you focus on your fears, or even on trying to move away from your fears, that is your dominant thought and you will be motivated by fear. If you focus on a positive goal or achievement, you will be motivated by it, and you will move in that direction.

Let's look at what happens when we change the dominant thought from a goal to a fear. Imagine that we placed a sixteen-foot-long plank on the floor with a $10 bill at the end and asked you to walk the plank to get the money. You would probably be more than happy to walk sixteen feet for $10. Your current dominant thought is the goal of $10. If we used the same plank but put it between two twenty-story buildings and placed a $100 bill at the end, the game would be changed. Now, would you walk the plank? Would your current dominant thought be the money or the fear of falling?

The winners in life can find something positive in every situation. There is an extremely successful executive who always says, 'That's great!' when his employees bring him bad news. Then he and his employees find the silver linings. Eddie Cantor went broke during the Depression but turned bad into good by writing a best-selling joke book that helped millions laugh their way through those difficult times. Don't let others contribute negative self-talk that can interfere with your positive self-talk. If someone says how bad things look, either ignore the comment or turn it around.

When you practice your positive self-talk, be sure to emphasize your goals and what you want to achieve. Use the following guidelines to help you practice and enjoy positive, goal-directed talking.

197

TALKING CALMLY WORD-BY-WORD TO COPE WITH ANXIETY

Preparing for Anxiety in Stressful Situations

Effective Self-Talk	*Less Effective Self-Talk*
What is it I have to do?	There's so much to do.
I choose to do it.	I have to do it!
If I do the thing I fear, the fear is sure to die.	This is always frightening, but I'll do it.
I know ways to deal with this.	I think I can handle it.
I am well organized and efficient.	I can't forget what I need to say.
I have succeeded in situations like this one before. I am confident.	I won't worry anymore.
Time for a few deep breaths and relaxation. I am comfortable, relaxed, and at ease.	Usually the deep breathing lessens the anxiety.

Coping When Anxiety Starts to Build

Effective Self-Talk	*Less Effective Self-Talk*
My muscles are partially relaxed. Time to relax even more.	My muscles are getting tense. I have to relax.
I *can* meet this challenge. Coping is my middle name.	This is frightening, but I think I'll be all right.
One step at a time. I can handle the situation.	I can't handle it unless I take one step at a time.
I'll just think about what I have to do.	Don't get distracted. Just do what you have to.
I'm in control. Relax and take a deep breath.	Don't get nervous. You are in control.

Coping When Anxiety Starts to Overwhelm

Effective Self-Talk	*Less Effective Self-Talk*
Right now I feel nervous. But that's not like me. I'm also calm and confident.	Don't get nervous. You'll blow it.
If I do the thing I fear, the fear is sure to die.	I can't get afraid. I have to be cool.
I'll just pause. I *can* handle it.	Don't slow down. You've just got to beat this.
I'll label my relaxation level from 0 to 10, so I keep it in a good range.	I'll label my fear from 0 to 10, so I can watch it rise.
It's okay to feel some fear. It motivates me to do my best.	I shouldn't be afraid.
I'll pay attention to the present.	I shouldn't let my anxiety show.
I won't try to eliminate fear totally. I'll just keep it manageable.	I've got to stop being afraid.

Coping When It's All Over and the Anxiety Has Passed

Effective Self-Talk	*Less Effective Self-Talk*
I didn't get everything I wanted. That's okay. I tried, and that's what really counts.	I didn't get everything I wanted. I should have done better.
I have succeeded in some ways, and I'll have these successes to draw on next time.	I wasn't a total success – maybe next time.
I did the right things for myself. The other person may be a little angry or sad, but that's okay.	I shouldn't have hurt the other person's feelings.
That wasn't as hard as I thought. Next time it will be even easier.	I didn't think I would make it. I hope next time it is easier.
I'm doing better at this. I'm making progress.	I'm not doing as well as I should.

17 The Second Feature: Anger

We have introduced some techniques of positive self-talk for reducing anxiety. Positive self-talk can also help us manage the stress of other emotions. Anger is a very common source of such stress.

Anger can lead to destruction of property, disruption of important interpersonal relationships, and termination of employment. There are many ways of dealing with anger, and in the next few chapters we will help you learn some assertiveness skills. For many of us, however, it is first necessary to temper our aggression or violence so that we are able to put assertiveness skills to use. Changing our self-talk can help us temper our aggression.

Don't 'Put up' but Don't 'Shut up' Either

You have been learning new ways of dealing with anxiety by positive self-talking. Our goal for this chapter will be to help you learn sentences and statements that will help you avoid impulsive and negative responses to anger-provoking situations. We will show you ways to avoid 'putting up your dukes' and fighting. At the same time, as you will see, we don't want you to 'shut up' either. At first, you will learn what to say to yourself. In the chapters on assertiveness training, you will learn what to say to others to help you feel more competent and meet more of your goals.

Some people do not have difficulty with 'the shoot 'em ups.' Everyone experiences anger, but some people have been taught in childhood never to fight with either their fists or their words. There are some advantages to this style of life in that we avoid landing in jail, but unless we learn assertive ways of meeting our needs, we may experience frustration and stress-related psychosomatic disorders.

In the last chapter, you learned to talk yourself through anxiety by breaking most events into four time phases. These include (1) preparing for the feelings we may have, (2) coping when feelings of anxiety start to build, (3) coping when these feelings start to overwhelm, and (4) coping when the situation is over and the feelings have passed. These same phases are important in controlling our aggression.

In some situations anger is the best signal to fight because fighting is necessary. As discussed in the early chapters of this book, however, we encounter very few situations in modern life that would make good use of our physical ability to overcome other people or objects.

Getting in Line for the Shoot 'Em Ups

A good example of how talking to ourselves affects us involves a salesman who had a flat tire. He was in the country far from any service stations. He had a spare tire, but he did not have a jack. The salesman walked until he came to a farmhouse. He began to talk to himself as he approached the farmhouse: 'I bet the farmer won't want to help me. He probably has been plowing all day and is tired. Farmers don't like city folk anyway. He's going to think I'm really stupid for not having a jack. He'll probably laugh at me and tell me to go to town. Farmers can really be resentful.'

The salesman got to the door of the farmhouse and knocked loudly. You can imagine the surprise on the farmer's face when he came to the door and the man in front of him turned and yelled, 'I didn't want your old jack anyway.' There is a big difference between positive self-talk and negative self-talk.

To prepare for stressful situations that may provoke aggression, we need to rehearse what we will do and replace negative thinking with positive thinking. You can think of this phase as learning what to talk about while you get in line for the shoot 'em ups. If you are going home and you know that the people in the apartment above you may play loud music and you have gotten into several fights in the past, your self-talk will affect what you do and feel. Some ways to reduce your anger can be reviewed and practiced while you are stopped at red lights on your ride home. Memorize your lines or write them on a note card for use at red lights.

One of the most important things to ask yourself is 'What is it that I have to do?' It is also helpful to say, 'This may upset me, but I know some ways to deal with it.' Other useful phrases include 'I'll try not to take it too seriously,' and 'There is no need for an argument.' As you approach the situation, remind yourself: 'Time for a few breaths and

201

relaxation. I feel more comfortable, relaxed, and at ease.' As you get out of your car, you may say, 'Easy does it. Remember, I need to keep my sense of humor.' The last phrase is very important. It is hard to be angry when one is laughing.

In this example, we could prepare for an encounter with people who are not respecting our rights and find that they are not home. Many times, what we expect never happens. By saying the positive statements we have just reviewed, you can keep yourself calm while you wait and prepare for the potential event.

What you tell yourself before you enter anger-provoking situations is just as self-fulfilling as what you may say before anxiety-evoking situations. We need to strive to make our prophecies full of calm assertiveness, rather than blood and guts.

And In This Corner . . .

Next we can learn to cope with aggressive feelings by knowing what to say if our anger starts to build. In a boxing match this buildup may start when the announcer says, 'And in this corner . . .' At this point, we start to feel tense and ready to fight. We may get still angrier when we wonder whether we will be disqualified or our opponent will not show up at the last minute. These pessimistic ideas not only increase our anger but also can become self-fulfilling prophecies.

Take the example of someone who is accusing us of something we did not do. As we start to feel tense, it is helpful to say, 'My muscles are starting to feel a little tight. Time to relax. Time to slow down.' In addition, we might repeat the words, 'My anger can remind me of what I need to do. Time to help myself.' If a person begins to tell us all the wrong things we have done, it is easy to get angry. It is more helpful to say, 'Let's take this point by point.' As a person goes into a tirade, you can often help keep your own anger from getting out of hand by saying, 'Maybe we are both right. Let's try a cooperative approach.'

As the person's behavior begins to get under our skin and we begin to think of words to put him in his place, it is useful to say to yourself, 'Arguments lead to more arguments. Let's work constructively.' Sometimes, however, we feel that our self-esteem is on the line, and we have difficulty admitting that we are wrong. This reaction can come from the irrational belief that we need to be perfect or right all the time. Remember usually it is a question of what is right not who is right. Sometimes it is helpful to remind the other person of this fact.

Often it is best to let the other person run out of steam before beginning a discussion. By taking this time to relax, we can decrease our stress and allow the other person to become more receptive to discussion and arbitration.

In some situations, people provoke us in order to show that we have poor self-control. Even if this is not the case, many people have helped themselves by saying, 'He may want me to get really angry. Well, I'm going to try to disappoint him.' These positive statements should help you cope better when your feelings start to build.

When Your Back Is Against the Wall

When someone provokes or insults you, you may find your feelings starting to overwhelm you. At times, we are all caught off guard. A driver can cut in front of us in traffic, for example, or someone may damage something that is important to us. Our feelings may overwhelm us before we have had a chance to prepare or even recognize that they are starting to build. In other situations, we may have been preparing for our feelings as they started to build, but in the middle of the event our feelings overwhelm us. Just as in anxiety management, we need to know what to say to manage anger.

One of the best things to say is 'The more I keep my cool, the more I'm in control.' We may believe our anger will help us control the situation, but it usually does just the opposite. In addition, others will respect your ability to keep cool and stay in control.

When someone insults us, it is important to remember that we don't have to prove or defend ourselves. Positive talking will help remind us. Try using 'I don't need to prove myself.' It will be helpful to have the following phrase at the tip of your tongue: 'I don't want to make more out of this than I have to.' Another way to deal with insults is to say, 'No need to doubt myself – what he says may not matter.'

Anger-producing situations may arise that do not involve insults or provocations. If someone is cheating us in business or sold us poor quality merchandise, our feelings of anger may become strong. In these cases, it is often helpful to say, 'I'll think of what I want to get out of this.' This self-talk helps us to focus on what we need to do in order to get what we hope for. Often it is helpful to remind ourselves,

'Look for the good parts of this. I don't want to assume the worst and jump to conclusions.'

One of the advantages of anger is that it alerts us to our need to change the situation. If we are being cheated, it is better to know about it now than later, so that we can protect our property or investment. But, if we jump to conclusions because of our anger, we may later regret having disrupted an opportunity or a relationship. If a girl friend seems to be paying a great deal of attention to another man, it is important not to assume the worst and jump to a conclusion that she is going to leave. It is best to say to yourself, 'Let me get more information. Perhaps she is speaking to her cousin or her friend.'

And the Winner is . . .

After the situation is over and your anger has passed, it is important to know how to reward yourself. Just as in anxiety management, this is a unique opportunity for positive self-talk. It helps us to put the situation in perspective and reward ourselves for our accomplishments. When we get a reward for doing something, we are more likely to meet future challenges in the same way. If we reward ourselves for positive self-talking, we are more likely to use this skill again and avoid blowing up in other situations.

An example is if someone fails to pay back a loan or return something he has borrowed. You have coped successfully with your anger and asserted your needs to this person. The final step is to reward yourself by saying, 'I'm doing better at this! I'm making progress!' If you have done well but not as well as you had hoped, say, 'I can be pleased with my progress.' If you have done even better than you had expected, you might say, 'That wasn't really as hard as I thought.'

There usually are still some small feelings left over or some difficulties that are not resolved. In these cases, it is helpful to say, 'I will try not to take it personally. These are difficult situations. They take time to straighten out.'

Common Problems: 'I Always Have and I Always Will'

Just as in managing your anxiety, managing your anger requires that you try a new approach. One of the common problems is to get angry, blow up, and say, 'I always have, and I always will.' This response rewards the old ways and is not a productive way of managing your anger.

Just as in anxiety management, sometimes we are so angry that we cannot think positively. That is why it is very important to memorize the coping statements for each time phase of the event. If we are angry, it is often more difficult to remember what we want to say. That is why we must master and overlearn phrases so that they will be at our fingertips when we are angry.

Just as in anxiety management, some people find the phrases we suggest are not right for them. Write down your own phrases for the situation in which you hope to improve your coping. Again, be sure to include phrases that will prepare you for the event, some to help remind you to relax as your anger builds, some to help you cope with the anger when it starts to overwhelm you, and some to keep the situation in perspective and encourage yourself for the future.

Learning Your Lines

It is very important that you put the ideas you have been reading about into practice. To do so, you will need to learn the phrases systematically and practice them.

Counting Your Talks (Are You Talking to Yourself Enough?)

Spend a little time each day going through the four phases for coping with anger on a different stressor. If you have only a few major stressors, you may want to spend more than a day on some of them. Go slowly, and use your skill at visual imagery, so that when you begin working on these situations in real life, you will recall the statements and be able to cope more successfully. Make your 'talkies' as clear and provoking as you can. It is helpful to exaggerate the anger-provoking events to test your skill. The more you practice your self-talk and imagery rehearsal, the better you will be able to cope with feelings in real life.

Helpful Hints

Try to use periods of time during the day when you are waiting for a bus or checking out in a supermarket or have other free time. These are good times to relax and review your new self-talk. Keep these phrases on a slip of paper or card in your wallet or pocketbook for review during your free time. Again, it is often helpful to learn these phrases just before you go to sleep and, for this reason, we recommend that you leave the list on your night stand.

Do not try to learn all the phrases or visualize all the scenes at one time. It is useful to read all of them through in the beginning, but it is best to practice only a few each day. Again, this is a little like taking a series of injections for an inoculation against a disease to build up antibodies. These techniques are sometimes called anger inoculation.

If you still have difficulty with a situation, break it into its time phases, pick the one you have the most trouble with, and go over the statements for that time phase again. By continuing to do this, you will find yourself better and better able to cope with the anger that some situations evoke.

TALKING CALMLY WORD-BY-WORD TO COPE WITH ANGER

Preparing for Anger in Stressful Situations

Effective Self-Talk	*Less Effective Self-Talk*
What is it that I have to do?	I have to win this one.
This may upset me, but I know some ways to deal with it.	This is going to make me angry.
There may not be any need for an argument.	I know there will be an argument.
I'll try not to take it too seriously.	This one's for real.
Time for a few deep breaths and relaxation. I feel more comfortable, relaxed, and at ease.	I'm really ready for him.
Easy does it. Remember, I need to keep my sense of humor.	He's going to find out I'm serious.

Coping When Anger Starts to Build

Effective Self-Talk	*Less Effective Self-Talk*
My muscles are starting to feel a little tight. Time to relax. Time to slow down.	I'm really getting uptight.

206

Effective Self-Talk	Less Effective Self-Talk
My anger can remind me of what I need to do. Time to help myself.	This makes me mad.
Let's take this point by point.	He's wrong.
Maybe we are both right. Let's try a cooperative approach.	He's against me.
Let's remember, it's not who is right but what is right.	Only one of us is right, and it's me.
Arguments lead to more arguments. Let's work constructively.	Now, he's in for an argument.
He may want me to get really angry. Well, I'm going to try to disappoint him.	I'll show him.

Coping When Anger Starts to Overwhelm

Effective Self-Talk	Less Effective Self-Talk
The more I keep my cool, the more I'm in control.	He can't do that.
I'll think of what I want to get out of this.	I'll get even.
I don't need to prove myself.	I can't let him get away with that.
I don't want to make more out of this than I have to.	I'll take it to the top.
No need to doubt myself. What he says may not matter.	He can't say that to me.
Look for the good parts of this. I don't want to assume the worst and jump to conclusions.	This is going to be awful.

Coping When It's All Over and the Anger Has Passed

Effective Self-Talk	Less Effective Self-Talk
These are difficult situations. They take time to straighten out.	That always happens.

Effective Self-Talk	*Less Effective Self-Talk*
I will try not to take it personally.	He still didn't see my point.
That wasn't really as hard as I thought.	That was awful.
I'm doing better at this! I'm making progress!	I should have said more.
I can be pleased with my progress.	I'll win the argument next time.

Part Five

I Can Relax Now, but Will the Bully Stop Kicking Sand in My Face? Communicating Your Needs and Feelings

18   What Is Assertiveness?

We have practiced a number of techniques for stress management. Some involved relaxing our bodies. Others involved changing our thoughts and feelings so we could better cope with stressful situations. Another way of managing stress is through assertiveness.

Sometimes we fail to draw lines, set limits, speak up, or say no to people and demands in our lives. This difficulty can lead to procrastination, suffering in silence, halfheartedness, sloppiness, or forgetfulness as we say no in unconscious or dishonest ways.

If we cannot refuse the requests of others, we may live our lives according to other people's priorities rather than our own. We then may have additional stress that can be harmful and unnecessary. If we fail to assert ourselves, we can stockpile anger and find ourselves mentally and physically uptight.

Sometimes we feel that the only way to get our needs met and keep from being pushed around is to fight for our rights. When we feel bullied or fear that we will be bullied, we may try to bully others. We may then find ourselves in a continuous and desperate struggle with a lion's share of stress from guilt and loneliness.

In living and communicating with others, we behave in many ways. It is helpful to look at our reactions to others and group them into three main ways of behaving. We can be assertive, aggressive, or passive. What do we mean by these words?

Passive Behavior

Passive behavior means giving up your rights by not expressing your honest feelings, thoughts, and beliefs. It often involves permitting others to 'walk all over' you. It can also mean expressing yourself in such an apologetic way that you are overlooked. We behave passively when we do what we are told, regardless of how we feel about it.

211

When we act passively, we often feel helpless, anxious, resentful, and disappointed with ourselves. The goal of passivity is usually to please others and to avoid conflict or rejection.

Not too long ago, one of the authors found himself slipping into passive behavior. He was attending a convention with his wife, who is also a psychologist. They were given a room directly beneath the disco bar. The music was loud enough that if his wife had not been pregnant and tired from a long drive, they might have enjoyed live entertainment in their room!

The author wanted to change the situation, but he hesitated, thinking (1) he was given the convention rate, (2) someone had to use the room, (3) the hotel staff would think he was pushy, and (4) the manager would not change the room at 9:00 P.M. Inside, he felt angry, anxious, and powerless.

Then he laughed at himself. He realized that if he did not do something, he would be practicing passive behavior. He would not be getting what he paid for or expressing his feelings. He would be preaching wine but drinking water. One of the alternatives he considered was aggressive behavior.

Aggressive Behavior

When we are aggressive, we stand up for our personal rights and express our thoughts and feelings. But we do this in dishonest ways, which usually are not helpful and almost always step on the personal rights of others. Examples of aggressive behavior are blaming, threatening, and fighting.

When we are aggressive, we usually feel angry, frustrated, or self-righteous. We often feel bitter, guilty, or lonely afterward. The usual goals of aggressive behavior are to dominate, protect, win, humiliate, and force other people to lose.

In the example above, the author thought about going upstairs and yelling at the band leader or pulling the plug to the amplifiers. This behavior would have violated the rights of the band to make a living and the patrons to enjoy the music they came to hear. If the author had gone upstairs, he might have felt guilty or his wife might have been so embarrassed that he might feel very lonely. Finally, he might still be stuck in the noisy room or be thrown out altogether. At this point, he thought about assertive behavior.

Assertive Behavior

Assertive behavior means standing up for your personal rights and expressing your thoughts, feelings, and beliefs in direct, honest, and helpful ways, which do not violate the rights of others. Assertiveness means respecting yourself, expressing your needs, and defending your rights. It also means respecting the needs, feelings, and rights of other people.

When we are assertive, we usually feel better about ourselves and more self-confident. Assertiveness does not guarantee winning, but it does increase the chances of a good compromise or a better result without making others angry.

The author decided to count down to relaxation and review his rights. He was able to relax and remind himself that he had paid for a comfortable place to sleep. He then called the desk, stated the problem, and expressed his discomfort. The clerk answered that she would have the bass turned down.

The author hesitated and then realized that he was skeptical about the effectiveness of this measure. He scanned his body for tension and made his need for another room clear. After a brief silence, the clerk gave him a new room. The author was pleased, the hotel gained a satisfied customer, and the couple got a good night's rest.

The first step in assertiveness training is learning to recognize passive, assertive, and aggressive behavior. Read slowly through the charts on pages 214 to 218. Notice that the first two charts clarify the verbal and nonverbal characteristics of the three types of behavior.

About 60 percent of all communication is nonverbal, so pay attention to these characteristics. To become aware of potential double messages, try to imagine using the verbal part of one type of behavior with the nonverbal part of another.

The third and fourth charts reveal what our goals, feelings, and payoffs may be. How do you feel most of the time? What are your goals and what are your payoffs?

The fifth chart shows the effects of the three types of behavior on others. What effects do you want to have on your family, friends, and fellow workers?

The last chart reveals the outcomes we can expect from such behaviors. Think of some recent events and their outcomes. Did your outcomes match the behaviors you used?

These charts can help you see meekness, withdrawal, attack, and

A COMPARISON OF PASSIVE, ASSERTIVE, AND AGGRESSIVE BEHAVIORS

VERBAL BEHAVIORS

Passive	Assertive	Aggressive
You avoid saying what you want, think, or feel. If you do, you speak in such a way that you put yourself down. Apologetic words with hidden meanings, a smoke screen of vague words, or silence are used frequently. Examples are 'You know,' 'Well,' 'I mean,' 'I guess,' and 'I'm sorry.' You allow others to choose for you.	You say what you honestly want, think, and feel in direct and helpful ways. You make your own choices. You communicate with tact and humor. You use 'I' statements. Your words are clear and objective. They are few and well chosen.	You say what you want, think, and feel, but at the expense of others. You use 'loaded words' and 'you' statements that label or blame. You employ threats or accusations and one-upmanship. You choose for others.

NONVERBAL BEHAVIORS

Passive	Assertive	Aggressive
You use actions instead of words. You hope someone will guess what you want. You look	You listen closely. Your manner is calm and assured. You communicate caring and	You make an exaggerated show of strength. You are flippant. You have an air of superiority.

as though you don't mean what you say. Your voice is weak, hesitant, and soft. You whisper in a monotone. Your eyes are averted or downcast. You nod your head to almost anything another person says. You sit or stand far away from the other person. You don't know what to do with your hands, and they are trembling or clammy. You look uncomfortable, shuffle, and are tense or inhibited.

strength. Your voice is firm, warm, and expressive. You look directly at the other person, but you don't stare. You face the person. Your hands are relaxed. You hold your head erect, and you lean toward the other person. You have a relaxed expression.

Your voice is tense, loud, cold, or demanding. You are deadly quiet. Your eyes are narrow, cold, and staring. You almost see through the other person. You take a macho fight stance. Your hands are on your hips, and you are inches from the other person. Your hands are in fists, or your fingers are pointed at the other person. You are tense and appear angry.

YOUR APPARENT GOALS AND FEELINGS

GOALS

Passive	Assertive	Aggressive
To please, to be liked.	To communicate, to be respected.	To dominate or humiliate.

FEELINGS

Passive	Assertive	Aggressive
You feel anxious, ignored, hurt, manipulated, and disappointed with yourself. You are often angry and resentful later.	You feel confident and successful. You feel good about yourself at that time and later. You feel in control, you have self-respect, and you are goal-oriented.	You feel self-righteous, controlling, and superior. Sometimes you feel embarrassed or selfish later.

YOUR APPARENT PAYOFFS

PAYOFFS

Passive	Assertive	Aggressive
You avoid unpleasant situations, conflicts, short-term tensions, and confrontations. You don't have to take responsibility for your choices.	You feel good. You feel respected by others. Your self-confidence improves. You make your own choices. Your relationships with others are improved. You have very little physical distress now or later. You are in touch with your feelings.	You get some anger off your chest. You get a feeling of control. You feel superior.

THE EFFECTS ON OTHERS

THEIR FEELINGS

Passive	*Assertive*	*Aggressive*
They feel guilty, superior, frustrated, or even angry.	They feel respected or valued. They feel free to express themselves.	They feel humiliated, depreciated, or hurt.

THEIR FEELINGS TOWARD YOU

Passive	*Assertive*	*Aggressive*
They feel irritated. They pity and depreciate you. They feel frustrated or disgusted with you. They lose respect for you because you are a pushover.	They usually respect, trust, and value you. They know where you stand.	They feel hurt, defensive, humiliated, or angry. They resent, distrust, and fear you. They may want revenge.

PROBABLE OUTCOMES OF EACH TYPE OF BEHAVIOR

Passive

You don't get what you want. If you do get your own way, it is by indirect means. You feel emotionally dishonest. Others achieve their goals at your expense. Your rights are violated. Your anger builds up, and you either push it down or redirect it toward other people who are less powerful. You may find yourself procrastinating, suffering in silence, doing things halfheartedly, being sloppy, or becoming forgetful. Others manipulate you. Loneliness and isolation may become common in your life.

Assertive

You often get what you want if it is reasonable. You often achieve your goals. You gain self-respect. You feel good. You convert win-lose to win-win. The outcome is determined by above-board negotiations. Your rights and others' rights are respected.

Aggressive

You often get what you want but at the expense of others. You hurt others by making choices for them and infantilizing them. Others feel they have a right to get even. You may have increasing difficulty with relaxing and unwinding later.

blame for what they are – sadly inadequate strategies of escape that create more pain and stress than they prevent. Before you can achieve assertive behavior, you must face the fact that passive and aggressive behaviors have often failed to get you what you want.

EXAMPLES OF COMMUNICATION STYLES

The situation you might be in	What you say and do
1. You are watching a movie, but people seated in front of you are making it hard to hear the sound.	You sit and fume, clearing your throat occasionally. (Passive)
2. At a meeting one person often interrupts you when you are speaking.	You look at the person and say firmly, 'Excuse me, I'd like to finish what I'm saying.' (Assertive)
3. You'd like a raise.	You shuffle into your boss's office and say, 'Do you think that, ah, you could see your way clear to giving me a raise?' (Passive)
4. You have talked with your boss about a helpful suggestion for organizing the work in the office. He says that he thinks it is a good idea and he will ask someone else to put the change into effect.	You put your hands on your hips and shout, 'This was my suggestion, and I'll not stand for someone else getting all the credit for it.' (Aggressive)
5. You are looking forward to a quiet night alone. A relative calls and asks you to babysit.	You communicate caring but strength as you say, 'I put aside tonight for myself, and I won't be able to babysit.' (Assertive)
6. Your parents or in-laws call and tell you they are dropping by. You are busy.	In a loud voice you say, 'You always call two minutes before you are here and expect me to drop everything.' (Aggressive)
7. Two workers in your office	You call the offenders together,

219

have been talking about personal matters. The work is piling up. Others have been complaining. You are their supervisor.

lean toward them, and say, 'I know how easy it is for time to slip by when you are relaxing and talking to your friends. But your work is piling up and I would like you to use the twenty-minute break for personal conversation.' (Assertive)

8. A good friend is always late for things you plan to do together. You have not said anything for several weeks.

When your friend arrives, you look as though you are ready to explode. You say, 'You're never on time!' (Aggressive)

9. A date and time is being set for a weekly meeting. The time is not convenient for you. The times are set when it will be next to impossible for you to make the meeting regularly.

When asked about the time, you look down and almost whisper, 'Well, I guess it's okay. I'm not going to be able to come very much, but if it fits everyone else's schedule, it's OK with me.' (Passive)

10. You are the only woman (or man) in a group of men (or women). You are asked to be the secretary at the meetings.

You respond, 'I'm willing to do my share and take the notes this time. In future meetings I'd like others to take their turn.' (Assertive)

19 When Do You Turn Aggressive and When Do You Turn the Other Cheek?

Now that you understand and can identify behavior that is aggressive, passive, and assertive, it is time to put the spotlight on your own life. By now, you probably have discovered that some of your behavior is aggressive or passive. Before you try to change these behaviors, it is best to pinpoint a large number of them so that you can start asserting yourself in situations that will have the greatest likelihood of success. This chapter should help you 'know thyself' a little better and identify some reasonable goals for assertiveness training.

To help you do this, find the chart on page 222. Notice that ten situations are given and seven categories of people are provided. For example, you may not have difficulty refusing requests from subordinates at work, but you may have great difficulty refusing requests from your spouse or from close friends. You may be able to give your opinions easily if they differ from those of friends but you may have much more difficulty doing so when you are in large groups.

The goal of categorizing your assertiveness in different interactions is to become aware of the situations in which you have the most difficulty. By rating them, you will know where to start practicing new assertive behaviors.

As you fill out the chart on page 222, note that in the first three categories of situations – refusing requests, handling criticism, and receiving from others – the interaction is begun by others. The list continues with situations in which passivity can result when we put off doing anything because we are not forced to act.

Your Inalienable Rights

Notice that each category of situation reflects one of the rights that we have as people. Many people do not realize that they have rights in

RATING YOUR ASSERTIVENESS IN DIFFERENT SITUATIONS WITH DIFFERENT PEOPLE

Directions: Fill in each of the blocks with a rating of your assertiveness from 0 to 10. A rating of 0 means you have no difficulty at all in asserting yourself. A rating of 10 means you are completely unable to assert yourself.

People: Situation:	Relatives	Friends	Strangers	Authority Figures	Subordinates	Service People	Groups
1. Refusing requests							
2. Handling criticism							
3. Receiving from others							
4. Stating your rights and needs							
5. Expressing negative feelings							
6. Giving negative feedback and confronting others							
7. Differing with others and giving opinions							
8. Making requests							
9. Expressing positive feelings							
10. Making social contacts							

their relationships with others. Some of us have full knowledge of a long list of obligations but are only dimly aware of our own rights.

Whether you make up a list of rights from the Declaration of Independence, the Bill of Rights, or the Universal Declaration of Human Rights, your rights are freedoms which people have sought and fought for. Your assertion keeps you free by upholding these rights.

What are some of your rights? You have the right to refuse a request. In fact, you have the right to say no to any request without feeling guilty. Other people's problems may be important and pressing, but you are not required to solve them. You also have the right to change your mind or decide on another course of action.

You have the right to handle criticisms without assuming or acting as if they are always correct. In addition, you have the right to make mistakes.

You have the right to receive from others and to accept gifts with no strings attached, and you do not have to reciprocate now or in the future. You have the right to state your needs and to stand up for your rights, even if it sometimes means putting yourself first.

More Rights

You have the right to express your true feelings whether they are positive, warm, and pleasurable or negative, angry, and dissatisfied. Part of assertiveness is the right to be the final judge of your feelings. By accepting and expressing your feelings you can avoid the loneliness that comes from either being unaware of these feelings or being unable to communicate them to others.

If your rights are violated, you have the right to give negative feedback so that the other person can choose to respect your rights. You have the right to protest unfair treatment or criticism.

You have the right to your own convictions. If someone proposes something you do not like, you have the right to differ with that person and give your opinions.

You also have the right to make requests in the hope that others will help you. Some of us have been taught to deny our own needs and never to ask for help or emotional support. Finally, you have the right to make social contacts, to start conversations with others, and to build friendships. Without these rights we would live in a dangerous and lonely world. Such a world would be full of distress.

223

The following chart will help you to assess your own behavior patterns. While you fill out the chart, it may be helpful to run through the past week or two and find situations in your life where you found yourself acting in either an aggressive or passive manner. The most important problems for stress management are the ones that occur over and over again. Even those to which you give a rating of mildly difficult are important if they happen often. They are also important because it is usually best to change your behavior on the easier tasks first so as to ensure success.

Now, rate your assertiveness in the situations categorized in the chart.

Mildly Difficult Situations Calling for Assertiveness

When you have rated your assertiveness in various situations, choose a few real-life examples in which you have mild difficulty asserting yourself. These should be rated around a 3 on the 0 to 10 scale. Write these situations down. For example, a teacher we worked with wrote down the following situations.

Example 1. *Refusing requests from friends: Jane Stoner asked me to help her with the United Fund*

Example 2. *Stating rights and needs with relatives: John borrows the family car but does not tell us when he will return it.*

Example 3. *Differing with others and giving opinions in groups; Speaking up at the faculty meeting when I disagree with curriculum changes.*

Moderately Difficult Situations Calling for Assertiveness

Next, make a list of situations in which you have moderate difficulty asserting yourself. These should be rated around 5 to 7 on the scale. Here is a list that a young lawyer gave.

Example 1. *Making social contacts with strangers:*
meeting the attractive girl in front of me in line at lunch

Example 2. *Handling criticisms from authority figures:*
Finding myself tongue tied when the boss points out a mistake

Example 3. *Giving negative feedback to subordinates:*
Pointing out a mistake to the older secretary who made it.

Very Difficult Situations Calling for Assertiveness

Finally, make a list of situations in which you have a great deal of difficulty asserting yourself. These should have a rating of 8 to 10. A homemaker had particular difficulty with situations outside of the home. Her list included the following examples.

Example 1. *Refusing request from service personnel:*
The waitress asked me to hurry up because there is a large group requiring seating.

Example 2. *Differing with others and giving opinions in groups. Expressing her concern for her children's safety when the issue of bussing came up at a meeting*

Example 3. *Making requests from authority figures.*
Asking Johnny's pediatrician about the treatment that he is recommending.

20 Rolling Up Your Sleeves and Becoming Assertive

You have taken the first steps toward assertive behavior. You have learned the differences between aggressive, passive, and assertive behavior. You have pinpointed the situations and the people that cause you difficulty being assertive. You have rated the difficulty of the situations, and now it is time to begin practicing assertiveness skills.

The following step-by-step approach to assertiveness training comes from the book *Your Perfect Right* by Robert Alberti, Ph.D., and Michael Emmons, Ph.D. Their book started the assertiveness training movement. The steps involve reviewing your behaviors and trying to be assertive in a situation with a high probability of success.

First, review the lists of mildly, moderately, and very difficult situations which you wrote for Chapter 19. Then, list and categorize your responses according to whether they were passive, assertive, or aggressive. Look at what you say verbally and how you say it non-verbally. Write down your goals by referring to the chart, Your Apparent Goals and Feelings, in Chapter 18.

Perhaps you are trying to avoid conflict, to please, dominate, or humiliate rather than communicate. Consider what you gain by being aggressive or passive and what you might gain by being assertive. You almost always have more to gain by being assertive. If necessary, review the effects on others of your behavioral options and their probable outcomes.

Planning Your Assertiveness

Now that you have reviewed what you are currently doing and have chosen to become more assertive, it is time to decide how you might handle the situations better. A good way of finding a better way of coping with the situation is to observe someone who is handling it effectively. You may wish to write down a variety of responses that might be more effective than ones you are currently using. Later in this chapter, we will suggest many different assertive techniques.

Imagining Your Assertiveness

The next step is to use visual imagery to imagine better ways of handling the problem. Imagine yourself acting in an assertive manner both verbally and nonverbally. Picture how the other person will react and your response. Envision a number of outcomes and how you can handle them.

Role-Playing Your Assertiveness

Rather than jumping from imagining your new behavior to trying it out in the 'cruel world,' it is best first to role-play your assertive solutions. Role-playing means taking the role of someone who is acting in an assertive manner. It is often helpful to use a mirror to check your nonverbal messages. Be sure that you are:

1. Facing the other person from a normal distance.
2. Looking directly at the other person without staring.
3. Keeping your head erect and body relaxed.
4. Leaning toward the other person.
5. Speaking distinctly and firmly, so as to be easily heard.

Try taking the role of yourself and then taking the role of the other person. Finally, try your role once again. Imagine and rehearse all the possible outcomes.

When you role-play, be sure to use your relaxation techniques to calm yourself. This will also help you learn a relaxed, calm, and firm approach to assertive communication. You may also want to practice your new skills with someone in your family or with a friend. Be sure to switch roles and practice both roles several times.

The Real Thing

The next step is to choose a situation that is likely to bring good results and build up your confidence. Talk over your difficulties with members of your family or a close friend. Ask them to help you deal with your problem by encouraging you and by praising you when you report back about your attempts. Then, relax and take the plunge. Afterward, do not be blind to your progress. Reward yourself for acting assertively.

Remember, you do not have to succeed all the time. Just be sure to learn from your mistakes and then practice more effective behaviors in your imagination, your role-playing, and your daily life. It will take a good deal of practice before you can practice these behaviors naturally and automatically.

Taking the Steps to Assertiveness

A young woman who was looking forward to graduating from college and getting married came to one of us for therapy because she was suffering from tension headaches. After she found some relief from relaxation training, it became clear that a major source of stress was her relationship with her fiancé, a senior medical student. Her fiancé often asked her to do more errands than she wanted to take on.

Following the steps suggested above, the woman, whom we will call Susan, began by reviewing her behavior. She described the situation that brought the problem to a head in the following way. The weekend before, her fiancé, whom we will call Bill, had spent one of his few days off fishing with his friends. He had been at her apartment a couple of hours before she returned from shopping with her mother. When Bill told her that he was hungry and asked why she was late, she was angry and disappointed that he had not started dinner, but she apologized and said she would begin cooking right away.

Susan correctly identified her behavior as passive. She had avoided saying what she thought, wanted, or felt. Her apology had a hidden meaning of anger, and she remembered being tense and hoping that he would see how tired she looked.

Susan realized how much she wanted to please Bill. At the same time, she felt resentful. Thinking back, she remembered how little respect Bill's father had for his wife, who never stood up to him or refused his requests before their divorce. She vowed not to fall into the same trap.

Susan started to think of assertive behaviors that she might use. She had a good friend named Kathy, who was married to a medical student and seemed to have a very healthy relationship with her husband.

Susan talked with Kathy and then began using visual imagery. She rehearsed new ways of responding to Bill's requests. She also imagined new ways of approaching Bill for a discussion about these issues.

At our next session, Susan reviewed this work but was advised to slow down. She had picked one of her most difficult situations, one that could seriously affect her personal happiness. She then found an easier situation that was not as critical and had a higher likelihood of immediate success. Susan chose a mildly difficult but common problem she had with her sister.

After imagining an assertive response to her sister's requests, she role-played the behavior. But with a weak voice and her eyes turned downward, she did not look as though she meant what she was saying. Susan then watched herself in the mirror, started to laugh, and agreed to use a mirror to practice her nonverbal behaviors at home.

After successfully asserting herself with her sister, Susan began role-playing some of the new approaches she wanted to use in her relationship with Bill. She practiced with her friend Kathy and then tried out her new skills with Bill.

As it turned out, Bill was very concerned that their marriage should not end the way his parents' had. He was surprised at his actions when Susan expressed her disappointment and described what he did that troubled her. At the next session of therapy, Susan reported that she was proud of her assertiveness and that their communication was steadily improving.

Responding Assertively to the Requests of Others

The step-by-step approach we just covered is effective in situations in which you need to initiate an assertive behavior. But there are many situations that require you to respond to the actions of other people. We nave found it important to practice these situations and role-play them repeatedly because in these stressful situations you may respond impulsively.

Let us take the example of a request made by an authority figure at work. Your immediate supervisor asks you to stay a few hours overtime and do extra work. You have special plans, and you do not want to give them up. First, you should ask for clarification. If you do not understand what is requested of you or its importance, it is difficult to make a decision either to fulfill the request or to refuse it. In this case, it would be important to clarify how pressing the work is and whether it is work you might be expected to accomplish.

The next step is to decide where you stand on the issue. You need to take time to process the request and make a decision. Even in a situation like the one just given, you may want to say that you need time to think it over and let your boss know when you will have an answer. Before responding, it is helpful to use a relaxation technique such as scanning or countdown.

Try to use the word 'no' when turning down a request. 'No' has a great deal of power and clarity. It is a lot better than 'Well, I just don't think so . . . ah . . .' Along the same lines, it is important to be as brief as possible. Give your reasons for refusing the request, but avoid long, elaborate justification or explanation. Long excuses can become accusations or reveal your tendency toward overresponsibility. The other person can use these excuses to manipulate you.

Try to use 'I' messages. In this case, you might say, 'I won't work overtime tonight.' This might be more effective than 'I can't work tonight' or 'I shouldn't work tonight.' Using an 'I' message makes it clear that you have made a choice.

The Broken Record Technique

You may find it necessary to refuse the request several times before the person 'hears' you. In this case, you can use a technique that has been popularized by Manuel Smith, Ph.D. He called it the broken record. To use the technique you calmly repeat your 'no,' with or without your original reason for declining. You do so as often as is required. You may find it helpful to practice the broken record technique in your role-playing.

One of the best situations to use the broken record is when you are trying to get what you have paid for. It is particularly useful with repairmen, waiters, waitresses, salespeople, and landlords. In these cases, you continue saying no to any compromise that is unsatisfactory. Be sure to speak in a firm, relaxed manner. Role-playing these situations can help you to realize how frequently you may have to play your broken record in a situation.

The Power of Silence

Silence is a very potent form of nonverbal communication. If someone continues to badger you after you have turned on your broken record, use silence. This technique is particularly useful on the telephone. If you recall the difficulty that one of the authors had because of the noise level in his hotel room, you may be interested to know that the author's silence seemed to be what finally led the clerk to make the decision to change the room.

Additional Approaches

You may also want to assert yourself about what is happening when you are being badgered. You may want to say, 'I really wish you would stop pressuring me.' Or you could try, 'I'm not going to change my mind.' If this does not work, you may need to tell the person what you are going to do next. You may say that you are going to change the topic, hang up the phone, or leave. And it may be necessary to follow through and do what you say you are going to do.

An additional approach, called the paradoxical statement, has the power of the unexpected. A paradox may lead to exactly the opposite of what you actually say. For example, just before you leave or hang up the phone, you may say, 'I hope you will write me a letter or call me several more times about this matter. It is really helping me to practice my assertiveness.' This response often disarms the person who is badgering you and leaves him without an offense.

The Fogging Technique

Another major technique popularized by Dr. Smith is called fogging. The person trying to be assertive repeats what the other person is saying or asking for. In this way, before he says no, the person acknowledges the other person's problem and shows that he understands what the other person is communicating.

In relationships with important people, it is helpful to acknowledge the feelings that the other person may have about your refusal. You may want to reflect his feelings after he has stated them, saying something like 'I know that you've been hoping that I would do it and that this may be a disappointment to you, but I won't be able to.'

Try to avoid using the words 'I'm sorry.' Apologizing is often unnecessary and dishonest. It also tends to compromise your basic right to say no. You may wish to offer a compromise, but it is important that you realize you have the freedom not to compromise and not to work an hour extra or come in early the next day. Be sure to refuse the major request clearly and without feeling guilty.

Finally, you have the right to change your mind and refuse a request that you may have originally agreed to. You have to weigh the consequences, but if you find yourself hedging or feeling manipulated, you may want to reconsider your initial decision.

Practice Saying 'No'

To practice saying no to requests and demands, use the following examples. First, try them in your imagination and then role-play them in front of a mirror.

1. A friend asks you for a loan until next pay day.
2. Your daughter asks if she may stay out until 3:00 in the morning.
3. You are on a committee and have done your work. Another committee member calls you at the last minute and tries to get you to do some of his work.
4. Your uncle tells you of his plan to visit you for a month. This is his third visit this year.
5. A person at work never seems to have a ride home. He asks you again for one.
6. A salesperson pressures you to buy when you are still undecided.
7. You and your wife are out with friends who want to go for a nightcap. You are tired and want to go home.
8. A friend asks you to make cookies for a bake sale, but you have planned an evening with another friend.
9. Your boss asks you again to postpone your vacation.
10. A friend expects you to help her plan a party.

Taking the Stress out of Criticism

Criticism you receive from others is another major category of situations for which you may need to practice responding to others in an assertive manner. When someone criticizes you, you may find it helpful to use a brief relaxation technique such as taking a deep breath and saying silently, 'Relax and let go.' This will help you to listen to what the person is saying. If the criticism is vague or ambiguous, it may be helpful to ask the person to be more specific. The next step may be to state the criticism in your own words. This allows you to check out what you have heard and shows the other person that you understood the criticism.

At this point, it is often helpful to take a moment to relax and decide whether the criticism is accurate or useful. You may also want to get in touch with your feelings so you can share them with the person making the criticism. You may feel annoyed, angry, or scared. It is often helpful to share these feelings with the other person so that the person will know the effect the criticism is having on you. You may want to express your feelings about the timing, frequency, or accuracy of the criticism.

If the criticism is fair, you may find it helpful to ask for specific suggestions and alternatives. It is important to avoid excuses that may turn out to be self-accusations. Try to move toward the future and turn the person criticizing you in the same direction. When sharing your feelings about the criticism, it is important to use 'I' statements so as not to put the other person on the defensive. Consider the difference between 'You don't understand anything' and 'It seems to me that you may not have understood what happened.'

By using a relaxation technique, you can avoid an escalating sense of urgency and anger. If you try to match the pace and volume of the person criticizing you, an argument may develop. Try speaking slowly, calmly, and quietly.

Here are some examples of criticisms to practice with:

1. Your boss says your work is sloppy.
2. Your supervisor says your work is never finished on time.
3. Your wife says you don't love her.
4. Your child says you don't understand him.
5. Your mother says you don't visit often enough.
6. Your girl friend says you are a cheat.
7. Your teacher says your paper was confusing and meaningless.
8. A new acquaintance says, 'Most women don't know what they're talking about.'
9. Your students say your lectures are boring.
10. A customer says that what you have done or what you sell is useless.

Common Problems and Their Solutions

Some people can recognize and categorize their behavior but have difficulty with the next step of vividly imagining better ways of handling the problem. They know what to imagine, but to do so makes them anxious. If you seem to be having trouble visualizing a situation without a great deal of anxiety, you may be conditioned to respond with fear in situations in which you might be disliked or rejected. If this is the case, it may be helpful to return to Chapter 12. Practice mental simulation and image rehearsal with relaxation so that you will be less sensitive to what others say and do.

Irrational Beliefs Supporting Passive Behaviors

Another way of handling difficulties with assertiveness is to examine potential irrational beliefs about assertiveness. Lynn Bloom, Karen Coburn, and Joan Pearlman, in their excellent book *The New Assertive Woman*, review irrational beliefs that support passive behaviors. One of their chapters is entitled 'What's the Worst That Could Happen – Irrational Beliefs.' These irrational beliefs can support passive behaviors whether you are a man or a woman.

You may have unrealistic beliefs about the possible outcomes of a situation involving assertive behavior. Even if the outcome is negative, you may be blowing it out of proportion or assuming that you could not handle it. Some of the irrational beliefs and their rational counterparts are listed below:

Irrational Belief	*Rational Counterpart*
1. As soon as I am assertive, others will become angry at me.	Others may react positively, neutrally, or negatively. If assertiveness involves legitimate rights, the odds are that you will have a positive response.
2. As soon as I assert myself, people will become angry and I will be devastated.	I will be capable of handling it, and I am not responsible for another person's anger. It may well be that person's problem.
3. I want others to be honest and straightforward with me, but if I tell others what I feel or want, I will hurt them.	People may or may not feel hurt, and most people prefer to be dealt with directly.

Irrational Belief	*Rational Counterpart*
4. If others are hurt by my assertive behavior, I am responsible for their hurt feelings.	Even if they are hurt, I can let them know I care for them in other ways, and they will survive.
5. If I turn down legitimate requests, other people will hate me.	Even legitimate requests can be refused. I can consider my own needs, and I cannot please everyone all the time.
6. I should always avoid making statements or asking questions that might make me look stupid.	I am a valuable human being. The people I want to associate with will accept me as a valuable human being.

Irrational Beliefs Supporting Aggressive Behaviors

Aggression is appropriate for situations in which we are physically attacked. Fearing harm, we strike back to protect ourselves. Unfortunately, we may misperceive a situation as dangerous and become aggressive in unnecessary and ineffective ways. What we think and say to ourselves can determine what we see and do. This is especially true when we jump to conclusions without considering all the evidence.

Just as there are irrational beliefs that support passive behaviors, there are irrational beliefs that support aggressive behaviors. If you are trying to substitute assertive behaviors for aggressive ones, consider some of the false beliefs that often support aggressive behaviors. The irrational beliefs that follow were held by people in a group we led to help them get better control over their tempers and aggressive behaviors. Some of the rational counterparts which the group members found useful are provided next to each irrational belief.

Irrational Belief	*Rational Counterpart*
1. It's either him or me, and it's not going to be me if I can help it.	We can both win. Let's look for a compromise.
2. If I'm not aggressive, they will be.	Others may respond in many ways – odds are the ways will be neutral or positive.

Irrational Belief	Rational Counterpart
3. It's a dog-eat-dog world.	What you expect is often what you get.
4. If I don't angrily turn this request down now, I'll have a flood of requests to contend with.	I can be assertive if people later try to take advantage of me.
5. If I don't let them know loud and clear, they won't do what they said they would.	First, I'll see what they say to my firm request. I can always use other assertive techniques if they refuse.
6. You can't teach an old dog new tricks. I always get angry.	Always? Few 'always' or 'never' statements are true.

Check and dispute your irrational beliefs. Some of them may be interfering with your right to be assertive. Review Chapter 15 about thinking and feeling better if you have trouble recognizing and disputing them.

When It Is Best Not to Be Assertive

Assertive communication is direct and honest. But there may be times when it is best to be aggressive or passive. When you are stressed, the fight-or-flight response may be appropriate. You do not want to talk about your rights when a saber-toothed tiger is running toward you. Likewise, when a robber puts a gun to your head, it may not be the best time to be assertive. Pick your battles carefully and weigh the costs against the benefits of being assertive, passive, or aggressive.

Part Six

Planning Your Days
and Your Years

21 Managing the Times of Your Life

The Faster I Go, the Behinder I Get

Time has fascinated men throughout the ages. 'Time, time, oh good, good time, where have you gone?' This has been the lament of the young and the striving. It has also been the lament of the old and the dying. If you have ever wondered where time has gone, you may have been using your time ineffectively. You may know the meaning of the words 'The faster I go, the behinder I get.'

Not Seeing the Forest for the Trees

One of the best stories we know concerning the ineffective use of time is about a lumberjack, or at least a very powerful young man who wanted to be a lumberjack. This young man wandered through a logging camp on his eighteenth birthday. He had been raised around lumbering communities and admired the strong lumberjacks. He told the boss that he wanted a job. Seeing that the boy was large, strong, and healthy, the boss quickly agreed. The first day this lad chopped down ten large trees entirely by himself. This was quite an accomplishment, and the boss was very pleased. He complimented the boy on his energy and strength.

The next day, the boy seemed to work just as hard and just as long, but he only chopped down eight trees. This was still a respectable showing. The rest of the week passed, and each day the boy worked just as hard and just as long, but each day he produced less. On Friday, the boss called the boy into his office after noticing that he had yet to fell one tree. The sun was going down. The boy had worked vigorously all day. He was ashamed because he had produced so little, and tears began to roll down his face as he went into the office.

239

'Sir,' he said, 'I'm working harder and harder, but I'm afraid I'm a disappointment to you. I have yet to fell one tree today.' 'Why do you do so little?' the boss asked. 'I'm really trying, Sir,' was the response. 'Have you taken the time to sharpen your ax, boy?' The boy answered, 'No, sir, I really haven't had time because I have been so busy working.' The lesson: work sharper, not harder.

Today, thousands of people everywhere in the world tirelessly pursue a fleeting thing called time. Yet time is the one thing that we are all given in equal amounts. The rich and the poor all have the same number of minutes in an hour, hours in a day, and days in a year.

What Is Time?

It has been said that your time is your life. If you waste your time, you waste your life. Saint Augustine said that we speak of time as though we understand it, but when we are asked to define it, our minds go blank. Time can be thought of as an endless series of decisions, small and large, that gradually shape our lives.

Not only do we have difficulty defining time, but we also have misconceptions about time. For example, we often say that time flies. Of course, time does not fly. Time moves at a predetermined rate. Another misconception is that we can save time. We cannot really save time. We cannot put time in a bank or collect interest on time that is saved. Can we make up time? No, once time is spent it is irretrievable. Some say time is money, but it is valuable only if it is productive or enjoyable.

We often feel that time and the clock are against us. But time can be on our side once we have the ability to organize our lives to use time to our benefit. If the use of time is an endless series of management decisions, inappropriate decisions can produce frustration, lower self-esteem, and increase stress levels.

Danger Signals of Poor Time Management

There are various danger signals that suggest a person can benefit from better time management. Read through the following list and discover if any of these warnings apply to you. Use the scale under the title to determine your score between 0 and 10 for each item. Record your score in the blank next to each statement and then add these scores to compute your total time management score.

TIME MANAGEMENT SCALE

0	1 2 3	4 5 6	7 8 9	10
Never	Sometimes	Frequently	Most of the Time	Always

—— 1. I am indispensable. I find myself taking on various tasks because I'm the only one who can do them.

—— 2. Daily crises take up all my time. I have no time to do important things because I'm too busy putting out fires.

—— 3. I attempt to do too much at one time. I feel I can do it all, and I rarely say no.

—— 4. I feel unrelenting pressure, as if I'm always behind and have no way to catch up. I'm always rushing.

—— 5. I'm working habitually long hours, ten, twelve, fourteen, even eighteen hours a day, five, six, and seven days a week.

—— 6. I constantly feel overwhelmed by demands and details and feel that I have to do what I don't want to do most of the time.

—— 7. I feel guilty about leaving work on time. I don't have sufficient time for rest or personal relationships. I take worries and problems home.

—— 8. I constantly miss deadlines.

—— 9. I am plagued by fatigue and listlessness with many slack hours of unproductive activity.

—— 10. I chronically vacillate between unpleasant alternatives.

—— Total Score

If you scored less than 35 total points, you may benefit from learning additional time-management techniques, but your stress level is probably not significantly affected by time pressure. If you scored 36 to 60, you probably could use time-management training to reduce the risk of potential stress disorders.

If you scored above 60, your life may feel dangerously out of control. People who score over 60 often 'don't have time' for training in stress or time management. They may put off indefinitely such important decisions as to stop smoking, begin exercising, spend more time with family and friends, or take vacations. We have a choice whether we wish to allow time to manage us, or we wish to manage time.

Time, Stress, and Productivity

Productivity can increase as we spend more time and energy, but only up to a critical point. Past this point, additional time and energy become counter-productive. Time management experts use a stress-productivity curve to demonstrate this finding. If you examine this curve, you will notice that there is a critical point beyond which increasing time, energy, and stress lead to decreasing productivity. This is the point of diminishing returns.

STRESS-PRODUCTIVITY CURVE

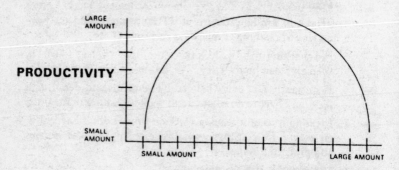

We mentioned earlier in this book that stress can be a motivator. Time can also be our friend. If you have too much stress or too little time, however, these can become enemies that lead to many of the problems we listed above. Time can be your master or your slave. Time management techniques are ways of gaining control over your life and finding solutions to various time wasters.

Time Wasters Are Time Robbers

An analysis of time wasters helps to build a firm foundation for good time management. A time waster is anything that prohibits us from reaching our objectives most effectively. Time is a perishable asset, and if we are not careful, it can be taken away without our even noticing it is being stolen. Time wasters are robbers. They can be divided into two major categories: major and minor time wasters.

Major time wasters stand between us and what we want to accomplish. They include problems with our attitudes, goals, objectives, priorities, plans, and abilities to make basic decisions.

Minor time wasters include distractions that hinder us once we are on the way to accomplishing what we want to accomplish. Minor time wasters can include interruptions that we face during the day, lengthy meetings of minor importance, needless reports, extended telephone calls, unexpected visitors, and many others.

Taking a Time Inventory

Before examining steps to effective time management and analyzing time wasters, it is useful to take your own personal time inventory. To do this, you should make a chart of the day, broken into fifteen-minute segments, or use an appointment book. Carry the chart or appointment book with you during a typical day and fill it in as you go along. It is most helpful to complete this inventory as you go through a normal day. If you try to recall accurately how you spent your time and how much work you actually accomplished in a particular day, you might find it difficult or impossible.

Categorize the activities that suit your particular business or daily routine. We would like to suggest certain categories that you may find useful. For example, categories that are often helpful in taking a time inventory of the working part of the day include socializing, routine tasks, low-priority work, productive work, meetings, and telephone calls. Helpful categories for when you are not at work include telephone calls, television, recreation, errands, commuting, shopping, household chores, eating, personal hygiene, and sleeping.

Modify or add any categories that will help you better understand how you spend your time. Taking a time inventory can help you separate and examine the various categories of time and how you use them. You can then determine whether you want to spend more or less time in particular activities.

The next step is to make a satisfaction column and indicate whether you were satisfied, unsatisfied, or neither next to each fifteen-minute segment.

By taking a time inventory, some people learn that they need to limit phone conversations to five minutes, reduce the amount of time spent on preparation for breakfast and eating, shorten the time spent showering and preparing for work in the morning, and restrict the time spent watching television. Some people, however, find that morning is their best time for relaxation. For them, a long, casual breakfast may be very effective in helping to manage stress.

Although every person is unique, the majority of people find that their most productive work hours and peak energy periods are in the morning. If there are many interruptions, lengthy meetings, or a lack of priorities and organized objectives in the morning, they may feel they have wasted the day before they reach noon. These people should schedule their most productive work in the mornings.

Complete your time inventory and then add up the amount of time spent in each category of activity. Following is a blank inventory chart as a sample.

PERSONAL TIME INVENTORY

List the activities you do during the next three days. Use the following Activity Codes and make up Personal Codes to describe how your time was spent.

In the *Satisfaction* column place a ' + ,' '0,' or ' – ' to indicate how satisfied you are with how you spent your time. If you are very satisfied or feel the time was spent productively, place a ' + ' in the column. If you are not satisfied with how you spent the time but feel that what you did was necessary, rate it '0.' If you are dissatisfied with how you spent your time or feel that what you did was unnecessary use the ' – ' for the rating.

Activity Codes:

Socializing: Soc.
Telephone Calls: Tel.
Meetings: Mtgs.
Low-Priority Work: LPW
Medium-Priority Work: MPW
Productive Work: PW
Commuting to Work: Com.

Passive recreation (reading, listening to the radio): PR
Active recreation (exercise, golf): AR
Errands: Err.
Shopping: Shop
Household Chores: HC
Eating: Eat

Date _____

Time	Activity	Satisfaction (+, 0, −)	Time	Activity	Satisfaction (+, 0, −)
5:00 A.M.	_____		10:00 A.M.	_____	
5:15 A.M.	_____		10:15 A.M.	_____	
5:30 A.M.	_____		10:30 A.M.	_____	
5:45 A.M.	_____		10:45 A.M.	_____	
6:00 A.M.	_____		11:00 A.M.	_____	
6:15 A.M.	_____		11:15 A.M.	_____	
6:30 A.M.	_____		11:30 A.M.	_____	
6:45 A.M.	_____		11:45 A.M.	_____	
7:00 A.M.	_____		Noon	_____	

Time Analysis

Group the activities according to category and record the time spent doing the activity. Total up the amount of time spent in each category of activity on your time inventory. Indicate whether you were satisfied or dissatisfied with how much time you spent for each activity. If you were dissatisfied, indicate in the adjustment column how much more or less time you would want to spend on a particular activity.

Activity	Time Spent	Satisfaction (+, 0, −)	Adjustment
Example: *Casual office talk*	*3 hours*	*−*	*2 hours less*

Job Descriptions

Now you have analyzed how you spend your time. We would like to encourage you to decide that you have a choice as to how you use your time. Taking responsibility for the way you use your time is no more and no less than taking responsibility for the way you live your life. Making this decision allows you to choose to spend your time in ways other than how you spend it now.

We have worked with many people who chronically complain about their jobs, constant interruptions, and a feeling of always being behind. It is true that some jobs involve coping with many inter-ruptions and 'putting out fires.' We certainly don't recommend such a situation, but if your job entails dealing with constant interruptions, it is easier to deal with them if you consciously chose the job. One clear way to add stress to an already stressful job is to adopt the 'I have to' attitude. Do you frequently find yourself saying or thinking, 'I have to take care of this because. . . .' or 'I have to work late because. . . .'?

Many people feel that their jobs are beyond their control. If you fre-quently feel this way, it helps to step back and assess the situation in the following way. Write out a realistic job description. Become aware of your authority and responsibility. Write down all the duties you take on. Do not be surprised if the job is not what you initially contracted for. Many people find that they are actually doing the wrong tasks – tasks that are unimportant or not even part of their jobs.

Once you have an accurate job description and a list of your duties, decide if this is really the job you want. If it is not, you may wish to use assertiveness to renegotiate the job description or duties and take better advantage of the skills and time of others over whom you have authority.

You may decide that your best choice is to change jobs. It may be wise to check the material about life-change management in Chapter 13 to plan an optimal time period for adding this change stressor. Most people find that the best time to land a new job is when they already have one.

Job searching requires skills many of us never learned or used. An excellent guide to finding a job is *The Trees Jobs Grow On* by Kurt Nathan, Ph.D. See the suggested readings and recordings listed in Appendix III.

The Job-Person Fit

Hans Selye points out that among people, 'There are racehorses and there are turtles.' Most of us fall somewhere between the two extremes. If you are a casual person, you probably do not want to be in a profes-sion that requires you to run a race. Your real pleasures may be at home in the evenings watching your children grow up or spending time with a few close friends. If you are a real racehorse, you may find it stressful to sit quietly in familiar surroundings. Different people have different values and pleasures.

Jimmy Buffet sings a song called 'It's My Job.' His words describe an attitude of contentment expressed by a street sweeper as he is sweeping the streets. He sings, 'It's my job and that's enough reason to go for me.' This street sweeper has resolved his values with his job, and he does the best at what he has chosen to do. We all have choices in life, although sometimes we are put into situations that allow us to choose only how we will react.

The prisoners of war (POWs) in Vietnam responded differently depending on their interpretations of their situation. Some became depressed and focused only on the horror around them. Others used it as a 'vacation' for self-improvement and practiced musical instruments, played golf, wrote books, or exercised. Some returned depressed, and some returned with new skills.

Many people feel that they, too, are POWs, but they mean prisoners of work. You probably have a choice in your vocational endeavours. Write down your job description and decide if it describes what you want to be doing. If you choose your present job situation, use the job stress as an opportunity for self-improvement. Follow the guidelines in this chapter to help you better manage your time and job stress. When you fill in your goals and priorities, be sure these are what you truly want. It is easier to reach the goals of your choice than goals chosen by parents, spouse, colleagues, or peers.

The Importance of Goals

Now, we want you to examine what many people discover is their major time waster: a lack of important goals. Goals reflect our purpose in life and have a widespread impact on our lives.

Victor Frankl is a Viennese psychiatrist who survived the horror of the Nazi death camps in World War II. In his book *Man's Search for Meaning*, he describes how those who had a purpose for living were able to withstand torture and starvation. The purpose for living could have been revenge, building a new homeland, or waiting for the Allied forces to arrive. Those without purpose, goals, or positive self-direction died quickly.

Dennis Waitley, in his book *The Psychology of Winning*, tells how the Vietnam POWs who adjusted most easily upon returning to freedom were those with goals. The goals could be as clear and uncomplicated as one POW's goal to become the world's record holder for the number of consecutive sit-ups.

It has been said that two of the greatest tragedies are never to have had a goal or to have reached it. Life is a series of ever-growing accomplishments, and few people have only one goal which they reach and then call it quits. Those who do so face a major change stressor. Consider the man who finally retires and has no new goals. The emptiness can be devastating. As you work through this section on goals, we would like you to consider your future in a number of different ways.

Lifelong Goals

First, imagine that you are very old and you overhear your grandchildren or relatives talking to their friends about you and your life. What would you want them to say about you and your accomplishments? Write down your thoughts on this subject.

Next, we would like you to write your own epitaph. An epitaph is an inscription on a tomb and is written as a tribute to the dead person. How would you want others to remember you?

As you list your future goals in this chapter, remember that people are goal-seekers by design. We constantly adjust our self-image and subconscious to help us reach goals. Often, our goals are not planned or they are dictated by negative self-talk such as 'I can't do this very well' or 'I just know she's not going to like me.' Many people actually program themselves not to reach goals by using negative self-talk, failing to define goals clearly, or neglecting to make plans for reaching well-chosen goals.

Most people spend more time planning a party or reading the newspaper than they spend planning their lives. Dennis Waitley describes winners as people with a definite purpose in life. He also says, 'If you don't stand for something, you'll fall for anything.' Keep his words in mind as you explore your goals and the value you place on them.

Goal-Getting

Goals must be obtainable, and objectives must be quantifiable. In addition, goals should be flexible in the event that they are blocked by other priorities. If you set as a goal acquisition of a luxury automobile, for example, you may find that you spend more per month than you had expected. That may or may not be compatible with your other goals.

On a different scale, you may have set researching a new project as a goal. If the boss comes in and says the budget has to go to committee tomorrow, your priorities may shift. Your long-term goal is starting the new project, but without money budgeted for it, you may be doing the research out of your own pocket and in your own time. That is why it is helpful to establish flexible plans for achieving long-term goals.

We would like you to do an exercise involving two-minute drills. Use the Goal Cues listed below to help you think of categories of goals.

GOAL CUES

New home	Increase earnings	Start exercising
Home improvement	New position	Stop smoking
Lose weight	Family activity	Family
Professional skill	Become more	communication
Long vacation	patient	New honor
Spiritual goals	Additional	Solve a problem
New hobby	education	More spontaneity
Closer friends	Short vacation	Play with children
Coworker	Increase savings	Community service
communication	Pay debts off	More marital
	Manage something	satisfaction
	better	

First, we ask you to spend two minutes writing down all the goals that you would like to accomplish in the next five years. Limber up your imagination and write down anything that comes to mind. Spend only two minutes on this task.

Next, list all the goals you hope to accomplish next year. Spend only two minutes.

Spend only two minutes writing down all the goals you want to accomplish for the next six months.

Spend another two minutes writing down all your goals for the coming month and include work priorities, self-improvement programs, recreational activities, social functions, family gatherings, and so on.

Top-Priority Goals

Now that you have created these four lists of goals, we would like you to go back and prioritize each goal. Use an A, B, C format.

A's will include all those items that you rank as being most essential and most desired. These are your 'must do's.' They are often innovative and require creativity.

B's will include all those items that could be put off for a while but that you feel are still important. These are your 'desirable to do' or routine duties.

C's are items that could be put off indefinitely with little or no harm. These are your 'can waits' and are often trivial.

After you have prioritized your list, combine the three lists into one by including two A items from each of your long-term, one-year, six-month, and one-month goals. Write these down under the heading 'A-Priority Goals.'

The list you just made should indicate the most important goals you would like to accomplish in the next year. To ensure that this list contains your *most* important goals, we want you to complete another list.

. For the next list, imagine you have been told that you have a terminal illness and you will die in one year. During your last year of life you will neither be incapacitated nor experience pain. You will be able to do everything you currently do. Now, write down your goals for the next year if you knew you would die at the end of the year. Title this list 'My Goals if Next Year Is the Last Year of My Life.'

Compare the last two lists you have constructed. If these lists are totally different, you may want to consider more seriously some of the 'Goals if Next Year Is the Last Year of My Life' list. Now, combine the A-Priority Goals and 'My Goals if Next Year Is the Last Year of My Life' lists to reflect your most important goals accurately.

Now that you have selected your current major life goals, it is essential to set up a timetable for each goal. Indicate time periods in which the goals can reasonably be attained.

You now have important goals to work toward and a timetable to guide you. These are your top priorities. Translate these goals and projects into monthly, weekly, and daily activities. Use these as a guide for your time management for a month.

At the end of the month, review your list to see if you need to make a new list. Sometimes goals are completed, and sometimes uncompleted goals remain high in importance. Other goals may drop in importance. Set aside time every day to work on your A-Priority goals. Emphasize the results that you want rather than the activity, and try to accomplish at least one step toward each goal every day.

Planning Today Means a More Relaxed Tomorrow

When a sailor is preparing for a voyage, he will chart his course toward his destination and determine what prevailing winds he may expect. Seldom will he be able to predict all the changes of weather, but the forethought of planning tells him which reefs to avoid. He will also plan and rehearse his actions should a sudden squall or a prolonged storm appear. We may take an example from the real-life sailor as we sail on the sea of life.

Anything that arouses a stress response can be called a stressor. How we plan our course with these stressors in mind will have an effect on how well we actually deal with the stress. First, we need to have a chart indicating where we are going and what dangers we may expect. Next, we need to know the strengths and weaknesses of the vessel on which we are sailing.

If you know that your vocational goal is to become a successful businessman, you should also know your port of destination. Being a successful businessman means many things to many people. Without a specific goal, you may not even know when your ship has come in. A chart does little good unless you set a course, estimate a time of arrival and determine a destination.

The vessel needs to be equipped to make the voyage. If the ship has a slow leak or battered sails, you may need to decide whether to pull into an intermediary port for repairs or continue. If the leak develops a day away from your destination, you may be able to keep the ship afloat until you reach port. So it is with living. If we know we have to finish a project by the deadline, we can often keep going. When the deadline is met, we can make our repairs by relaxing and taking time off.

The need may arise to look once again at our chart and see how far we are from our long-term goals. At this point many people have problems. First, they were not certain how much they have accomplished. With a sense of time urgency, they decide to set off once again without planning a period of time to repair the ship. Something in the back of their minds may be saying, 'It's better to be doing something without a plan than doing nothing.' They forget that making the ship seaworthy and studying the chart to find a plan is far from doing nothing.

Knowing what your goals and plans are gives you a better chance of recognizing the stressors you will encounter and how long you may be exposed to them. Without plans and goals, people never know when they have done enough or where they are on their voyage. It is very hard to relax and take a break if you don't plan for one or forget when it is break time.

An Ounce of Planning Is Worth a Pound of Work

The best way to work effectively toward your A-Priority goals is to plan your day successfully. Here is one of the most powerful rules of time management: *One hour spent in effective planning saves three to four hours in execution*. Crises can often be avoided with proper planning. Proper planning will also ensure that the efforts you make during the day are directed at your main priorities, the major goals that you have set in your life. Without a plan, without a road map, or without a chart for navigation, a person is left adrift on a sea of stress.

Making mistakes is part of being a fallible human being. But remember the saying, 'If you don't have the time to do it right, when will you have the time to do it over?' Plan enough time to do quality work the first time.

The only alternative to personal planning is reacting to the demands of others. In effect, the decision of how you use your time is made by others who are not likely to have as their goals the same business or personal goals that you have just listed. You can end up on Friday wondering where the week went or on your deathbed wondering where your life went.

Work before Play or Guilt without Gain

We often find that people with whom we work experience a great deal of guilt about how they spend their day. Many of these people have goals, but they get involved in recreational activities before they have advanced toward their goals and earned their recreation. When they do this they feel guilty.

We emphasize play and recreation as part of effective stress management. When you feel subconsciously or consciously that you have not earned the right for recreation or play because of wasted time during the day, guilt is the price you pay. This can become a pattern, and the feelings of guilt can become attached to play even after a productive day's work. Recreation and play that become strongly associated with negative emotions such as guilt no longer provide the intended and needed relief from work.

Scheduling Your Time

Allocate your time according to your priorities. Part of doing this means planning your time every day of your life. Schedule appointments and time to stay abreast of what is new in your field. Schedule time to enjoy recreational activities. It is very important to schedule time to take care of yourself physically, and each day we should strive toward taking care of ourselves in the best way we can. The winners in life know that they have only one vehicle, and that is their body. Unless they maintain that body, they will grow old too soon and lose the energy needed to enjoy and accomplish their goals in life.

You may also want to look back over your important goals and note whether you included a satisfying family life. If you are a workaholic, revise your list of goals and plans to include family and personal goals. Many successful people are very lonely.

To-Do Lists

As you work toward the accomplishment of your goals, one technique to help you keep focused on important goals is to keep a daily 'To-Do' list. Break your larger goals into very small, short-term goals. Meeting some of these attainable short-term goals can be very reinforcing. It gives you an important sense of accomplishment and momentum.

The 'To-Do' list includes all the small, short-term goals you would like to accomplish for a particular day. Rate each item as A, B, or C. If you find yourself doing a C item such as cleaning out your desk, and your A items aren't finished, you can be certain that you are wasting your time. Work your way down from the A items to the C items.

Many individuals begin with little tasks that are inconsequential or unrelated to the day's goals. These may include filing old memos, checking the sports pages in the newspaper, talking to the secretary about a movie, putting away books, or many other activities. Often we do these little tasks as a way of putting off what causes us anxiety – our A items.

Find ways to overcome your anxieties and try to tackle the tough, important jobs first, not last. The following sections describe additional ways of managing your life to help you manage your time.

Not-to-Do Lists

When you have a particularly tight timetable, you may find it helpful to write down specific things you do *not* plan to do. Write down the time wasters and time robbers you will avoid. For example, you may write down that you will not answer phone calls unless they are truly urgent, you will not accept visitors, or you will not file anything today. Not-to-Do lists can be almost as important as To-Do lists.

Saying 'No'

One of the best things we can do for ourselves is to learn how to say no. This is so important that we have devoted an entire section in the chapter about assertiveness training to refusing requests.

Poorly considered commitments may force you to spend time on low-priority items. You may also find yourself doing other people's high-priority items, which, for you, are not very important. Often people will try to convince you to do their work for them. You must be able to say no if work is delegated unfairly to you.

The 80/20 Rule

The 80/20 rule is a very important concept in time management. It is also called the 'Pareto Principle.' This principle will help you to become more comfortable not doing C items. Simply stated, only 20 percent of the tasks that we do produce 80 percent of the rewards. Another way of putting this is that most people spend 80 percent of their time doing duties that are related to only 20 percent of the total job results.

If you are in sales, this principle can mean that only 20 percent of your customers or calls produce 80 percent of your sales. On the home front, it is likely that 80 percent of the washing is done on the 20 percent of the wardrobe that is worn most often.

In a list of ten tasks, doing two of them will yield 80 percent of the rewards. Find these two tasks because they are prime candidates for your top A priorities.

If you are trying to meet a deadline, the 80/20 rule means that unless you manage your time, you are faced with doing the important 80 percent of the job in 20 percent of the little time left before your deadline!

This is a general rule but one that has been demonstrated time and time again. Remembering this concept will help you concentrate your efforts on the 20 percent of the tasks that will produce 80 percent of the benefits. The C items and the B items that you have listed will probably not produce what you want to accomplish. Setting your sights on your A items and their related tasks will provide you with the best plan for reaching your true goals. The solution is not in learning how to do everything more efficiently but in learning how to do less more effectively.

Delegation

When you have many B and particularly C items to do, delegate them. Often they can be delegated to a secretary, hired help, spouse, parents, or children.

Diana Silcox, a professional time management consultant and author of *Woman Time*, kept a time inventory when she was beginning to expand her consulting service. She found that she was answering every phone call, cleaning her house, doing her own laundry, and handling her own typing and filing. She reset her priorities so as to establish her right to a rich personal life as well as challenging professional life. She then hired a maid as well as a secretary and began sending out her laundry, shopping by phone or mail, and eating out more often.

Before you delegate, determine the time necessary to do the task and the time required to explain, instruct, and coordinate. Delegate tasks for which the time needed to complete the work is long in relation to the time required to instruct and supervise. Avoid doing things you should delegate, but be sure to avoid delegating jobs you should do yourself.

When you delegate work, give clear, simple instructions and deadlines. Try to assign activities that will stretch the capabilities of others, share the responsibilities, and make everyone feel like a useful member of a team. When these activities have been completed, give

255

feedback to your subordinates. Plan ahead for vacations as well as shorter absences and delegate the work to be done while you are away.

Avoiding Reverse Delegation

Another important part of effective delegation is to follow up periodically on each task that you have delegated. Write down reminders in your appointment book. If a task is given back to you in unfinished or unacceptable form without a reasonable explanation or without sufficient time for redelegation, you are experiencing reverse delegation. Periodic follow-ups can help prevent reverse delegation and procrastination.

Do You Want to Delegate?

For delegating to work, you have to want to do it. You may need to ask yourself some tough questions. Do you see delegation as a loss of power? Can you trust others? Perhaps you need to look at your hiring and firing policies or your management styles.

One of the Best Places to Delegate

The garbage can is often the best place to delegate something. How many of us can remember poking through routine work, straightening our desks, or doing trivial tasks instead of doing our A items? We get a temporary feeling of satisfaction, but even with a neater desk, we still have to face the important items. There are some C's that are better left undone or delegated to the garbage can. Ask yourself, 'How terrible would it be if I just threw this away?' If your answer is 'Not too terrible,' delegate it to your garbage can.

If you find that you can't discard certain C items, set aside a special drawer or file for them. When the drawer or file gets full, file everything in an envelope or box and label it 'C items' along with the date. January 2 every year is a good time to go through these C files. Usually it is easy to throw things away when they have aged. If you still cannot throw them away, transfer them back to your selected drawer or file. Maybe you can delegate them to the wastebasket next year.

The Once Over

It is not always best to file your C's. To avoid accumulating paper-work, look at each item when you receive it. If at all possible, make a decision at that time.

The best example is dealing with mail. Throw away any mail you feel you can do without. Once you have scanned a piece of mail or paperwork, you should be able to make a decision about it, write out the decision, immediately turn it back in, mail it out, or throw it away.

Not all mail and paperwork lends itself to quick and final action. Some papers and projects need many revisions and polishing. Some decisions require a great deal of thought. If you cannot take quick and final action at least do something to advance a project. This may mean nothing more than recording the date and your thoughts after reviewing a project.

Often people become overwhelmed by paperwork simply because they do not make the decisions that need to be made the first time. We are a country of people who tend to collect papers, always thinking that we will need them at some point in the future. Remember to throw away any and all the pieces of mail that you possibly can.

Creative Time Management

One of the most enjoyable ways of managing time is to combine information you have gained from taking a time inventory and from pinpointing your goals. For example, several years ago, when one of the authors first read about time management, he took a time inventory and found that he spent about one and a half hours daily in work-related commuting. The author drove to and from work and traveled to various places where he consulted. He enjoyed listening to music on the radio while he drove, but sometimes he found this boring.

One of the goal cues the author used to establish his long- and short-range goals was additional education. He not only wanted and needed to keep up with new discoveries but found continuing education very exciting. In response to the 'publish or perish' pressures of academia, he was putting off this activity and complaining that he never had enough time.

The author considered increasing his commuting enjoyment by installing a stereo tape deck so that he could listen to music tapes of his choice. At that point, he remembered how much he had enjoyed listening to taped lectures from a conference that a colleague had attended. He knew he could not afford to buy enough conference tapes to fill even half of the eight hours of weekly commuting time.

The author went to the library and discovered that the audiovisual department had a large assortment of conference tapes and a series called *Audio-Digest Psychiatry*. The audio-digest series is available in every medical specialty and has been providing monthly or twice-monthly excerpts of medical conferences for more than twenty-seven years.

Advertisements in a weekly magazine introduced him to *Books on Tape* (P.O. Box 7900, Newport Beach, CA 92660, or call 800-854-6758) and some mail order rental libraries. He then subscribed to an excellent monthly program called *Insight* by Earl Nightingale (7300 North Lehigh, Chicago, IL 60648, or call 800-323-5552). He even learned about a business news magazine on tape, *Newstrack*, available from the Executive Tape Service (Box 1178, Englewood, CA 80150). A combination of music, lectures, and books has not only taken the boredom and frustration out of driving but has provided a great deal of continuing education and enjoyment.

We have discussed this example in detail for several reasons. It reveals an effective planning process that anyone can use to find hundreds of valuable hidden hours. Homemakers who want to learn additional skills or a profession after their children grow up often make obtaining an education a goal. They can use the same planning process to optimize time spent in repetitive tasks such as ironing, dusting, or other housework, and chauffeuring the children to and from their activities. These times can be used for home study courses or university homework.

Perhaps one of your goals is to increase your correspondence with friends and family. Make use of odd moments of time spent in beauty shops, waiting rooms, and restaurants by keeping post cards and note paper in your purse or briefcase. You may want to conserve time and meet some of your goals by learning how to speed read. You may also decide to carry reading matter with you to make the most of small chunks of time. Combining the results of setting your goals and taking a time inventory can yield exciting possibilities.

The Perfect Person

We have yet to find the perfect person. We have found many people who are perfectionists; and these are the same people who tend to slow down the works. These people never seem to be able to 'see the forest for the trees.' *We will never be perfect.*

The role of man is not consistent with any concept related to the perfectionist. In fact, about 20 percent of everything we do is a mistake. Everyone makes about two mistakes for every ten decisions, and you must realize that you too will bat about two for ten. Mistakes are the best tools we have to help us learn. If you are a perfectionist, you should etch in the back of your mind the words, 'Just get it done,' or 'Do it!' Too often we tend to want the first draft to be perfect. And that same perfectionism will prevent us from ever getting started on the tasks that will lead to our true goals.

Vary the quality of your efforts. Trying to do your best at everything can lead to doing everything adequately but nothing brilliantly. Said another way, you cannot be anything if you want to be everything. Allocate your best efforts to your A-priority tasks and strive for acceptable performances in your B- or C-priority tasks.

If you are an executive, match the quality of your efforts to the quality and demands of the project. If you are a homemaker, save energy from housework so you can enjoy quality time with your spouse and children. With this end in mind, ask yourself, 'What will happen if I don't do this chore immediately and perfectly?'

Scheduling Interruptions and Quiet Periods

Build time into your daily schedule for interruptions, unforeseen problems, and the inevitable fires that must be put out. If you schedule times for these, you can avoid rushing and feeling pressured.

It is also very important to make reasonable time estimates for the length of various events. If you schedule yourself for thirty-minute lunch breaks between important appointments, you probably will have difficulties keeping within those time boundaries and enjoying lunch.

You should also be able to set aside periods of time during each day for quiet times when you can focus on relaxing and unwinding. These are times when you should be interrupted only if there is an emergency. Schedule quiet times in your appointment book or you may not take advantage of them.

A Practical Lesson Worth $25,000: Sleep on It!

Dr. George Crane, a business journalist, recently wrote about a little-known incident in which $25,000 was paid for a practical lesson in time management. Charles Schwab, the chairman of the Bethlehem Steel Company, once consulted a New York-based time management expert named Ivy Lee. Schwab said, 'My friend, I'll pay you any price if you will just show us how to get more things done.' Lee accepted the challenge and gave Schwab the following advice:

'At night, spend five minutes analyzing your problems of the following day. Write them down on a sheet of paper, but place them in the order of their importance.

'Then tackle the first item as soon as you reach the office. Stick to it until it is finished; then shift to No. 2. Test this plan as long as you like; then send me a check for whatever you consider it worth.'

Shortly thereafter, Lee received a check for $25,000 and a brief note from the steel magnate. Schwab wrote, 'This is the most practical lesson I have ever learned!' Schwab added that he had been putting off an important phone call for nine months, but after seeing Lee he had put it at the top of his first list. The call, he wrote, 'netted us $2 million because of a new order for steel beams.'

To optimize your performance, make a list of the five most important tasks that you want to accomplish during the next day. Make up this list before you leave work. Schedule quiet time during the last half hour of work. Review what you have accomplished for the day and decide on five important jobs that you want to do during the next day. Take this list home with you and review it before you go to bed.

The mind, particularly the subconscious mind, has an amazing capacity to work and plan at night while we sleep. Often people who are starting a new job will wake in the middle of the night with a nightmare of themselves working at the new job and perhaps feeling overwhelmed. This simply indicates that the unconscious mind is working on the new task and practicing and rehearsing during sleep. You can mentally prepare yourself on a nightly basis by knowing what your goals are and having a plan for what you want to do the next day.

Remember to plan your play time and your weekend to make the most of your leisure time. Early in the week, write down your weekend plans and begin the necessary preparations. In this way you won't be left alone or bored when the weekend comes. This is very important for workaholics. On Friday, review your weekend plans just before you go to sleep.

Five Minutes in the Morning

If you have set your priorities for the day, filled out your To-Do list, and slept on the five most important things to do, you are ready at the beginning of the day to involve other people who will help you in executing your tasks. Spend five minutes in a priority-setting conference in the morning. Set aside time to review your plans with the people who are working with you so that they can also plan their days. Often secretaries feel overwhelmed because they see work coming from many different directions and do not know where to start.

The five-minute priority-setting conference allows the secretary as well as the boss to decide which task needs to be done first. Secretaries should not have to guess what the boss's priorities are. If you are a secretary, be sure to ask your boss the order of things to be done. Use the techniques from the assertiveness training chapter to help you establish which items can and cannot be done in a reasonable day's work.

Always limit the five-minute priority-setting conference to five minutes. Do not allow it to turn into a staff meeting. A small number of key people should be standing, and there should be no chairs, coffee, or Danish. It should be a work-oriented and planning-oriented session with a numbered agenda to keep the meeting focused.

Planning Other Meetings

Limiting the length and purpose of meetings can make a large cumulative difference over the course of weeks and months. There is no reason why most meetings have to take an hour, and yet most are scheduled to start and end on the hour. Generally speaking, work will expand to fill the time appropriated. Unfortunately, this additional work is seldom productive.

Block Interruptions

It is often considered proper to have an open-door policy at work. Businesses have also been adopting open-space policies in response to economic and environmental pressures. Space in businesses costs money, and private offices are less and less the norm. Movable partitions are sometimes employed to provide some measure of privacy. The overall effect, however, is that people are now physically working very closely together and in open spaces that increase the chances for interruptions. Any time you are working in an atmosphere that permits other staff members to contact you at any time, your productivity may be threatened.

It has been reported that the typical manager in the United States is interrupted an average of once every eight minutes. The interruptions may be from a visitor or from the boss buzzing on the intercom. Phone calls are common forms of interruption. When people take time inventories, they often find that they are involved in only two hours of essential work in an eight-hour day. This low productivity can result in working overtime and eliminating needed hours for recreation and family.

Quiet Work Time for Office and Home

There are several different ways you can eliminate interruptions. One approach taken by large businesses is to schedule two hours of quiet work time into the high-productivity period of the day. This period is usually in the morning. Perhaps you can schedule one hour of quiet work time in the early morning when there will be no contact between members of your staff. Workers would not be available to each other at that time. Later in the morning, you could have a coffee break or a period during which staff members are available to each other. Still later in the morning, you could resume the quiet time for an hour.

Some people find that they can be especially productive in the day if they come in very early before other people are there. This is not always practical or healthy, and scheduling quiet work time can be an effective way of accomplishing the same result. This technique also works for the housewife who experiences constant interruptions. Let friends and relatives know that you are not available at certain times except for emergencies.

Time-Saving Techniques for the Telephone

To block the interruption of phone calls, you can make yourself unavailable during part of the day. Phone calls can break up your concentration, and many of them are not important. The person who answers the phone is the critical person in this technique. If this is a receptionist, that person needs to know which calls you want to take directly, which you want referred elsewhere, which you want the receptionist to provide information to the caller, and which to take messages from. It is incumbent upon the person who is unavailable to return the calls later in the day so as to maintain credibility.

Check your time inventory to see how much time you spend on the phone when you return, initiate, or accept telephone calls. You may find that you spend more time returning or initiating a call than accepting one. Analyze the reasons. You may want to set a conscious time limit for each call and use a call timer or pretend you are making a long distance call at your own expense. When you have used up your allotted time or have completed your intended discussion, use your assertiveness skills to close the conversation politely.

If you are placed on hold frequently, you may want to purchase an inexpensive amplifier to hold the receiver while you continue working. These devices are very useful for homemakers who enjoy talking while they work.

Visitors

Visitors are a source of interruption at work and can break up your concentration on an important task. If a quiet work period is in operation for two hours during the morning, this could be an ideal time to be unavailable to visitors.

To make this technique work for you, you need to inform key people that you will not be available during particular hours. An appointment system may be necessary. When you work on an appointment-only basis, no one will have cause to complain if he or she drops in and you are unavailable.

Remember that blocking out time for yourself will save time. Thirty percent more productivity is gained by having a period without interruptions. What if your job is handling interruptions? If that is your situation, you can practice limiting the length of each interruption.

The First Day of the Month and Your Daily Calendar

The first day of each month can be a very important time to take aim toward your goals. Family and social events can be planned at that time, and you can put birthdays or anniversaries on your calendar. You

263

can also plan time for educational programs that you may wish to attend during the month. You may wish to set a goal to attend at least one educational program each month. You can schedule this activity during the first part of the month. You should also put company activities on your calendar so that you can plan for these when you make out your schedule.

Your appointment book or daily calendar can be a powerful tool for time management if you expand its uses. Consolidate all miscellaneous notes, phone messages, and memos in your book or calendar. The information will then be readily available for use now and retrieval later. List your activities and quiet periods for the following week.

Part of your appointment book can serve as a place for your To-Do lists, relaxation cues, and meeting agendas. You can also use it to schedule follow-ups on delegated tasks. Car and other maintenance schedules can be written in for the coming year with reminders to make appointments and follow up on work that has been delegated. Anniversaries, birthdays, and other important dates can be entered with notes a week before to purchase gifts or cards.

Summing It All Up

The main thrust of this chapter is how to manage your time more effectively. Time is a major asset, and it should be managed just as we manage any other valuable asset. Perhaps one of the most important things that we covered was setting up your goals so that you know where you are going. Having a plan and working toward it is an important part of life. It is also an integral part of learning how to manage time.

Before you go on to the next chapter, we would like to review the major points about setting goals. These are the steps that we feel you have to read and reread, practice and practice again. Remember that rehearsal and practice will help to accomplish your goals. The following list is a summary of what you need to do to ensure that you are spending most of your time getting where you want to go and enjoying what you want to experience in life.

1. Put your goals in writing. If you did not complete that section as you went through this chapter, you probably do not have any goals. You have only wishes. If you have not put a goal into writing, it is not a goal – it is just a wish.

264

2. Goals must be better than your very best, but they must be believable. If you did not jog and set a goal to run a marathon in two weeks, you would not believe you could do it, and you would probably become frustrated and stop trying. If you were to set a goal that you would run one mile in two weeks, you could believe it was realistic and work toward it every day. Your goals must be better than where you are now, but they must be believable.

3. Set short-term goals. It is very rewarding to have reached a goal. If you set only long-term goals you will become discouraged because you are less likely to receive short-term rewards and reinforcements.

4. Goals should be set for all areas of your life. Set business and professional goals, but also set goals related to family, physical health, and spiritual growth. If you set only work goals, you are sitting on a stool that is balanced on one leg, and if anything should happen to that leg, you will end up sitting on your tailbone.

5. Set long-term goals and personal accomplishments as well as short-term goals. You should know who you want to be and what you want. If you read magazines about cars because your goal is to have a faster car, you will be pulled toward that goal subconsciously. If your goal is to have a nice house, and you read magazines such as *Architectural Digest*, you will be drawn toward that goal. If you read travel brochures about distant parts of the world, you will probably travel more than if you read only magazines about gardening.

6. Vividly imagine the accomplishment of your goals. See yourself accomplishing what you set out to accomplish. The winners in life rehearse time and time again seeing themselves being successful and attaining their goals.

When the astronauts first landed on the moon, they described it as being just as they had imagined and rehearsed. One astronaut, as he stepped onto the moon, described it as 'old home week' because he had simulated being there so many times before.

When the recent space shuttle was launched, the physiological stress response of the astronauts was minimal. They had practiced time and time again doing just what they were doing. Any of us who had not practiced being in the space shuttle would have had such great increases in blood pressures and pulse rates that we would have been able to feel our hearts pounding. But the astronauts had rehearsed time and time again and vividly imagined the accomplishment of their goal. This is what the winners in life do. They not only set their sights on their goal, but they imagine themselves acquiring that goal.

7. Goals must be ardently desired. If you just want something a little bit, you may not work and strive to attain it, and, in all probability, you will not accomplish it. You really need to want the goals that you are working toward. This is why we have emphasized the importance of establishing personal long-term and short-term goals.

You have to make a commitment such as 'I want to be the best salesman in the company in eighteen months,' or 'I want to have my house decorated beautifully in one year.' If you want to be a world traveler, you have to commit yourself to seeing at least one foreign country a year.

A perfect example of a commitment to a goal is reflected in what Jack La Lanne, a world-famous physical fitness expert, does on each birthday. Each birthday he establishes a different goal. Recently, he swam in icy waters pulling a rope that was attached to several boats full of people, one person for each year of his life. He is committed to the goal of physical fitness, and he expresses that goal in everything he does.

Time management is not a skill that you will acquire from reading this chapter or from reviewing the suggested materials listed in Appendix III. You must practice and live some of these techniques of time management. This may take you two months, or as long as six months. Remember, as long as you are striving toward a goal, and as long as you are practicing the necessary techniques, you will accomplish what you are working toward.

Part Seven

*Enhancing Health
and Preventing Disease:
When Your Body Wears
Out, Where Are You
Going to Live?*

22 Keeping Your Body 'Tuned Up' and Safe

The benefits of regular exercise and good nutrition are popular topics of conversation today, and science is providing a growing body of knowledge to make possible a separation of fact and fancy. Exercise and nutrition can be of importance in the prevention of illness and in the enhancement of health. The next two chapters offer some reasonable guidelines to help you incorporate proper nutrition and regular exercise into your life. These are essential ingredients in combating the wear and tear of stress.

Regular exercise has both physiological and psychological benefits. Advantages that have been associated with regular exercise include a greater ability to concentrate, a reduced risk of heart attack, more energy, a firmer appearance, reduced anxiety and hostility, elevated mood, improved immune response, better sleep, and better control of body weight.

The Stress Response

In the first chapter of this book, we reviewed the sympathetic nervous system's response to stress. If you recall, the body responds with preparation for fighting or fleeing. Our heart beats faster, our blood pressure soars, our breathing quickens, our perspiration increases, our muscles tense, and our body pours stored sugars and fats into the bloodstream. In addition, a signal originating from the hypothalamus contributes to the secretion of adrenalin.

Exercise provides a way of releasing a great deal of the muscle tension and general physical arousal accumulated in our responses to stress. Rather than fighting a tiger or fleeing from a bear, we can hit a punching bag or jog around the track.

Exercise as Relaxation

One very important benefit of exercise is muscle relaxation. In response to stress, our bodies often become tense. This tension can accumulate, especially after a long day. One way to relax after a tense day is to engage in exercise. You will find that after exercising, your muscles are relaxed and calm.

Using exercise to relax is far better than another common release used at the end of a day's work – alcohol. Drinking alcohol adds another stressor and can ultimately lower your ability to manage stress.

Exercise Helps Vitamins Fight off Disease

Recent research explored the effects of exercise and vitamins on the body's immune system in its constant fight to ward off disease. Vitamins C and E improved immune functioning, but exercise strongly augmented these effects. In this research, the exercise group had more infection-fighting cells regardless of whether they took the vitamin supplements.

The Role of Exercise Today

As man became industrialized, he developed more and more labor-saving devices. Physical activity was no longer necessary for survival and became a form of recreation. When we rediscover play and enjoy body movement, we restore a sense of control and wholeness to our lives. Since you are the sum of physical and mental activities, exercise can be self-enhancing and improve your responses not only to physical stressors but to social and mental stressors as well.

Exercise as a Mental Release

Exercise can be used to clear your mind. One frustration you may face during the work day is having your mind become so cluttered that you cannot concentrate. Problems may seem impossible to solve. This is an excellent time to go for a walk, jog, or swim. People who exercise report that time away from working diligently on a problem gives them a chance to sort everything out in a more relaxed way.

For example, a nurse reached an impasse while working on the development of a new health program. After working on crucial scheduling problems for several hours, she seemed no closer than when she started. In an effort to solve these problems, she went to a coworker to discuss the schedule. Still, no solution was reached.

At this point, the work day was over, and the two workers decided to exercise together. During their twenty minutes of jogging, they discussed the scheduling problem. By the end of the run, they had solved the problem. It is not clear whether this happened because the pressure was off or simply because their minds were more creative in another environment. But it worked! This is a common response among people who exercise regularly.

Exercise and Self-Image

Many people find that their body image is a stressor. Whether they are overweight, too flabby, or not as muscular as they would like to be, the end result is that they are unhappy with themselves. As Richard Simmons says, 'Plastic surgery may tighten up a few things, but exercise is Mother Nature's cheapest body lift.' People who begin an exercise program find that their self-image improves and they get an emotional lift as well.

How Does Exercise Physically Help Us to Manage Stress?

When we are in good physical condition, we have a greater capacity to resist stress and strain. We react more slowly and less drastically to environmental, physical, and psychological stimuli. Physiologists have repeatedly shown that a regular exercise program will improve endurance, reduce total peripheral resistance in blood circulation, lower systolic and diastolic blood pressure, increase the inner size of arteries, increase the number of capillaries, lower blood lipids, and improve lung capacity and muscular strength. This all adds up to an increase in endurance and a greater resistance to fatigue.

The heart becomes more powerful and more efficient with appropriate exercise. A conditioned heart beats more slowly at rest and during work. It also acquires a greater pumping capacity.

A simple way to express this effect is summed up in the old phrase, 'Use it, or lose it!' Approximately 80 percent of the adult population today is not active enough to arrest physiological decay. Such an inactive lifestyle is said to be a slow form of suicide. It actually requires very little time to obtain and maintain an adequate level of fitness. This is often misunderstood because when óne thinks of a physically fit person, too often the athlete comes to mind. It is not necessary to spend the number of hours and endure the strenuous training of a professional athlete to be considered physically fit. How, then, does one define physical fitness?

Components of Physical Fitness

A person is considered physically fit if he or she is engaged in activities that bring about three fitness components: cardiorespiratory endurance, flexibility, and muscular function. These can be remembered as the three S's: stamina, suppleness, and strength.

Cardiorespiratory endurance is the ability to perform moderately strenuous, large muscle exercises for relatively long periods of time. Large muscle exercises include walking, cycling, swimming, or jogging. A relatively long period of time is defined as twenty to thirty minutes. The word 'cardiorespiratory' represents the knowledge that these activities depend a great deal on the capacity of the heart and lungs.

Flexibility is defined as the range of motion about a joint, or simply the ability to move a body part from one extreme position to another. Touching your toes is an example of the range of motion about the hip joint.

Muscular function includes muscular strength, muscular endurance, and muscular power. Muscular strength is the force that a muscle can exert against a resistance. Muscular endurance is the ability of that muscle to resist fatigue. Muscular power is the result of strength and the speed at which the force can be applied.

If you perform the same exercise every day, you will not increase your strength or endurance. This goal is reached only by stretching your abilities a small increment each day. The isometric exercises that Charles Atlas made famous increased strength, but only in the skeletal muscles. The heart and lungs were left out of many of these fitness programs.

All three fitness components are important. For adults, however, cardiorespiratory endurance is considered the most important fitness component. The work of Dr. Kenneth Cooper in the area of aerobics is an example of an approach to exercise that emphasizes cardiorespiratory fitness. Because of the importance of cardiorespiratory

272

fitness, the remaining discussion will deal largely with exercises and activities that bring about improvement in this area. These activities are also helpful in reducing stress.

Cardiorespiratory Endurance

There are several activities that improve cardiorespiratory endurance. Examples include basketball, cycling, jogging, racquetball, jumping rope, ice and roller skating, snow and water skiing, swimming, tennis, and vigorous walking and dancing. All of these activities have something in common that causes an increase in cardiorespiratory endurance – they are 'aerobic.'

An aerobic activity is one that uses oxygen to produce energy. An 'anaerobic' activity takes place in the absence of oxygen. An example of an anaerobic activity is running at top speed but for only a short period of time. In reality these two systems work simultaneously. Any activity that is continued for several minutes will be using oxygen and is therefore considered aerobic.

A pioneer in the area of exercise, Dr. Kenneth Cooper, used this knowledge in writing a number of books and tape programs. These are highly recommended for anyone interested in beginning an exercise program. All the information you need for a variety of activities is included in the material, as well as a system to help the beginner measure his or her improvement.

How Much Exercise Do I Need?

What about the 'how hard,' 'how often,' and 'for how long' of exercise? Exercise specialists refer to these as the frequency, duration, and intensity of exercise. It may surprise you to learn how little time and effort are needed to obtain an adequate amount of exercise to develop cardiorespiratory endurance.

The recommended frequency of exercise is a minimum of three times per week. These three days should not be continuous but scheduled with a day of rest between the days of exercise. Once you have increased your cardiovascular endurance, however, you may want to exercise five or six days a week to enjoy the recreation and help relieve stress.

The recommended duration of exercise or the amount of time one should exercise each time is twenty to thirty minutes. This time should be continuous rather than ten minutes in the morning, ten minutes at noon, and ten minutes in the evening.

The intensity of the exercise session is not as easy to define as the frequency and duration. A simple test of intensity is how a person feels. If it is not possible to talk while exercising because you are breathing too hard (known as the 'talk test'), you are exercising too vigorously. A more scientific and individualized indicator is your heart rate or pulse.

The heart rate is an excellent measure of how much stress a person is undergoing. The heart rate will increase in direct proportion to the intensity of the exercise. First, you must learn how to take your pulse. This requires practice. To learn, follow the directions below.

The average heart rate is approximately seventy-two beats per minute. This rate varies a great deal from one individual to another, and it depends on many factors such as age, sex, level of fitness, and medications. How high should your heart rate be during exercise?

To achieve cardiorespiratory benefits, a person should work at 70 percent to 85 percent of his or her MAXIMUM HEART RATE. The MAXIMUM HEART RATE can be estimated (as shown below) and then used to calculate the TARGET HEART RATE for exercise (which is 70 percent to 85 percent of the MAXIMUM HEART RATE).

To calculate maximum heart rate:

220 minus *your age in years* equals MAXIMUM HEART RATE.

Example: If you are fifty years of age:

220 – *50 = 170 beats per minute.* Your MAXIMUM HEART RATE is 170 beats per minute.

Now fill in the blanks and calculate your MAXIMUM HEART RATE.

220 – _____ = _____ beats per minute

To calculate target heart rate range:

The TARGET HEART RATE RANGE is 70 percent to 85 percent of the MAXIMUM HEART RATE. Using the example above:

70 percent of MAXIMUM HEART RATE equals _____ beats per minute.

.70 × 170 = 119 beats per minute.

85 percent of MAXIMUM HEART RATE equals _____ beats per minute.

FOUR PLACES TO TAKE YOUR PULSE

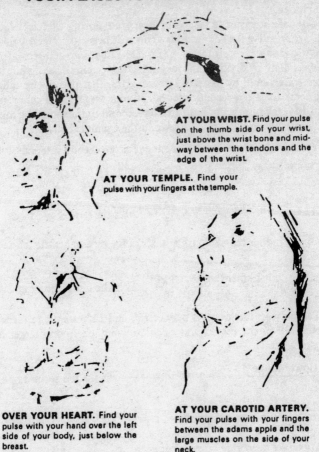

AT YOUR WRIST. Find your pulse on the thumb side of your wrist, just above the wrist bone and midway between the tendons and the edge of the wrist.

AT YOUR TEMPLE. Find your pulse with your fingers at the temple.

OVER YOUR HEART. Find your pulse with your hand over the left side of your body, just below the breast.

AT YOUR CAROTID ARTERY. Find your pulse with your fingers between the adams apple and the large muscles on the side of your neck.

.85 × 170 = 144 beats per minute.

The example's TARGET HEART RATE RANGE is between 119 and 144 beats per minute.

Now fill in the blanks and calculate your TARGET HEART RATE RANGE:

.70 × _____ = _____ beats per minute.

.85 × _____ = _____ beats per minute.

During exercise, your heart rate should remain in your target heart rate range.

To make it easier to take your heart rate during exercise, you can take your pulse for ten seconds. You will need to convert your one-minute (sixty second) target heart rate range into ten-second rates. This is done by dividing the lower and upper numbers of your target heart rate range by six and remembering that this is the range of numbers for a ten-second interval. If your target heart rate range is 120-144, the number of beats in a ten-second count should be roughly between 20 and 24. This is shown in the example below.

To calculate target heart rate range for ten-second intervals:

Divide lower range of target heart range by 6 to get the ten-second rate.

Example: $\dfrac{\text{lower range}}{6} = \dfrac{119}{6} = 20$ is the ten-second rate.

Divide higher range of target heart range by 6 to get the ten-second rate.

Example: $\dfrac{\text{higher range}}{6} = \dfrac{144}{6} = 24$ is the ten-second rate.

Target heart rate range is between 20 and 24 beats per ten seconds. Now fill in the blanks and calculate your ten-second target heart rate range:

$\dfrac{\text{lower range}}{6} = \dfrac{\rule{2cm}{0.4pt}}{6} = \rule{2cm}{0.4pt}$ is the ten-second rate.

$\dfrac{\text{higher range}}{6} = \dfrac{\rule{2cm}{0.4pt}}{6} = \rule{2cm}{0.4pt}$ is the ten-second rate.

My target heart rate range is between _____ and _____ beats per ten seconds.

If you are just beginning an exercise program, it is a good idea to exercise in the lower part of the target heart rate range so that you will be able to exercise the recommended duration of twenty to thirty minutes. You may be surprised at how little exercise it takes to elevate your heart rate to the target range if your life has been sedentary.

A few words of caution are necessary. Too much exercise, too soon, not only will discourage you but will add another stressor to your life.

If you are over thirty-five years of age, it is advisable to have a physical examination and a treadmill stress test before beginning an exercise program. This test of physical working capacity is performed while one walks on a treadmill. During this test, the physician administering the test is able to observe how your heart responds to various exercise loads. *Remember, if you are over the age of thirty-five or in poor physical condition, do not begin an exercise program without first consulting your physician.*

Earlier, we pointed out that it is often good to exercise soon after you experience a stress response. This advice does not apply to severe emotional stress. When you have experienced a major stressor, you may not be able to benefit or survive the added physical stressor of exercise. If you get angry at your boss and go out jogging, you may overdo it. Do not let this happen. Have an exercise specialist give you an exercise prescription, and be sure to use moderation!

Becoming More Fit: Getting Started

If you have not yet begun a formal fitness program, increasing your general activity level is an excellent place to begin. Small changes are significant. Just as the goal of fitness training is not to make you a star athlete, the goal of getting started is not to make you a fitness fanatic. Our goal is to help you take the first step toward becoming fit, avoid tripping over common problems, and continue your efforts.

There are probably as many reasons as there are people to explain why so many who are well informed procrastinate about starting an exercise program. Research from the surgeon general's 1979 report, *Healthy People*, showed that although individuals knew that regular exercise was an important health habit, few were practicing regular exercise. If you feel you are too busy to exercise, refer to Chapter 21 and apply the time management techniques to help you get started.

Let's discuss some of the reasons frequently given for not exercising. Memories of pain after exercise keep some people from beginning to exercise again. Pain from exercise is unnecessary and is usually brought about by exercising incorrectly. If one properly warms up and cools down after exercise, and does not do too much too soon, there will be little or no pain. You can improve your body's strength and endurance without causing pain. Use pain as a signal that you are doing too much. Stiffness and muscle pain should not be considered signs that you are getting stronger.

Expense is another reason often used for not starting an exercise program. Although some sports and activities do require an investment or a fee, not all exercise programs are expensive. In fact, many of the best exercises are free. It is important to remember when you are selecting an activity that the lower the costs in time, money, or inconvenience, the more likely you will be to continue the program.

Lack of knowledge on how to exercise properly is another concern of people who do not exercise. The information in this chapter is sufficient to help you start exercising. The books listed in Appendix III provide additional information from many experts. Another suggestion is to enroll in an exercise class. This has the advantage of providing you with information, as well as involving you in a support group of others who are also beginning an exercise program.

The more fun the exercise is for you, the more likely you will be to continue it. Fitness does not have to be a lonely, tortuous activity. In fact, finding another person with whom you can enjoy exercising helps tremendously. So find a buddy and arrange to meet this person on a regular basis. Not only will this person be a support for you, but you will provide support for him or her.

Some people feel embarrassed when starting an exercise program. Find others at your same level of fitness with whom to exercise. Avoid being competitive and afraid of not winning. If you tend to be competitive, avoid competitive events at the beginning of a fitness program. Competition often brings out a blind determination that may not be safe.

It is important to remember that if weather or scheduling problems force you to miss a day of exercise, *do not give up altogether*! Instead, return to the regular schedule as soon as possible. Exaggerating your 'failure' and criticizing yourself will only add another emotional stressor.

A common misconception about exercise is that it will bring about fatigue. If approached sensibly, this is not true. People report that incorporating regular exercise has increased their level of energy, increased their alertness, and made them more relaxed.

Incorporating Exercise into Your Regular Activities

Listed below are several ways to increase your activity level even if you are not ready to begin a formal exercise program. These suggestions will help you manage stress by giving you healthy breaks.

278

1. Become a 'stair person' by taking the stairs for at least a few flights instead of relying entirely on the elevator. Try going down stairs first and then up stairs.
2. Stand instead of sitting.
3. Walk the longer distance rather than taking a short cut.
4. Park the car farther away from your workplace or the shopping center and walk the distance.
5. If you use public transportation, get off a stop earlier and walk the extra distance.
6. Walk to a nearby restaurant instead of driving or having food delivered.
7. If you have a pet, walk the pet farther, faster, or more often.
8. Walk or cycle to a nearby store instead of driving.
9. When playing golf, do not use a golf cart for all the holes.
10. In department stores, take the stairs instead of an escalator.
11. Take a walk rather than sitting down for a coffee break.
12. Use a distant restroom rather than the one closest to your desk.

One of the authors remembers getting a call from the telephone company encouraging him to buy still another telephone extension so he 'wouldn't run the little woman ragged'. He was told that it could save as much as seventy miles of walking each year. After discussing this idea, they decided they could save the money for sporting equipment and use the walking to burn off as much as three pounds every other year!

This concept can apply not only to telephone extensions but also to many labor-saving devices. The exercise machines that can be purchased are simply labor-making contraptions that compensate for the reduction in physical activity caused by labor-saving machines. Home robots are around the corner and will place even more importance on the recreational exercise and energy-increasing ingenuity we have been talking about.

To make any of these suggestions a permanent part of your life, you will need to make exercise a real priority. Make it as convenient as possible. Remember, if you are too busy to exercise, you are too busy.

How to Stick to Your Exercise Plans

In choosing an exercise plan or a sports activity, consider some of the obstacles to getting started and some of the ways you can help yourself stick with the plan. For example, you may not have the money to buy expensive sports equipment that you want such as a tennis racket, a bicycle, or a pair of hiking boots. This is an obstacle, but it can also be an aid to fitness.

You may find it helpful to consider the equipment a reward to be earned by increasing everyday activities that you are capable of doing without a financial expense. This is a far better alternative than waiting until you can afford the expensive sports equipment. For example, it is usually better to begin brisk walking before jogging or skiing, so walk everywhere you can and make a chart to show your progress in scheduled walking. Reward yourself after a certain number of days of such activity.

One author's wife joined a health spa and chose to pay for it in monthly installments. In this way, she knew she would be reminded every month to make full use or even increase her use of the membership.

Try to find a companion to share your chosen activity. As we suggested earlier, try to find someone at your own level of ability. Agree to meet on a regular basis and make a commitment to keep these dates. If you cannot find a partner, try to make your walking or jogging more fun. Bring along a pocket radio or cassette tape recorder and find a place with pleasant scenery. Be sure to pat yourself on the back for every move in the direction toward better health.

The time you spend thinking of the right activity with the right company will pay off in the long run. Beware of the 'four-day phenomenon.' The researcher who coined this term found that most dieters and exercisers take on too much too soon and give up after roughly four days. Try to find activities that you can imagine doing regularly.

An Example of a Formal Exercise Program

Included below is a sample exercise plan. Because walking is convenient, inexpensive, and a good starting point, it is used as an example. When beginning an exercise program, be sure to keep detailed records. For each time that you walk, you should note the time, distance, and heart rate achieved. It is also important to record any feelings that are associated with the exercise; for example, leg pains, stomach cramps, and more pleasant feelings such as 'felt great today.'

Several calendars are available that provide a record-keeping form which details the information just mentioned. You may want to put a mark and the number of minutes for each exercise session on the

Home Practice Chart next to the corresponding day. It is also easy to construct your own form of record keeping.

Remembering to take it leisurely at first, a good objective for the first week of exercise is to walk three times for thirty minutes each time. After each walk, return home and record the time, the distance, how you felt, and the heart rate that you achieved during exercise. If you consistently fall below your target heart rate range this first week, do not be too concerned. It is more important to establish the habit of being outdoors or on a track three times a week for thirty minutes each time. As you become more comfortable in spending that time walking, you can walk at a faster pace or you can jog a little to get the heart pumping within the target heart rate range. An example of record keeping for the first few weeks of exercise is shown below.

Week 1

SUNDAY

Walked: 30 minutes
Heart Rate: 110
Distance: 1½ miles
Felt a little tired.

TUESDAY

Raining – did not walk

THURSDAY

Walked: 30 minutes
Heart Rate: 110
Distance: 1½ miles
Not tired at all today.

Week 2

SUNDAY

Walked, jogged: 30 minutes
Heart Rate: 130
Distance: 2 miles
Breathing a little harder today, but felt good.

TUESDAY

Walked, jogged: 30 minutes
Heart Rate: 130
Distance: 2 miles
Feeling great!

THURSDAY

Walked, jogged: 30 minutes
Heart Rate: 130
Distance: 1¾ miles

281

Tired today, was walking slower. A little disappointed that I didn't go the full 2 miles – but
on second thought, I'm doing great!

Week 3

SUNDAY Jogged: 30 minutes
        Heart Rate: 135
        Distance: 2½ miles
        Felt stronger today than ever!

TUESDAY Party after work, so I wasn't able to jog. Will try
         to jog tomorrow.

WEDNESDAY Jogged: 30 minutes
           Heart Rate: 135
           Distance: 2½ miles
           Felt OK while jogging, but really pleased, since
           I missed yesterday, that I was flexible enough to
           exercise today.

THURSDAY Jogged: 20 minutes
          Heart Rate: 135
          Distance: 1½ miles
          Feeling tight today, so I didn't go as far.

Week 4

SUNDAY Jogged: 30 minutes
        Heart Rate: 140
        Distance: 3 miles
        Feeling great!

TUESDAY Jogged: 30 minutes
         Heart Rate: 140
         Distance: 3 miles
         Feeling great!

THURSDAY Jogged: 30 minutes
          Heart Rate: 140
          Distance: 3 miles
          Feeling great!

If this person totaled the distance covered each week, it would be
obvious that the distance increased from Week 1 to Week 4. The total

distance for Week 1 was 3.0 miles; for Week 2, 5¾ miles; for Week 3, 6½ miles; and for Week 4, 9 miles. If you were to graph this record, you would see a gradual increase in the distance that could be covered in the same amount of time. Also, if you had been noting how you felt each time you returned from walking, you would probably begin to notice that the walking became easier with less pain and with more enjoyment as time went on. Dr. Kenneth Cooper, in his books and tape programs on aerobics, has devised an excellent point system, which is based on heart rate and distance covered. We recommend it for anyone who is beginning an exercise program.

Habits for a Safe and Healthy Lifestyle

Keeping your body fit cannot be overemphasized, but keeping your body safe is equally important in preventive medicine. For example, research clearly supports the use of seat belts by every passenger in a car at all times, and we recommend that you follow this advice. For most people, buckling or not buckling is a habit. Remember, habits of this sort die hard or die with the person. One highway patrol officer says, 'I have never unbuckled a dead man.'

Fortunately, more and more Americans are keeping their bodies safe and 'tuned up.' The government issued its annual report on the nation's health in January of this year. We are living longer despite bad habits. The diagnosis is clear, however, according to Health Secretary Margaret Heckler. Lifestyle is still our greatest health risk. Americans have become their own worst enemies through cigarettes and drug abuse. Some good news is that the percentage of adult smokers has decreased by 25 percent. Unfortunately, smoking is still the largest single preventable cause of illness and premature death in this country.

Helping to keep your body tuned up through stress management and proper exercise may help one to stop smoking. But many people need a more organized program for this. If you are a smoker, we strongly recommend that you contact the American Cancer Society or the American Heart Association and inquire into their inexpensive or free stop-smoking clinics and written self-paced programs. You can find these organizations in your telephone directory.

Therefore, if you are a heavy smoker now, the single most important thing that you can do to begin living a lifestyle of wellness would be to reduce the number of cigarettes that you smoke and ultimately

23   Stress Management through Nutrition and Weight Control

The relationship between exercise and stress has been studied for years, but the relationship between nutrition and stress has only recently received the attention it deserves. Much of the interest in this area has come from the knowledge that stress imposes additional demands on the body. First, let us review how our eating habits are related to stress.

The Relationship between Stress and Eating Habits

People respond to stress in different ways: some smoke, some drink alcohol, and some increase or decrease their food consumption.

How do these behaviors relate to our stress cycle? Consider the example of overeating. The net effect of overeating is weight gain. In our society, weight gain can be still another source of stress. Thus we begin to see a vicious cycle:

> stressful situation – overeating – weight gain – more
> stress – more overeating – more weight gain –

The most important thing to realize about this cycle is that the episode of overeating did not solve the problem unless the stressor was hunger. In most cases, the stressor that triggered the person to eat probably still exists. We recommend all of the coping techniques discussed in this book for helping individuals through stressful situations. As you will learn, maintaining a proper diet is also an important technique for managing stress.

Another response to stress is consumption of alcoholic beverages. Using alcohol to manage or avoid managing stress is similar to overeating. Alcohol just adds another stressor. Not only does it fail to solve the original problem, but it brings other problems with it!

Stress is often used as an excuse for not eating properly. A common example is the person who complains of not having enough time to take a lunch break. Instead of taking a break, he consumes candy bars or potato chips from the vending machines or skips the meal altogether. If you find yourself saying, 'I don't have time to eat,' we recommend that you study the chapter on time management. Make good eating habits and regular meals a priority.

Advertising plays a tremendous role in our eating habits. Unfortunately, foods that are heavily advertised and easiest to sell, transport, and manufacture are not always best for our bodies. Can improper eating habits actually cause stress? Yes. If, over a period of time, one does not consume adequate amounts of nutrients, the stores of these nutrients become depleted. The person is then more susceptible to disease and less able to adapt to other stressors.

Pregnancy is an example of a positive change in a woman's life, but it is also a stress on the body. If the woman has not adequately prepared for the pregnancy by eating properly during the months before conception, there is a greater risk associated with the pregnancy. Maintaining good eating habits prepares the body for additional demands made upon it.

Proper nutrition can be used to help cope with stress. Exercise has often been used this way, but only recently have scientists begun to consider proper eating as a coping strategy. We feel strongly that it is. All too frequently, we see people who are stressed or feel depressed and have a low self-esteem because of their body image. In this situation, the individual's concern over his or her body weight is a stressor, and proper eating habits can be a coping strategy.

There is another advantage to eating properly. People who exercise regularly and eat properly feel good about themselves. These positive feelings are an important part of other coping strategies, especially those we presented in the chapter on thinking and feeling better. When your self-esteem is high, other parts of your life seem less stressful because you view the world through the eyes of a winner.

What Makes up a Healthy Diet?

In the pages that follow, you will find guidelines for healthy eating. These are consistent with the 1980 *Dietary Guidelines for Americans* by the U.S. Department of Agriculture and by the U.S. Department of Health and Human Services. There is a great deal of controversy about nutrition today; but all agree that these guidelines are sound and safe.

These guidelines are intended for the general population, specifically those who are free from disease. They may not be specific enough for people who are on a special diet for a diagnosed condition. Remember, no guidelines can guarantee health or well-being because health depends on many factors in addition to diet. Food alone will not make a person healthy – but good eating habits, combined with regular exercise and stress management, can improve your health.

Dietary Guidelines for Americans

The seven dietary guidelines are as follows:

1. Eat a variety of foods.
2. Maintain your ideal weight.
3. Avoid too much fat, saturated fat, and cholesterol.
4. Eat foods with adequate starch and fiber.
5. Avoid too much sugar.
6. Avoid too much sodium.
7. If you drink alcohol, do so in moderation.

Eat a Variety of Foods

You need about forty different nutrients to stay healthy. These include vitamins and minerals, as well as amino acids (from proteins), essential fatty acids (from vegetable oils and animal fats), and sources of energy (calories from carbohydrates, proteins, and fats). These nutrients are in the foods you normally eat. Water is also an essential nutrient.

Research has shown that the body uses nutritional reserves when a person is under stress. The reserves most clearly depleted are protein, B-vitamins, vitamin C, and vitamin A. But it is important to realize that these reserves can be replaced and maintained by consuming balanced meals. Supplements are seldom necessary.

Most foods contain more than one nutrient, but no single food item supplies all the essential nutrients in the amounts you need. Therefore, you should eat a variety of foods to ensure an adequate diet that will replace nutrients lost while you are under stress.

The greater the variety of foods you consume, the less likely you are to develop either a deficiency or an excess of single nutrients.

Variety also reduces your likelihood of being exposed to excessive amounts of contaminants in any single food item.

One way to assure variety and a well-balanced diet is to select foods each day from each of several major groups. Eat fruits and vegetables; cereals, breads, and grains; poultry, fish, and lean meats; dried peas and beans; and cheese, yogurt, and skimmed or low-fat milk.

Fruits and vegetables are excellent sources of vitamins, especially vitamin A (dark green vegetables and yellow vegetables such as carrots, squash, and sweet potatoes) and vitamin C (citrus fruits, peppers, baked potatoes, and strawberries). Whole grain and enriched breads, cereals, and grain products provide B-vitamins and iron. Meats supply protein, fat, iron, and other minerals, as well as several vitamins, including thiamine and vitamin B_{12}. Dairy products are major sources of calcium and other nutrients. A regular intake of balanced meals based on the above foods is a preventive measure in avoiding the effects of stress.

Caffeine, on the other hand, has been shown to affect the central nervous system, often making people nervous and putting them on edge. Some nutritionists have called coffee a stress-packed beverage. It is the worst offender with up to 155 mg. of caffeine in each cup; instant coffee is next with about 70 mg.; and tea, cola, or some other soft drinks are runners-up, with 30 to 65 mg. per twelve-ounce can. So limit or avoid caffeine, especially when you are under stress. If you want to drink something warm, try a grain-based beverage such as Postum or decaffeinated herbal teas.

If you decide to change your diet to decrease stress-packed foods and increase health-enhancing foods, try to find foods that you enjoy eating, so that you will be more likely to eat them for a lifetime. Consider variety, texture, taste, smell, and visual attractiveness. Schedule time to explore new sources of food or even to grow a garden. Observe what others eat and see if you can make choices that are nutritious and that you might also enjoy eating.

Maintain Your Ideal Weight

If you are overweight, your chances of developing some chronic disorders are increased. Obesity is associated with high blood pressure, increased levels of blood fats (triglycerides and cholesterol), and diabetes. All of these are associated with increased risk of heart attacks and strokes. In fact, people who are 25 percent or more over their ideal weight are two and a half times more likely to have a heart attack than those at or below their ideal weight. Thus you should try to maintain an 'ideal' weight. For most people, their weight should not be more than it was when they were young adults (twenty to twenty-five years old). Later in this chapter, we will discuss techniques for weight control.

For those of you who are now at your suggested body weight, it is important to know that the average American gains one-half to one full pound per year between the ages of twenty and fifty. Keep an eye on these creeping pounds resulting from what some have called our country's 'thorn of plenty'! It may be helpful to adopt some of the suggestions on weight control as a preventive measure.

Do not attempt to reduce your weight too far below the acceptable range. Severe weight loss may be associated with nutritional deficiencies, menstrual irregularities, infertility, hair loss, skin changes, cold intolerance, severe constipation, psychiatric disturbances, and other complications.

If you lose weight suddenly or for unknown reasons, see a physician. Unexplained weight loss may be an early sign of an underlying disorder.

Avoid Too Much Fat, Saturated Fat, and Cholesterol

Americans, whose diets are high in saturated fats and cholesterol, tend to have high blood cholesterol levels, which increase the risk of heart attack. There are wide variations among people's blood cholesterol levels, however, which are related to heredity and the way a person's body uses cholesterol. Some people can consume diets high in saturated fats and cholesterol and still maintain a normal blood cholesterol level. Other people, unfortunately, have high levels of blood cholesterol even if they have low-fat, low-cholesterol diets.

There is controversy about the best recommendations for healthy Americans. But for the U.S. population as a whole, a reduction in our current intake of total fat, saturated fat, and cholesterol is sensible. This suggestion is especially appropriate for people who have high blood pressure, smoke, or have a family history of heart disease.

To avoid too much fat, saturated fat, and cholesterol,

1. Choose lean meat, fish, poultry, dried beans, and peas as your protein sources.
2. Limit your intake of eggs and organ meats such as liver.

3. Limit your intake of butter, cream, hydrogenated margarines, shortenings, palm oil, coconut oil, and foods made from these products.
4. Trim excess fat off meats, and remove skin from chicken.
5. Grill, bake, or boil rather than fry foods.
6. Read labels carefully to determine both the amount and types of fat contained in foods.

Eat Foods with Adequate Starch and Fiber

The major sources of energy in the average American diet are carbohydrates and fats. To a lesser extent, proteins and alcohol also supply energy. While decreasing your fat intake, you should increase your calories from carbohydrates so as to supply your body's energy needs.

A common misconception about carbohydrates is that they are high in calories. This is not true. In trying to reduce your weight to an 'ideal' level, carbohydrates have an advantage over fats: carbohydrates contain less than half the number of calories per ounce as do fats.

Complex carbohydrates are better than simple carbohydrates. Simple carbohydrates, such as sugars, provide energy but little else in the way of nutrients. Complex carbohydrate foods, such as beans, vegetables, whole grain breads, cereals, and grain products, contain many essential nutrients.

Increasing your consumption of certain complex carbohydrates can help increase dietary fiber, which is advantageous because the average American diet is relatively low in fiber. Eating more foods high in fiber tends to reduce the symptoms of chronic constipation and other gastrointestinal disorders. There is also concern that low-fiber diets might increase the risk of developing cancer of the colon, but evidence is inconclusive at this time.

To be sure that you eat enough fiber, you should consume fruits, vegetables, and whole grain breads and cereals. There is no reason to add fiber to foods that do not already contain it.

To eat more complex carbohydrates daily,

1. Substitute starches for fats and sugars. For example, eat whole-grain crackers for a snack instead of candy.
2. Select foods that are good sources of fiber and starch, such as whole-grain breads and cereals, fruits, vegetables, beans, and peas.

Avoid Too Much Sugar

The major health hazard from eating too much sugar is tooth decay. The risk of tooth decay is not simply a matter of how much sugar you eat. The risk increases the more frequently you eat sugar and sweets, especially if you eat between meals and if you eat foods that stick to the teeth. Small but frequent snacks of sticky candy or day-long consumption of soft drinks, for example, may be more harmful to your teeth than a large amount of sugar consumed at one time.

Contrary to widespread opinion, sugar consumption alone has not been proven to cause diabetes. The most common type of diabetes occurs in obese adults. For these people, avoiding sugar without losing weight will not solve the problem. There is also no convincing evidence that sugar causes heart attacks or blood vessel diseases.

Estimates indicate that, on the average, Americans consume more than 130 pounds of sugar a year, not only sugar in the sugar bowl but the sugars and syrups in jams, jellies, candies, cookies, soft drinks, cakes, and pies. Sugars are also found in breakfast cereals, catsup, flavored milks, and ice cream. The ingredient label frequently provides a clue to the amount of sugar in a product. Ingredients are listed in descending order from the greatest to the smallest quantity. So if a product lists sugar as the third of fifteen ingredients, you can be sure it is high in sugar.

To avoid excessive sugar,

1. Use less of all sugars, including white sugar, brown sugar, raw sugar, honey, and syrups.
2. Eat fewer foods containing sugar, such as candy, soft drinks, ice cream, cakes, and cookies.
3. Select fresh fruits or fruits canned without sugar rather than fruits canned in syrup.
4. Read food labels for clues on sugar content. If sucrose, glucose, maltose, dextrose, lactose, fructose, or syrups appear first, the product contains a large amount of sugar.
5. Remember, how often you eat sugar is as important as how much sugar you eat.

Avoid Too Much Sodium

Table salt contains sodium and chloride. Both are essential elements and should not be avoided altogether. Sodium is present in many beverages and foods that we eat, especially in processed foods, condiments, sauces, pickled foods, salty snacks, and sandwich meats. Baking soda, baking powder, monosodium glutamate (MSG), soft drinks, and even many medications (many antacids, for instance) contain sodium.

Excessive sodium is a major hazard for persons who have high blood pressure. Not everyone is equally susceptible. Although sodium intake is but one of the factors known to affect blood pressure, it is one that we can control.

At present, there is no good way to predict who will develop high blood pressure, though certain groups, such as blacks, have a higher incidence. Individuals with a family history of high blood pressure are also more susceptible. Low-sodium diets may help to prevent high blood pressure.

Most Americans want more sodium than they need. Consider reducing your sodium intake, and use less table salt. Eat foods that are high in sodium sparingly. Remember that up to half of sodium intake may be hidden, either as part of naturally occurring food or, more often, as part of a preservative or flavoring agent that has been added.

To avoid too much sodium,

1. Learn to enjoy the unsalted flavors of foods.
2. Cook with only small amounts of added salt.
3. Add little or no salt to food at the table.
4. Limit your intake of salty foods, such as potato chips, pretzels, salted nuts and popcorn, condiments (soy sauce, steak sauce, garlic salt), cheese, pickled foods, and cured meats.
5. Read food labels carefully to determine the amounts of sodium in processed foods and snack items.

If You Drink Alcohol, Do So in Moderation

Alcoholic beverages are high in calories and low in other nutrients. Even moderate drinkers may need to drink less if they wish to achieve ideal weight.

Heavy drinkers face additional problems. They often lose their appetite for food, so they do not obtain essential nutrients. Vitamin and mineral deficiencies occur commonly in heavy drinkers. This is, in part, because of poor intake but also because alcohol alters the absorption and use of some essential nutrients.

Heavy drinking may also cause a variety of serious conditions, such as cirrhosis of the liver and some neurological disorders. Cancer of the throat and neck is much more common in people who drink and smoke than in people who do not. Impotence is common in men with a history of consuming large quantities of alcohol.

Sustained or excessive alcohol consumption by pregnant women has been associated with birth defects. Pregnant women should avoid alcohol or limit their intake to the amount their physician recommends.

One or two drinks daily appear to cause no harm in adults. If you drink, you should do so in moderation.

Weight Control

Is there a proven method to help one obtain and maintain one's ideal body weight? Yes! It is a three-step formula, and it is simple.

1. If caloric use is greater than caloric intake, weight loss occurs.
2. If caloric use equals caloric intake, weight is maintained.
3. If caloric use is less than caloric intake, weight is increased.

Do not let anyone try to fool you – calories *do* count! All diets that cause a loss of weight do so because the caloric intake is less than the person's caloric expenditure. Some diets cause a faster weight loss than others, but this is often because the loss is of body water, not body fat.

Although the formula above is simple, it would be misleading to assume that the problem is simple. Losing weight and maintaining that weight loss is a major problem for American people today. Why?

1. Eating habits are learned. To maintain weight loss permanently, poor eating habits must be changed to new and good ones. Only diets that bring about a change in eating habits will be successful on a long-term basis.
2. To lose one pound of body fat, one must take in 3,500 calories less than one expends. A reasonable goal is to reduce caloric intake by 500 calories per day. This will produce a loss of one pound each week (7×500 calories = 3,500 calories or one pound). Avoid the harmful effects of near starvation and its companion, stressful malnutrition.
3. Because Americans are so sedentary, it is difficult for the

caloric expenditure to exceed the caloric intake (thereby bringing about a weight loss) without restricting calories and increasing activity. Both of these require a change in behavior.

4. People are often unrealistic in their expectations about how many pounds can be lost and in what period of time. Be patient! Here is an example. A thirty-year-old woman consuming 1,400 calories was maintaining her weight. She had tried a 1,000-calorie diet given to her by her doctor and became frustrated after one week because she had not lost any weight. Why?

If 1,400 calories are required to maintain weight, and you begin a *1,000-calorie* diet, you have a 400-calorie deficit per day.

$$3,500 \div 400 = 8.75 \text{ days}$$

With a 1,000-calorie-a-day diet, it would take eight to nine days to lose one pound. Because she was sedentary, her weight loss occurred very slowly. By following the recommendations in the chapter on exercise (aerobic exercise thirty minutes three times per week), she could lose one pound in approximately six days.

It is helpful to remember that weight gain does not occur overnight, so it is unrealistic to expect pounds to disappear overnight. It is helpful to keep in mind that a weight loss of any amount is better than a weight gain. Remember, the average American gains fifteen to thirty pounds between the ages of twenty and fifty years.

5. Most people underestimate the number of calories in food and overestimate the calories they burn off during exercise. For example, if you drink one eight-ounce glass of your favorite soft drink, you probably have consumed about 100 calories. If you wanted to burn off your soda, you would have to run about a mile, bicycle for two miles, play tennis for a quarter of an hour, or garden for about a third of an hour. If you eat six potato chips, plan on swimming for about ten minutes, playing golf for about twenty minutes, or running for about seven minutes.

A very useful exercise for losing weight was described by one of our high school coaches and health teachers: take both arms and push yourself away from the table!

Behavior Modification and Weight Control

This highly successful approach to weight loss concentrates on changing eating behaviors. New eating behaviors are the keys to the maintenance of any weight loss. These techniques must be practiced just like any of the techniques for stress management. Four categories of techniques are included in most behavior modification programs.

1. Self-monitoring: Record keeping is an essential part of becoming aware of your eating habits. Where? With whom? Doing what? At what time? Under what conditions? Answering these questions will familiarize you with the 'why' of your eating patterns.
2. Stimulus control: Keeping records usually divulges that there are various stimuli other than true hunger that trigger or bring about your desire to eat. Control of these stimuli will help you reduce your intake of food. Some of the most powerful stimuli for eating are actually food cues. Avoid leaving food in sight and avoid stocking your pantry with attractive snacks that are not nutritious.
3. Goal setting: Short-term and long-term goals are important in helping you to approach weight loss realistically. It is important to reward yourself for achieving goals because this positive reinforcement is motivating in itself. Some of the best rewards are to give yourself clothing in your new size and equipment for hobbies other than cooking and eating.
4. Relaxation: Just as relaxation techniques help you manage stressful situations, they can also help you get through the times when you are tempted to eat in response to anger, frustration, boredom, depression, and other negative emotions. Try to eat slowly, chew your food thoroughly, and relax between bites. Breathing from your stomach area will not only relax you but also help you to become aware of cues that you are full.

Caloric Restriction and Weight Control

Americans are actually consuming about 3 percent less food than during the early 1900s, yet an estimated 80 million Americans are overweight. Why? Because we are more sedentary.

Another reason is the kind of food we eat. Compared to the early

1900s we now consume fewer calories but more fat, fewer complex carbohydrates and more simple carbohydrates. Why is this important? A diet higher in fat and lower in carbohydrates contains a smaller quantity of food. In other words, we are consuming a smaller amount of food, and yet it has a higher concentration of calories.

Recommendations for controlling weight:

1. Learn new eating behaviors through self-monitoring, stimulus control, and reward. Avoid the 'rhythm method of girth control' by making changes you can live with the rest of your life. Remember, small caloric changes can have a major impact over a year or a lifetime.

2. Reduce caloric intake. It is possible that if you reduce your fat intake, you could successfully reduce total caloric intake without reducing total quantity of food eaten. A study comparing obese and nonobese doctors showed that the major difference between the two groups was their fat intake.

3. Increase physical activity. Muscle is heavier than fat, so if you reduce your caloric intake and increase your exercise, your weight may be an underestimate of your health. New findings in obesity research suggest that a man's waistline or the amount of fat in skin-fold measurements for women may be the best measures of obesity.

4. Practice stress management to help decrease eating in response to stressful situations.

5. When you have trouble sticking to the above guidelines, do not give up and tell yourself you are a failure. Tell yourself you are human and start following your plan again, right away.

24 Putting It All Together and Making It Work for You

Falling Down and Picking Yourself Up Again

The habits of a lifetime cannot be changed overnight. Change takes time, sometimes a year or two of dedicated practice. But if you do not change sometime during that year or two, your blood pressure elevations could become chronic, your stomach lining could open in a painful ulcer, you could be plagued with headaches, or you could suffer any number of other stress-related disorders.

There is no magic to transform you instantly into a successful stress manager. But we have seen hundreds of people make tremendous progress when they apply and practice the techniques presented in this book.

What will happen if you stop practicing your stress management techniques? Will you immediately return to the chronic stress responses of your old lifestyle? First, even if you have dedicated yourself to practicing these techniques, there will probably be times when you forget to 'relax and let go.' We all get overconfident at times.

Both authors have been practicing, teaching, and researching various stress management techniques for more than a decade. They still find themselves tense and rushing at times. They recognize their stress faster now, more than ever before, by listening to their bodies, and then they return to regularly scheduled stress management practice. The stress spiral can be broken!

Do not get discouraged if you find that you occasionally fail to handle certain stressors in the best way. If life is to be judged, it should be judged on a best efforts basis. You may wish you had done something better. You can imagine, plan, and practice toward doing better. But looking back with discouragement is not a realistic way to approach life. Don't let initial failures or temporary setbacks stop you from trying.

299

Is Failure a Part of Success?

All of science is based on failures. Thousands of unsuccessful experiments were necessary to produce such discoveries as the light bulb and pasteurized milk. Behind most successful people are numerous failures. The winners in life try to learn something from every experience.

The following is the history of one of life's winners who overcame many failures and personal hardships. He lost his job; suffered defeat in a campaign for the legislature; faced failure in business; won an election for the legislature; lost his sweetheart to a fatal disease; experienced a nervous breakdown; lost an election for Speaker in the legislature; lost in a race for congressional nomination; won an election to Congress; lost renomination; was rejected for a land officer; lost an election for the Senate; lost in a race for the vice-presidential nomination; and suffered a second defeat in a Senate election. Two years after his last defeat, Abraham Lincoln was elected president of the United States.

We can all benefit from adopting the 'stick-to-it' attitude of Lincoln. Accept initial failures or setbacks as part of the trial and error process that will bring you a little closer to being a successful stress manager. Most people don't fail, they just give up trying.

Positive Self-Control

Dennis Waitley, the psychologist who wrote *Psychology of Winning*, lists the ten characteristics of successful people. He means much more than financial success. He studies people who succeed in managing stress and living satisfying lives. Dennis Waitley's emphasis is on mental health and not mental illness. His ten qualities of a winner include

1. Positive self-awareness: understanding where you are coming from
2. Positive self-esteem: liking yourself
3. Positive self-control: making it happen for yourself
4. Positive self-motivation: wanting to and deciding you can
5. Positive self-expectancy: deciding that next time you will do even better
6. Positive self-image: seeing yourself changing and growing
7. Positive self-direction: having a game plan

8. Positive self-discipline: practicing mentally
9. Positive self-dimension: valuing yourself as a person
10. Positive self-projection: reflecting yourself in how you walk, talk, and listen.

All of these characteristics are important for successful living, and we highly recommend Dr. Waitley's books and tapes. His characteristic of positive self-control means that winners say, 'I make it happen to me.' Losers say, 'It always happens to me.' Dr. Waitley's proverb for living is 'Life is a do-it-to-myself project. I take the credit or the blame for my performance.'

The Freedom to Choose

Self-control means that you have the freedom to choose alternatives. If you believe your life is dictated by luck, fate, or circumstances, you are open to doubts and fears. You don't *have* to do anything in life. Hunger strikers, for example, decide they do not even have to eat. You can make the best choices among the available alternatives to help you reach your goals.

We hope you decide to break out of the habit of stressful living and into the skills of stress management. We know that you can. Positive self-control is a stress management skill and habit that puts you in control of your life. Not managing stress is also a habit. Habits take years to form, and habits die hard, or they die with the person. Nearly everything you do is a habit.

One of the best ways to break a bad habit is to replace it with a good one. Rather than concentrating on which stressful habits you are not going to do, begin to concentrate on which stress management habits you will practice and develop.

Making Excuses Versus Taking Responsibility

If you are like most people, there will be times when you encounter difficulty in exchanging familiar habits for new ones. If you slack off practicing your new stress management skills, examine your excuses. We often hear excuses such as 'I'm too busy today,' 'I'm too tired,' or 'This isn't working.'

Do not be lured by these excuses. Of course, they are partially true. You may be busy, tired, or progressing slowly. These excuses are also partially false. It is not because you are busy, tired, or progressing slowly that you cannot practice the exercises. Take responsibility for your decision to choose one activity over another by saying, 'I am busy closing out the books for the end of the month. I could do the exercises, but I *choose* not to.' Remember, you are in the driver's seat in your life.

The excuses you give for not rehearsing stress management techniques are probably the same excuses you have used for years to keep yourself locked into a stress cycle. Sometimes these excuses are based on faulty premises and misunderstood need systems.

Understanding Your Needs: Survival and Safety

In order to feel comfortable, most people have certain needs that must be met. If your car leaked gasoline and caught fire, your strong need for safety would supersede any need to get to the destination toward which you were driving.

Psychologists, particularly Dr. Abraham Maslow, have helped us to understand that our needs are often hierarchical. Food and shelter are usually considered to be at the top of our need hierarchy. Next comes the need for physical safety. Most people in today's world can fulfill these basic needs. It may be helpful to acknowledge the role other needs play and how we try to fulfill them.

When we fail to recognize our other needs, we begin to feed into our stress spiral. Recognizing your other needs will also help you to attack any excuses for not practicing your stress management skills.

The Needs for Security and Belonging

The need for security and stability motivates people toward stable relations, insurance policies, and dependable jobs. A strong need for affiliation and belonging means we would value family, avoid disagreements, and attempt to have everyone like us.

Could strong needs for security and affiliation interfere with stress management? Yes. A middle-aged woman we worked with believed her family would reject her if she did not have all of her housework done before she practiced relaxation. Since the work of the housewife is never done, she found little time to relax. She had a strong need to be appreciated. She wanted to be secure, not 'rock the boat,' and have everyone like her.

302

Taking positive self-control of her life, she was able to examine her needs and discussed them with her family. She reread the chapters on assertiveness training. She discovered that her family did not reject her if she took time for herself, but instead they wanted her to do so. In fact, her family had felt guilty because she was always doing things for others instead of for herself. She met her needs for relaxing and replenishing her store of energy, and she sacrificed none of her needs for a secure family relationship.

Believe it or not, a strong need for the respect of others can also interfere with stress management. We worked with a lovely woman in her middle thirties who was in an important management position. Her need for the respect and admiration of others nearly prevented her from learning more about managing stress. She was not able to join the stress management class until she explored this need and brought it into balance with her other needs for a healthy body. Why? She was afraid someone would find out she was in the class, think she could not manage stress, and lose respect for her.

The Needs for Esteem

If you are an energetic person who likes to succeed, you may have a strong need for achievement and accomplishment. Enthusiasm may push you to take on too many stress management exercises at once. You may overdo your practice at first, as you strive toward a goal of perfect stress management in ten days. You may find that you have set unrealistic goals and your program is too rigorous. The over-achiever often feels guilty about not reaching goals, begins to lose interest, and makes excuses about already being overextended. Soon practicing the techniques is put off indefinitely, and the person has burned out before even getting a good start.

If you have a strong need for achievement, be sure to take stress management practice slowly. Don't expect too much too soon. You will begin to feel more energy as a result of relaxation training. Consider your long- and short-term goals. You may wish to use this energy for recreation and hobbies rather than funneling it back into still more work.

Another strong need that may interfere with stress management is the need for power and control. If you find that you cannot delegate enough responsibilities to give you time to practice relaxation, review the time management and assertive chapters.

Rate the strength of your various needs. Use a number from zero (no need) to ten (extremely strong need), and put your rating next to each need listed below.

     _____Power and control
     _____Achievement and accomplishment
     _____Esteem and respect
     _____Affiliation and belonging
     _____Security and stability
     _____Health and physical well-being

Now, ask yourself if, and how, your strongest needs may help or interfere with practicing what you have learned in this book. How strong is your need for a healthy body? For some people, the need for a healthy body is not stronger than the need for the things they gain by having a stress symptom!

In some cases, a spouse has to do the cooking, take out the garbage, or keep the house quiet if the person with the symptom is tired, suffers from a headache, or has elevated blood pressure. For others, a backache or an ulcer can offer power and control. How would your life be different if you did not have your stress-related problems? Is there anything you might have to give up?

The Highest Need on the Hierarchy

If one has fulfilled the needs we have reviewed, then what is left to strive for? The highest need on Dr. Maslow's hierarchy is the need for self-actualization. This is the need for self-fulfillment, for realizing one's potentials, and for becoming the person one is capable of becoming. As you learn to meet your other needs, strive to find the joy of self-fulfillment.

Reviewing Your Progress

Have you already gained a great deal from practicing the techniques in this book? Could you gain more? Review this book and underline the techniques that worked for you. Review your scores on the self-assessment scales that helped you analyze the specific areas of stress in your life.

Do you need more work on relaxing your muscles? Could you benefit from biofeedback for headaches? Do you want to break a habit such as smoking? Is now the time to begin exercising? Should you select books from the reading list to gain further knowledge of time management? What about the *Psychology of Winning* books and tapes?

You may find it helpful to set aside a few hours at the first of every month to review your stress management progress. Spend some time identifying the frequency and intensity of your stress responses. Look for the sources of your stress. These may be changes in your life such as new situations you are facing, new feelings you are experiencing, or new foods or drinks you have added to your diet.

Once you have reviewed your progress, develop a plan to cope with or to avoid the stressors. Consider using some or all of the techniques you have learned in this program. Finally, put your stress management plan into action.

This book and other books or recordings may not be sufficient to help you with all situations. You may want to become involved in an ongoing support group or obtain professional counseling to help you become a successful stress manager.

Support Groups to Help you through Crises in Living

In the past few years, many support networks have broken down. This is probably one of the reasons why we are experiencing such increases in stress today. Years ago, for example, people could count on a consistent and faithful family network that would help in times of crises. In addition, we were much less mobile, and people tended to become very friendly with neighbors. The neighborhood was once a support network within itself.

Because support groups are often very important in helping people manage their stress, we have included in Appendix II a list of support groups. You may wish to refer to it during particular life crises and for stress-related disorders you face.

Religion – A Source of Strength

Religious fellowship, spiritual principles, and faith in something greater than man can be major sources of strength for daily living and times of crisis. A sign we saw in front of a church reads, 'If God seems far away, who do you think moved?' Once again, the choice is ours.

Perhaps you could benefit from becoming more involved in a

305

church or synagogue. If you have moved recently and need to find one in your new community, call the leader of the one you left and ask for a referral; most have national directories if you are not referred to one in your area. You can also look in the yellow pages of the telephone book under churches or synagogues. If you are traveling, most hotels have a directory of nearby places of worship and the hours of their services.

Most churches and synagogues have groups for single people, teenagers, and others in the congregation. These groups can provide new social contacts and be sources of lasting friendships. Service groups affiliated with various religious denominations are listed in the *Encyclopedia of Associations*, which can be found in most libraries.

Professional Counseling

If you find that you are continuing to struggle with serious conflicts and problems, we strongly recommend that you seek professional counseling or therapy. There are a number of mental health professions whose members offer the help you may need.

Not all psychologists provide clinical services. The authors are clinical psychologists. After completing a liberal arts college education, clinical and counseling psychologists are trained in a psychology graduate program for a minimum of four years before interning for a year and receiving the Ph.D. Following this work, clinical psychologists must be supervised in most states for at least one and sometimes two years in a health care facility before taking an examination to become certified or licensed by the state board of examiners. Clinical psychologists offer personality, intellectual, and vocational testing as well as psychotherapy.

Psychiatrists complete a general curriculum in a medical school and then do a specialized psychiatric residency for about four years. Psychiatrists conduct psychotherapy, but they do not provide psychological testing. They prescribe medications, and psychologists do not.

Other mental health professionals include social workers, nurses, ministers, and counselors. Not all the members of these professions are trained to provide direct clinical services. It is best to inquire whether a social worker or a nurse is specifically a psychiatric social worker or a psychiatric nurse. Many counselors are primarily involved with vocational or spiritual work and are not trained in psychotherapy.

Mental health professionals may be listed under their specialty in the yellow pages. Some work in mental health clinics or other institutions, which are also listed in the telephone book.

To find the community mental health center in your area, you may need to look in the white pages of your telephone book under state department of human resources. The division of mental health may be listed under the name of your state. These centers are federally funded and are required to provide mental health services at a cost based on your ability to pay.

Most communities are also served by an institution which is a member of the Family Service Association of America. These institutions also provide professional mental health services and can be found by looking in the white pages under family and children's services or family counseling and children's services. To find still other sources of both professional and para professional help, consult the yellow pages under social service organizations.

Recommendations of friends or professionals who have knowledge of the therapist or institution are more informative and helpful than telephone listings. Most psychotherapists are listed in national registries. In addition, local county or state associations list names of their members by geographic areas and specialties. Local universities may also be a source of information.

It is wise to ask what training the counselor or psychotherapist has had and what his or her speciality is. Never hesitate to explore the credentials of the professional you are interviewing. Be certain that the counselor is licensed to ensure at least a minimal level of competency. Make sure, as well, that the counselor has experience in dealing with your type of problem and is comfortable working in that area. If your counselor wants to learn more about relaxation training you might suggest a book we have written for fellow clinicians, entitled *Stress Management: A Conceptual and Procedural Guide.*

An Invitation

We would very much appreciate hearing from you. One of the ways you can do this is to write us about this book. If there are parts you found difficult, let us know. If there are parts you found particularly helpful, let us know this as well. We would also like to learn about any additional ways you have found to manage stress and enhance your wellness.

A friend of ours shared with us the words of an eighty-five-year-old woman:

> If I had my life to live over, I'd dare to make more mistakes next time. I'd relax. I'd limber up. I would be sillier than I have been this trip. I would take fewer things seriously. I would take more chances. I would take more trips. I would climb more mountains and swim more rivers. I would eat more ice cream and less beans. I would perhaps have more actual troubles, but I'd have fewer imaginary ones.
>
> You see, I'm one of those people who live sensibly and sanely hour after hour, day after day. Oh, I've had my moments and, if I had it to do over again, I'd have more of them. In fact, I'd try to have nothing else. Just moments, one after another, instead of living so many years ahead of each day. I've been one of those persons who never goes anywhere without a thermometer, a hot water bottle, a raincoat and a parachute. If I had to do it again, I would travel lighter than I have.
>
> If I had my life to live over, I would start barefoot earlier in the spring and stay that way later in the fall. I would go to more dances. I would ride more merry-go-rounds. I would pick more daisies.

Nadine Stair
Louisville, Kentucky

This is not the end but the beginning. The winners in the game of life have a game plan. We hope your plan includes finding excitement every day of your life.

Good luck – and may your stressors always be manageable.

Appendices
&
Home Practice Charts

Appendix I Music for Stress Management

The power of music to promote change is not a new concept. The Bible, Greek and Roman literature, and Egyptian records discuss music as a therapeutic device. Wild beasts and trees were charmed by Orpheus. Ulysses had his crew put wax in their ears to avoid hearing the song of the sirens, which could lead them to destruction. The poets have written about the power of music to calm or stir the emotions and to inspire or suppress desire. Men march off to war with a song on their lips. We respond affectively to music.

The ways in which music affects us are varied. There are many studies demonstrating the relaxing physiological responses to music, including changes in breathing, cardiac blood pressure, blood supply, and galvanic skin responses. The first observations on the physiological effects of music are attributed to a French musician, Gretry (1741–1813), who took his pulse by placing the fingers of one hand on the artery in the wrist of his other hand and noted accompanying changes as he sang at different tempos. In 1880, Dogiel tested the influence of music on the circulation of blood in humans by means of a device called a plethysmograph. In 1927, Schoen and Gatewood reported data from twenty thousand persons that demonstrated changes in mood which were produced by music.

According to Diserens, the following effects of music are generally accepted. Music increases bodily metabolism, changes muscular activity, affects respiration, produces marked effects on pulse and blood pressure, and affords the physiological basis for the creation of different emotions.

Possibly the greatest importance of music, as it relates to the study of stress management, is the range and intensity of its associational value. It can serve as a stimulus for a wide variety of reactions, both pleasant and unpleasant. Music and the images it evokes are far more specific to the unique experiences of the listener than is language.

Farnsworth claims that, for most people, the real essence of music lies in the fact that it gives each person an opportunity to project his private experience through his own personal images. Therefore, appropriately selected music can enhance the relaxation experience through calming images and can also promote physical relaxation.

We suggest that you try some of the selections listed below because research has shown that they can help most people to enhance their relaxation experiences. Since everyone responds differently, you should make your own evaluation of each recommendation. We have also included natural environmental sounds which many people find calming.

CLASSICAL-INSTRUMENTAL MUSIC BY J. S. BACH

Concerto in D minor for Two Violins and Strings BWV 1043, 'Largo'.
Harpsichord Concerto in F Minor, BWV 1056, 'Largo'.
Solo Harpsichord Concerto in F Major, BWV 978, 'Largo'.

MEDITATIVE LISTENING EXPERIENCES

Healing Sounds of the Ancients
Serenity by David Sun
Crystal Cave by Upper Astral

ENVIRONMENTAL SOUNDS

Restful Sounds (seashore and country sounds)
Garden of Dreams (stream, rainfall)
Tropical Island

(The tapes listed for meditative listening experiences and environmental sounds are available from New World Cassettes, whose address is given below.)

Some taped music suitable for meditation is available in high street record shops, but there are also several organisations that specialise in supplying it. Others provide spoken courses of various kinds, which readers may like to consider if they find difficulty in obtaining the specific American recordings mentioned in Appendix III. The following are some examples:

Lifeskills, 3 Brighton Road, London N2 8JU. Tel. (01) 346 9646. Tapes for relaxation, stress management, self-presentation, assertiveness skills, examination technique and habit control.

Matthew Manning Centre, 39 Abbeygate Street, Bury St Edmunds, Suffolk, IP33 1LW. A range of self-help holistic healing tapes, using relaxation and visualisation techniques.

New World Cassettes, Box 15, Twickenham, TW1 4SP. A selection of music for relaxation and meditation, and self-help courses on a variety of subjects. The company offers a personally tailored selection service.

Readers who experience difficulty in obtaining particular tapes in the United Kingdom or from America may find the information available from the National Sound Archive, 29 Exhibition Road, London SW7 2AS. Tel. (01) 589 6603.

Appendix II A Guide to Self-Help Groups

What is a Self-Help Group?

A self-help group can provide valuable assistance and support to its members in dealing with their mutual problems and in improving their psychological well-being. Most self-help organizations were started by people who shared common life experiences and problems. Groups are usually controlled by their members and rely on the efforts, skills, knowledge, and concern of their members as their primary source of help.

How Effective Are Self-Help Groups?

A recent survey of one thousand eight hundred outpatient psychiatric facilities in the United States found that about half (48 percent) make either frequent or occasional referrals to self-help groups. In evaluating the usefulness of self-help groups, about 85 percent of the professionals rated the effectiveness of the groups as very high, high, or average. This rating suggests that professionals generally view self-help groups favorably.

Self-help groups provide a social treatment that can not only improve the quality of life for their members but also help prevent further difficulties. The groups offer their members information, comfort, emotional support, and a sense of belonging. Making a public commitment to change often motivates members to succeed. The desire to avoid letting one's friends down and the hope of gaining the group's approval for success can be very positive and very powerful forces for many people.

Self-help groups also sponsor public information programs designed to remove commonly held prejudices and prevent discrimination against their members. In addition, they often support legislation and research of benefit to their members.

How Can I Find a Self-Help Group?

There are several ways to find a self-help group that will meet your needs. If you know the name of the group, look it up in the telephone book. Many groups are also listed in the yellow pages under the section 'social service organizations'. Some newspapers have a calendar of events section in which they announce the times and places of the local weekly meetings. Other sources of referral are friends or local professionals, who are usually familiar with area resources.

Citizens' Advice Bureaux can often help with information, and main Post Offices keep lists of local organizations. Each area will also have a local council for voluntary organizations, to co-ordinate activities, although they go under different titles in different areas.

Another excellent source of information about local groups and activities is the public library, which often has not only a directory of local social services but a notice board open to the public. Groups advertising often include housewives' friendship groups, single or divorced clubs, baby-sitting circles, and all kinds of common-interest groups.

If these sources fail, two useful reference books are the *Charities Digest* and the *National Directory of Voluntary Organizations*, both likely to be in your local library. The latter is also obtainable at £5.95 plus postage from the National Council for Voluntary Organizations, 26 Bedford Square, London WC1B 3HU.

If you are still unable to find a group, consider forming one. Find other people with the same problem and/or local mental health professionals who can help you start a group.

NAMES AND ADDRESSES OF SOME OF THE LARGE, NATIONWIDE SELF-HELP GROUPS

Many of the following organisations have branches all over the United Kingdom. If you have not been able to find a local branch, the national headquarters, listed below, will be able to put you in touch with the one nearest you.

Age Concern England
Bernard Sunley House, 60 Pitcairn Road, Mitcham, Surrey CR4 3LL. Tel. 01–640 5431

Age Concern Wales
1 Park Grove, Cardiff, South Glamorgan CF1 3BJ. Tel. 0222 371566
Age Concern Northern Ireland
128 Great Victoria Street, Belfast 2. Tel. 0232 45729
Age Concern Scotland
33 Castle Street, Edinburgh EH2 3DN. Tel. 031–225 5000

A registered charity with the declared aim of 'promoting the welfare of the aged.' Age Concern operates in two complementary ways – campaigning, and organizing services. There are local groups all over the United Kingdom (950 in England alone), which provide services such as day care, visiting services, lunch clubs, over-60s clubs and specialist services for physically and mentally frail elderly people. The Age Concern movement as a whole campaigns with and on behalf of elderly people on such issues as public transport and housing; it stimulates innovation and research, having a facility to provide small grants to local groups; and it works in partnership with other relevant statutory and voluntary bodies.

Alcoholics Anonymous
11 Redcliffe Gardens, London SW10 9BO. Tel. 01–353 9779

This is a voluntary worldwide fellowship of men and women from all walks of life who meet together to attain and maintain sobriety. There are at present 2,100 groups in mainland Great Britain, with a total membership of about 35,000 people.

Al-Anon Family Groups UK & Eire
61 Great Dover Street, London SE1 4YF Tel. 01–403 0888 (24-hour service)

Al-Anon is a worldwide fellowship providing understanding and support for relatives and friends of problem drinkers, whether the alcoholic is still drinking or not. Nearly 900 groups meet in the United Kingdom and Eire. Everything is confidential and there are no dues or fees. Al-Anon is entirely self-supporting through the sale of its literature and members' voluntary contributions. Alateen is a part of Al-Anon especially for teenagers who are or have been affected by an alcoholic parent.

BACUP (British Association of Cancer United Patients and their families and friends)

121/123 Charterhouse Street, London EC1M 6AA. Tel. 01–608 1785. Cancer Information Service 01–608 1661

A new charity, founded in 1984 to help patients and their families to cope with cancer, BACUP provides a national information service on cancer, the practical and emotional aspects of living with the illness, and the services available to cancer patients. It also provides emotional support and advice, and aims to involve as many cancer patients as possible in helping each other in this. BACUP is in touch with cancer support groups all over the country, and hopes to set up regional branches where there is a need for them.

Divorce Conciliation and Advisory Service
38 Ebury Street, London SW1W 0LU. Tel. 01–730 2422.

Two services are offered. *Conciliation* offers divorced or separated parents help in negotiating and maintaining workable arrangements concerning their children. It also helps renegotiate arrangements which have already broken down or need changing due to altered circumstances. The *counselling service* is available at any stage of the process of divorce or separation, offering emotional support and practical advice before, during and after separation.

Gamblers Anonymous
17/23 Blantyre Street, London SW10. Tel. 01–352 3060

Formed in 1964, this is a fellowship of men and women who have joined together in order that they may stop gambling and help other gamblers to do the same. There are about 120 groups meeting weekly in the United Kingdom and Eire, each autonomous and self-supporting through voluntary contributions from members. The membership is around 1,500 at any one time and the age range is from 13 or 14 to over 70.

Gam-Anon is a fellowship run by relatives and friends of compulsive gamblers for their own mutual encouragement and support. Groups meet weekly on the same night as Gamblers Anonymous. Address and telephone number as for Gamblers Anonymous.

317

Heart to Heart
Mrs. J. Richardson, Box No 7, Pershore, Worcestershire. Tel. 0905 840446

This is a national network of telephone contact provided voluntarily by people who have undergone heart surgery, to give advice, support and encouragement to anyone about to undergo a similar experience. Patients can often be put in touch with someone who has undergone the same operation as they face themselves, and be helped through the trauma of surgery, recovery and getting back to a normal, healthy life.

Incest Crisis
32 Newbury Close, Northolt, Middlesex UB5 4JF. Tel. 01–422 5100 or 01–890 4732

Incest Crisis is a registered charity offering a 24-hour telephone counselling service to anyone involved in an incest situation. There are five major telephone lines in the UK and Eire and 120 volunteers on call, all with first-hand experience of sexual abuse by someone they would otherwise have trusted. Incest Crisis encourages abusers to ring, but its services are equally available to victims, families, social workers, and anyone else who may have become involved. Legal, psychiatric and medical advice are offered, drawing on sympathetic sources in the Great Ormond Street Hospital for Sick Children and Scotland Yard, among others.

La Leche League (Great Britain)
BM3424, London WC1V 6XX. Tel. 01–404 5011

This international charitable organization was founded in 1956 and now has more than 100,000 members in approximately 4,000 groups in 42 countries. The organization appoints leaders who arrange monthly discussion meetings of women interested in breastfeeding their infants. The goals are 'to foster good mothering through breastfeeding and thus to encourage closer and happier family relationships.' Each group maintains a lending library of books and leaflets on childbirth, breastfeeding and childcare.

National Children's Home
85 Highbury Park, London N5 1UD. Tel. 01–226 2033

A registered charity founded in 1869, the National Children's Home is in the process of changing its emphasis from the provision of traditional residential care, to concentrate more on providing services of all kinds to children, adolescents and their families facing a variety of difficulties and dangers. They operate at present 123 centers throughout the country, including adolescent independence units, family support centers and counselling advice services as well as children's homes and schools. The NCH Family Network offers a phone-in service for people who want to talk about a family problem. The number given above is for the London area, but there are 13 others in Great Britain, including Birmingham, Cardiff, and Glasgow.

Parents Anonymous
6–9 Manor Gardens, London N7 6LA. Tel. 01–263 5672 (Helpline 01–263 8918)

Parents Anonymous operates a strictly confidential telephone service offering comfort, sympathy and advice to parents who are distressed by their relationships with their children. Organized by someone who was herself a child batterer, the service is manned by volunteers, all parents, who have undergone a basic training course, and is backed up by professionals (doctors, barristers, etc.) on call to give advice when needed.

Take Heart
c/o George Morland, 55 Flaxpiece Road, Claycross, Chesterfield, Derbyshire. Tel. 0246 862462, evenings

Take Heart is the name of a small group started in Mansfield by heart attack victims who joined together for mutual support and encouragement, and to pool advice and experience in order to help new heart attack victims. Supported by the British Heart Foundation and the Chest, Heart and Stroke Association, its success has led to the formation of similar groups elsewhere in the country, and it is hoped that the movement will continue to spread. Each group functions autonomously, but a central register is kept, and action packs for people starting their own group can be obtained from the above address.

Volunteer Stroke Scheme

Mrs. P. Oswin, Manor Farm, Appleton, Abingdon, Oxon OX13 5JR. Tel. 0865 862954

This scheme was founded in 1973 to help stroke patients with speech and associated problems. It is run by volunteers who visit stroke patients regularly, establish a relaxed, neighborly relationship with them, and use common interests, games, puzzles and other simple methods to stimulate and help overcome the difficulties of speech, memory, handling money, numbers, telling the time, etc. Regular club meetings and occasional outings are also arranged. The scheme is supported by the DHSS, operates at present in over 60 Health Districts in the United Kingdom, and is still expanding.

TO GIVE IS ALSO TO RECEIVE

It is worth remembering that sometimes helping others can do as much good as helping oneself, if not more. The community spirit of working with others and the sense of being needed can be very rewarding, and most voluntary organizations are always glad to receive new volunteers. You may well be aware of groups in your area that need help and know what work you would be best suited for and most enjoy doing; but if you want to seek further information, the sources given on page 315 should again prove helpful.

Appendix III   Suggested Books and Recordings

We have listed below books, prerecorded relaxation tapes, and other recommended listening materials which you can use to extend, deepen, and practice the material in most of the chapters in this book.

RECOMMENDED RELAXATION TAPES

First, we recommend a cassette stress management program developed by a team of psychologists, including the authors of this book. It consists of three cassettes with musical and environmental backgrounds and a step-by-step fifty-two-page guide to stress management.

The contents of this program include Tape 1: *Progressive Relaxation and Deep Muscle Relaxation*; Tape 2: *Autogenic Relaxation: Arms & Hands and Legs & Feet*; and Tape 3: *Visual Imagery Relaxation and Image Rehearsal Practice*.

You may test this program for a fifteen-day money-back trial period. The cost is $34.95 plus $5.00 postage and handling for the complete *Relaxation and Stress Management Program* or $12.95 plus $5.00 postage and handling for individual tapes. Send to **Stress Management Research Associates, Inc., P.O. Box 2232-B, Houston, TX 77251**. For more information about these tapes and workshops by the authors, you may call (713) 890-8575.

Also available for children's stress is the *Family Relaxation and Self-Control Program*. It consists of Tape 1: *Parents' Relaxation Exercises and Parents' Trip to the Mountains*; Tape 2: *Children's Relaxation Exercises and Children's Slow-Relax*; Tape 3: *Trip to the Beach and Yes I Can, I Know I Can*. To order the family program, you may send $34.95 plus $5.00 postage and handling, or $12.95 plus $5.00 postage and handling for individual tapes to the address given above.

321

Chapter 4

Books

Brown, B. *New Mind, New Body*. New York: Harper & Row, 1974.
Goldberg, P. *Executive Health*. Maidenhead: McGraw-Hill, 1978.
Levinson, H. *Executive Stress*. New York: Mentor, 1975.
Pelletier, K. *Mind as Healer, Mind as Slayer*. London: Allen & Unwin, 1978.
Selye, H. *Stress without Distress*. London: Hodder & Stoughton, 1974.

Recordings

Charlesworth, E., and Peiffer, A. *Stress Management Training Program: Hospital Edition – Introduction*. Houston: Stress Management Research, 1977.
Stroebel, C. *Quieting Response Training – Introduction*. New York: BMA, 1978.

Chapter 5

Books

Jacobson, E. *Progressive Relaxation*. Chicago: University of Chicago, 1974.
——. *You Must Relax*. London: Souvenir Press, 1977.

Recordings

Budzynski, T. *Relaxation Training Program – Tense – Slo – Relax*. New York: BMA, 1974.
Charlesworth, E. *Relaxation and Stress Management Program – Progressive Relaxation*. Houston: Stress Management Research, 1981.
Charlesworth E., and Peiffer, A. *Stress Management Training Program – Progressive Relaxation*. Houston: Stress Management Research, 1977.
Stroebel, C. *Quieting Response Training – Relaxing Skeletal Muscles*. New York: BMA, 1978.

Chapter 6

Recording

Hartmann, C. H. *Mixed Scanning Relaxation Program.* New York: BMA, 1976.

Chapter 7

Books

Benson, H., with Klipper, M. *The Relaxation Response.* London: Collins, 1976.

LeShan, L. *How to Meditate.* Wellingborough: Turnstone Books, 1983.

Recordings

Budzynski, T. *Relaxation Training Program – Forehead and Facial Relaxation.* New York: BMA, 1974.

Charlesworth, E. *Relaxation and Stress Management Program – Deep Muscle Relaxation.* Houston: Stress Management Research, 1981.

Charlesworth, E., and Peiffer, A. *Stress Management Training Program: Hospital Edition – Deep Muscle Relaxation.* Houston: Stress Management Research, 1977.

Chapter 9

Recordings

Budzynski, T. *Relaxation Training Program – Limb Heaviness, Arms and Legs Heavy and Warm.* New York: BMA, 1974.

Charlesworth, E. *Relaxation and Stress Management Program – Autogenic Training.* Houston: Stress Management Research, 1981.

Charlesworth, E., and Peiffer, A. *Stress Management Training Program: Hospital Edition – Autogenic Training.* Houston: Stress Management Research, 1977.

Stroebel, C. *Quieting Response Training – Relaxing Smooth Muscles.* New York: BMA, 1978.

Chapter 10

Books

Masters, R., and Houston, J. *Mind Games*. London: Turnstone Books, 1972.

Ornstein, R. *The Psychology of Consciousness*. London: Jonathan Cape, 1975.

Recordings

Lupin, M. *Family Relaxation and Self-Control Program*. Houston: Biobehavioral, 1981.

Lazarus, A. *Personal Enrichment through Imagery*. New York: BMA, 1982.

Charlesworth, E. *Relaxation and Stress Management Program – Visual Imagery Relaxation*. Houston: Stress Management Research, 1981.

Charlesworth, E., and Peiffer, A. *Stress Management Training Program: Hospital Edition – Island Journey – Visual Imagery*. Houston: Stress Management Research, 1977.

Chapter 12

Book

Olson, K. *I Hurt Too Much for a Band-Aid*. Phoenix, Arizona: O'Sullivan Woodside, 1980.

Recordings

Budzynski, T. *Relaxation Training Program – Stress Management*. New York: BMA, 1974.

Charlesworth, E. *Relaxation and Stress Management Program – Image Rehearsal Practice*. Houston: Stress Management Research, 1981.

Charlesworth, E., and Peiffer, A. *Stress Management Training Program: Hospital Edition – Stress Management*. Houston: Stress Management Research, 1977.

Miller, J. *Taking the 'Ouch' out of Headaches*. Atlanta, Georgia: Atlanta Headache Clinic, 1981.

Stroebel, C. *Quieting Response Training – Ten Steps to the Integrated Quieting Response*. New York: BMA, 1978.

Chapter 13

Books

Levinson, D. *The Seasons of a Man's Life*. New York: Knopf, 1978.
Sheehy, G. *Passages: Predictable Crisis of Adult Life*. London: Bantam. 1977.
——. *Pathfinders*. London, Sidgwick & Jackson, 1982.

Recordings

Cetron, M., and O'Toole, P. *Encounters with the Future*. Chicago: Nightingale-Conant, 1983.
Jones, A. *How to Get an Emotional Divorce*. Clute, Texas: Individual Success, 1980.
Sheehy, G. *Passages*. Waco, Texas: SMI, 1982.

Chapter 14

Books

DeBakey, M., and Grotto, A. *The Living Heart*. New York: McKay, 1977.
Friedman, M., and Rosenman, R. *Type A Behaviour and Your Heart*. London: Wildwood House, 1974.

Recordings

Galton, L. *How Long Will I Live?* Waco, Texas: SMI, 1980.
Zimbardo, P. *Shyness: What Is It? What to Do About It?* New York: BMA, 1980.

Chapter 15

Books

Ellis, A., and Harper, R. *A New Guide to Rational Living*. Los Angeles: Wilshire, 1975.
Lazarus, A., and Fay, A. *I Can if I Want To*. New York: Warner, 1978.

Recordings

Ellis, A. *Rational Emotive Self-Help Techniques*. New York: BMA, 1980.

Emery, G. *Controlling Depression through Cognitive Therapy: Self Management Guide and Clinical Procedure.* New York: BMA, 1982

Chapter 16

Goldfried, M. *Self-Modification of Anxiety: Client Instructions.* New York: BMA, 1975.

Chapter 17

Ellis, A. *Anger Management: How to Live with – and without – Anger.* Pleasantville, N.Y.: Reader's Digest Press, 1977.

Chapter 18

Book

Alberti, R., and Emmons, M. *Your Perfect Right: A Guide to Assertive Behavior.* San Luis Obispo, California: Impact, 1970.

Recording

Rakos, R., and Schroeder, H. *Self-Directed Assertiveness Training.* New York: BMA, 1976.

Chapter 19

Books

Alberti, R., and Emmons, M. *Your Perfect Right: A Guide to Assertive Behavior.* San Luis Obispo, California: Impact, 1970.
Jakubowski, P., and Lange, A. *The Assertive Option: Your Rights and Responsibilities.* Champaign, Illinois: Research Press, 1978.

Recording

Rakos, R., and Schroeder, H. *Self-Directed Assertiveness Training.* New York: BMA, 1976.

Chapter 20

Books

Alberti, R., and Emmons, M. *Stand Up, Speak Out, Talk Back!* New York: Pocket Books, 1975.

——. *Your Perfect Right: A Guide to Assertive Behavior.* San Luis Obispo, California: Impact, 1970.

Blanchard, K., and Johnson, S. *The One Minute Manager.* London: Fontana, 1984.

Bloom, L., Coburn, K., and Pearlman, J. *The New Assertive Woman.* New York: Dell, 1976.

Smith, M. *When I Say No, I Feel Guilty.* London: Bantam, 1975.

Recordings

Blanchard, K., and Johnson, S. *The One Minute Manager.* Chicago: Nightingale-Conant, 1983.

Rakos, R., and Schroeder, H. *Self-Directed Assertiveness Training.* New York: BMA, 1976.

Chapter 21

Books

Bliss, E. *Getting Things Done.* London: Elm Tree Books, 1979.

Lakein, A. *How to Get Control of Your Time and Your Life.* New York: Signet, 1973.

Winston, S. *Getting Organized.* New York: Warner Books, 1978.

Young, P., and Jones, P. *Sidetracked Home Executives.* New York: Warner Books, 1981.

Recordings

Lakein, A. *How to Get Control of Your Time and Your Life.* Waco, Texas: SMI, 1980.

Nathan, K. *The Trees Jobs Grow on and How to Find the One for You.* Concord, Massachusetts: Heinle & Heinle, 1984.

Raygor, A. ed. *Rapid Reading and Comprehension Skills.* Gainsville: International Institute for Reading, 1981.

Chapter 22

Books

Anderson, R. *Stretching*. New York: Random House, 1980.

Cooper, K. *The New Aerobics*. London: Bantam, 1970.

Cooper, M., and Cooper, K. *Aerobics for Women*. London: Bantam, 1973.

Fixx, J. *The Complete Book of Running*. London: Chatto & Windus, 1979.

Sussman, A., and Goode, R. *The Magic of Walking*. New York: Simon & Schuster, 1967.

Recordings

Cooper, K. *Fitness for Life*. Chicago: Nightingale-Conant, 1983.

——. *Run for Your Life*. Waco, Texas: SMI, 1975.

Mahoney, M. *Comprehensive Exercise Guide*. New York: BMA, 1982.

Main, S., and Sample, B. *The Joy of Fitness*. Victoria, British Columbia: Joy of Fitness Production, 1981.

Chapter 23

Books

Berland, J., and the editors of *Consumer Guide*. *Rating the Diets*. New York: Signet, 1980.

Deutsch, R. *Realities of Nutrition*. Palo Alto, California: Bull, 1976.

Ferguson, J. *Habits Not Diets*. Palo Alto, California: Bull, 1976.

Mahoney, M., and Mahoney, K. *Permanent Weight Control: A Total Solution to the Dieter's Dilemma*. New York: W. W. Norton, 1980.

Methodist Hospital Diet Modification Clinic. *The Help Your Heart Eating Plan*. Houston: Methodist Hospital, 1979.

Pritikin, N., and McGrady, P. *The Pritikin Program for Diet and Exercise*. New York: Grosset & Dunlap, 1979.

Smith, N. *Food for Sport*. Palo Alto, California: Bull, 1976.

Stuart, R., and Davis, B. *Slim Chance in a Fat World. Behavioral Control of Obesity*. Champaign, Illinois: Research, 1978.

Cook books

Jordan, J. *Wings of Life*. London: Souvenir Press, 1980.

Lampen, N. *Fat-Free Recipes*. London: Faber & Faber, 1977.

Leonard, J., and Taylor, E. *The Live Longer Now Cookbook*. New York: Grosset & Dunlap, 1977.

Stafford, J. *Taste of Life*. London: Souvenir Press, 1985.

Recordings

Danaher, B., and Lichtenstein, E. *Comprehensive Smoking Cessation Program*. New York: BMA, 1980.

Marston, A., and Marston, M. *Comprehensive Weight Control Program*. New York: BMA, 1980.

Chapter 24

Books

Lazarus, A., and Fay, A. *I Can if I Want To*. New York: Warner Books, 1978.

Nathan, R., and Charlesworth, E. *Stress Management: A Conceptual and Procedural Guide*. Houston: Biobehavioral Press, 1980.

Recording

Waitley, Dennis. *Psychology of Winning*. Chicago: Nightingale-Conant, 1978.

HOME PRACTICE CHART

DIRECTIONS: For each week of your stress management program, record the date in the blank next to the week number. Space is provided to record your practice twice a day. The codes are defined below. Write the code of the technique you practiced in the appropriate blank next to session(1) and session(2) for each day. Next to the code, write in the number of minutes you practiced. In the last two columns, write in your relaxation ratings. Remember, 0 means total relaxation and 100 means total tension.

CODES FOR WHAT YOU PRACTICED:

Name of Technique	Code
Progressive Relaxation	PR
Scanning Relaxation	SR
Deep Muscle Relaxation	DM
Countdown Relaxation	CD
Autogenic Training	AT
Imagery Training	IT
Mental Simulation	MS
Other Training	OT

WEEK 1   DATE _____

Day/Session		What You Practiced	Minutes Practiced	Relaxation Ratings (0-100) Before	After
1	(1)				
	(2)				
2	(1)				
	(2)				
3	(1)				
	(2)				
4	(1)				
	(2)				
5	(1)				
	(2)				
6	(1)				
	(2)				
7	(1)				
	(2)				

WEEK 2   DATE _____

Day/Session		What You Practiced	Minutes Practiced	Relaxation Ratings (0-100) Before	After
1	(1)				
	(2)				
2	(1)				
	(2)				
3	(1)				
	(2)				
4	(1)				
	(2)				
5	(1)				
	(2)				
6	(1)				
	(2)				
7	(1)				
	(2)				

HOME PRACTICE CHART

DIRECTIONS: For each week of your stress management program, record the date in the blank next to the week number. Space is provided to record your practice twice a day. The codes for what you practiced are defined below. Write the code of the technique you practiced in the appropriate blank next to session(1) and session(2) for each day. Next to the code, write in the number of minutes you practiced. In the last two columns, write in your relaxation range. Remember, 0 means total relaxation and 100 means total tension.

CODES FOR WHAT YOU PRACTICED:

Name of Technique	Code
Progressive Relaxation	PR
Scanning Relaxation	SR
Deep Muscle Relaxation	DM
Countdown Relaxation	CD
Autogenic Training	AT
Imagery Training	IT
Mental Simulation	MS
Other Training	OT

WEEK 3   DATE _____

Day/Session		What You Practiced	Minutes Practiced	Relaxation Ratings (0-100) Before	After
1	(1)				
	(2)				
2	(1)				
	(2)				
3	(1)				
	(2)				
4	(1)				
	(2)				
5	(1)				
	(2)				
6	(1)				
	(2)				
7	(1)				
	(2)				

WEEK 4   DATE _____

Day/Session		What You Practiced	Minutes Practiced	Relaxation Ratings (0-100) Before	After
1	(1)				
	(2)				
2	(1)				
	(2)				
3	(1)				
	(2)				
4	(1)				
	(2)				
5	(1)				
	(2)				
6	(1)				
	(2)				
7	(1)				
	(2)				

HOME PRACTICE CHART

DIRECTIONS: For each week of your stress management program, record the date in the blank next to the week number. Space is provided to record your practice for what you practiced are defined below. Write the code of the technique you practiced in the appropriate blank next to session (1) and session (2) for each day. Next to the code, write in the number of minutes you practiced. In the last two columns, write in your relaxation ratings. Remember, 0 means total relaxation and 100 means total tension.

CODES FOR WHAT YOU PRACTICED:

Name of Technique	Code
Progressive Relaxation	PR
Scanning Relaxation	SR
Deep Muscle Relaxation	DM
Countdown Relaxation	CD
Autogenic Training	AT
Imagery Training	IT
Mental Simulation	MS
Other Training	OT

WEEK 5   DATE _____

Day/Session		What You Practiced	Minutes Practiced	Relaxation Ratings (0-100) Before	After
1	(1)				
	(2)				
2	(1)				
	(2)				
3	(1)				
	(2)				
4	(1)				
	(2)				
5	(1)				
	(2)				
6	(1)				
	(2)				
7	(1)				
	(2)				

WEEK 6   DATE _____

Day/Session		What You Practiced	Minutes Practiced	Relaxation Ratings (0-100) Before	After
1	(1)				
	(2)				
2	(1)				
	(2)				
3	(1)				
	(2)				
4	(1)				
	(2)				
5	(1)				
	(2)				
6	(1)				
	(2)				
7	(1)				
	(2)				

332

HOME PRACTICE CHART

DIRECTIONS: For each week of your stress management program, record the date in the blank next to the week number. Space is provided to record your practice twice a day. The codes for what you practiced are defined below. Write the code of the technique you practiced in the appropriate blank next to session (1) and session (2) for each day. Next to the code, write in the number of minutes you practiced. In the last two columns, write in your relaxation range. Remember, 0 means total relaxation and 100 means total tension.

CODES FOR WHAT YOU PRACTICED:

Name of Technique	Code
Progressive Relaxation	PR
Scanning Relaxation	SR
Deep Muscle Relaxation	DM
Countdown Relaxation	CD
Autogenic Training	AT
Imagery Training	IT
Mental Simulation	MS
Other Training	OT

333

WEEK 7 DATE _____

Day/Session	What You Practiced	Minutes Practiced	Relaxation Ratings (0-100) Before	After
1 (1)				
(2)				
2 (1)				
(2)				
3 (1)				
(2)				
4 (1)				
(2)				
5 (1)				
(2)				
6 (1)				
(2)				
7 (1)				
(2)				

WEEK 8 DATE _____

Day/Session	What You Practiced	Minutes Practiced	Relaxation Ratings (0-100) Before	After
1 (1)				
(2)				
2 (1)				
(2)				
3 (1)				
(2)				
4 (1)				
(2)				
5 (1)				
(2)				
6 (1)				
(2)				
7 (1)				
(2)				

HOME PRACTICE CHART

DIRECTIONS: For each week of your stress management program, record the date in the blank next to the week number. Space is provided to record your practice twice a day. The codes for what you practiced are defined below. Write the code of the technique you practiced on the appropriate blank next to session (1) and session (2) for each day. Next to the code, write in the number of minutes you practiced. In the last two columns, write in your relaxation rating. Remember, 0 means total relaxation and 100 means total tension.

CODES FOR WHAT
YOU PRACTICED:

Name of Technique	Code
Progressive Relaxation	PR
Scanning Relaxation	SR
Deep Muscle Relaxation	DM
Countdown Relaxation	CD
Autogenic Training	AT
Imagery Training	IT
Mental Simulation	MS
Other Training	OT

WEEK 9   DATE _____

Day/Session		What You Practiced	Minutes Practiced	Relaxation Ratings (0-100) Before	After
1	(1)				
	(2)				
2	(1)				
	(2)				
3	(1)				
	(2)				
4	(1)				
	(2)				
5	(1)				
	(2)				
6	(1)				
	(2)				
7	(1)				
	(2)				

WEEK 10   DATE _____

Day/Session		What You Practiced	Minutes Practiced	Relaxation Ratings (0-100) Before	After
1	(1)				
	(2)				
2	(1)				
	(2)				
3	(1)				
	(2)				
4	(1)				
	(2)				
5	(1)				
	(2)				
6	(1)				
	(2)				
7	(1)				
	(2)				

334

HOMEOPATHIC MEDICINE AT HOME
by Maesimund B. Panos M.D. and Jane Heimlich

Alternative Medicine the natural way in your own home

HOW TO CHOOSE AND USE HOMEOPATHIC
TREATMENT

Homeopathy has long been recognised as an effective
alternative to modern medical techniques, with the bonus
that homeopathic remedies are non-toxic, safe for children and pregnant women and do not cause side-effects.

Homeopathic Medicine at Home is a comprehensive and
practical guide to self-help homeopathy and tells you
how to treat minor ailments, deal with emergencies and
how to prescribe for yourself and your family.

* Your Home Remedy Kit
* What to do for Accidents
* A Happier Baby with Homeopathic Care
* How to Prevent and Treat Colds, Coughs, Ear-ache,
  Indigestion
* Your Growing Child
* What Homeopathy can do for Women
* Keeping your Pets Healthy

0 552 99244 5

THE HEADACHE AND MIGRAINE HANDBOOK
by D. J. N. Blau

This comprehensive book should help those troubled by headaches or migraine attacks. Instead of reaching for pills — some of which may have harmful side-effects — you can diagnose the cause of your headaches or migraines, learn how to prevent them and how far to treat yourself safely.

The Headache and Migraine Handbook tells you what symptoms you should look for, which trigger factors to avoid, when to seek medical advice and what you should tell your doctor. Pain in the head is a warning signal, so headaches cannot always be avoided, but by understanding their root causes you can reduce their frequency and severity.

Dr J. N. Blau is a distinguished British authority on the types and causes of all varieties of headaches and migraines and writes with clarity, sympathy and commonsense on this all too widespread problem.

* Tension headaches
* Pre-menstrual headaches
* Hangovers
* The weather and migraine
* Chinese restaurant headaches
* Warnings of migraine
* Nitrites and nitrates in food
* Cluster headaches

0 552 12815 5

THE PATIENT'S COMPANION
by Dr Vernon Coleman

'Definitely a worthwhile buy'

Woman's Own

'. . . a useful reference tool for the medicine cupboard'
The Times

'A mine of highly readable, well-organised information'
Company

The Patient's Companion was first published as *The Good Medicine Guide,* and has now been completely revised and updated for this new paperback edition.

Dr Vernon Coleman is one of Britain's bestselling writers on medicine and this excellent reference book has been written to help everyone to get the very best health care for themselves and their families.

* how to read a prescription
* what to stock in your medicine cupboard
* what to do when someone dies
* what to take to hospital
* what a form FP 95 is (and 35 others forms that doctors hand out to patients)
* how to leave your body to a medical school
* how to change your doctor
* how to seek advice when going abroad
* what vaccinations you and your child need

0 552 12734 5

STRESS WITHOUT DISTRESS
by Hans Selye

Hans Selye knows more about stress than any other scientist. Here, taking off his lab coat and speaking simply to all of us, he offers a lifetime of learning about how to survive in a pressure-ridden society.

'*Stress Without Distress* is not only a helpful book. It is thoughtful, wise, and moral in the best sense of that word'

Alvin Toffler, author of Future Shock

'Stress is the spice of life,' says Dr Selye. Without it you would be a vegetable — or dead. Then why can stress be destructive, causing ulcers, heart disease, and so many other ailments of modern society?

To those and other vital questions about health and self-fulfilment, Dr Selye in *Stress Without Distress* offers reassuring answers, based on a lifetime of pioneering biological research.

He explains the physiological mechanisms of stress and offers specific advice on avoiding stress that is harmful. He tells you what to do if you're baffled by a problem, why procrastination is dangerous, how to enjoy leisure, why aimlessness causes distress. He discusses the concept of work as rewarding and satisfying play,and the relationship between work, stress and aging.

Stress Without Distress shows how you can increase your potential in a practical and natural way without endangering your health with harmful stress factors.

0 552 13002 8

NEW WAYS TO LOWER YOUR BLOOD PRESSURE
by Claire Safran

Learn How To Control Your High Blood Pressure

High Blood Pressure, or Hypertension, is widely recognised as one of the major risk factors in causing heart disease or strokes.

New Ways to Lower your Blood Pressure by award-winning writer Claire Safran will tell you everything your doctor may not have time for and sorts out current research, new ideas, approaches and treatments in a clear, easy-to-follow style.

Should you or shouldn't you cut out salt? What about your diet? What about different drugs? Will meditation help you? Today there are more answers and more choices open to you than ever before. Claire Safran has information on what the best doctors say, and examines the range of treatments and the full repertory of cures and remedies. Let this valuable book help you choose the ways that will work for you. The more ideas you try, the quicker your blood pressure will come down and the healthier you'll be.

* New approaches to exercise
* New ways of looking at your diet
* New ideas about salt
* Most self-help methods will work within thirty days
* Includes a diet plan and recipes
* New healthy ways to reduce stress
* New relaxation techniques

0 552 12822 8

RUNNING WITHOUT FEAR
by Dr Kenneth H. Cooper

SAFE GUIDELINES FOR EXERCISE

At what point do you put your health at risk in the course of exercise? Is there a way to exercise safely? Yes, says Dr Kenneth H. Cooper, whose landmark book *Aerobics* coined that term and started America running. Now, in this timely and important book, Dr Cooper presents a safe, sensible programme that takes the fear out of exercise. Whether you run, swim, cycle, ski, dance, or perform any aerobic exercise, the guidelines in this book are all you will need for a lifetime of worry-free physical fitness. Inside you will learn:

* How to reduce the eleven 'rules of risk' for development of heart disease
* The danger and fallacy of the myth of invulnerability: that the more we exercise, the healthier we are
* What constitutes a safe and effective stress test — plus, the new Cooper Protocol, the state-of-the-art procedure in stress testing developed at the Institute of Aerobics Research
* Why the cool-down is the most dangerous phase of exercise
* How to avoid the Jim Fixx Syndrome
* How, when, and where you are at risk during exercise
* How to develop your own personalized and safe exercise programme
* Complete with illustrations, charts, self-evaluation tests, references, glossary and index

'A well-considered and authoritative answer to the anti-exercise lobby and no one is better qualified than Dr Cooper to write such a book'

Bruce Tolloh, Running

0 553 17356 1

GETTING WELL AGAIN
by O. Carl Simonton, M.D.
   Stephanie Matthews-Simonton
   James L. Creighton

Why do some patients get well and others dies when the prognosis is the same for both?

From experience with hundreds of patients at their world-famous Cancer Counselling and Research Centre in Dallas, Texas, the Simontons have found a scientific basis for the 'will to live'

In *Getting Well Again* they profile the typical 'cancer personality': how an individual's reaction to stress and other emotional factors can contribute to the onset and progress of cancer — and how positive expectations, self-awareness and self-care can contribute to survival.

This book offers the same self-help techniques the Simontons' patients have used so successfully to reinforce usual medical treatment — techniques for learning positive attitudes, relaxation, visualization, goal setting, managing pain, exercise and building an emotional support system.

0 553 17272 7

NON FICTION AVAILABLE FROM PATHWAY

The prices shown below were correct at the time of going to press. However Transworld Publishers reserve the right to show new retail prices on covers which may differ from those previously advertised in the text or elsewhere.

☐ 17275 1	**MAKING LOVE DURING PREGNANCY**	*Elizabeth Bing & Libby Colman*	£3.50
☐ 12815 5	**THE HEADACHE AND MIGRAINE HANDBOOK**	*J.N. Blau*	£3.50
☐ 12734 5	**THE PATIENT'S COMPANION**	*Vernon Coleman*	£3.95
☐ 99238 0	**ADDICTS AND ADDICTIONS**	*Vernon Coleman*	£3.50
☐ 17356 1	**RUNNING WITHOUR FEAR**	*Kenneth Cooper*	£3.95
☐ 12798 1	**THE BITTER PILL**	*Dr. Ellen Grant*	£3.50
☐ 99242 9	**JUDITH HANN'S TOTAL HEALTH PLAN**	*Judith Hann*	£2.95
☐ 99246 1	**COMING TO TERMS**	*Roberta Israeloff*	£3.50
☐ 17362 6	**RECIPES FOR ALLERGICS**	*Billie Little*	£3.95
☐ 17274 3	**RECIPES FOR DIABETICS**	*Billie Little & Penny L. Thorup*	£3.95
☐ 17273 5	**THE HERB BOOK**	*John Lust*	£4.95
☐ 99244 5	**HOMEOPATHIC MEDICINE AT HOME**	*Maesimund B. Panos &*	
		Jane Heimlich	£4.95
☐ 12829 5	**THE A FOR ALLERGY DIET**	*Barbara Paterson*	£2.95
☐ 12822 8	**NEW WAYS TO LOWER YOUR BLOOD PRESSURE**	*Claire Safran*	£3.95
☐ 13002 8	**STRESS WITHOUT DISTRESS**	*Hans Selye*	£2.95
☐ 17272 7	**GETTING WELL AGAIN**	*Carl & Stephanie Simonton*	£3.95
☐ 99263 1	**LEARNING TO LIVE WITH DIABETES**	*Dr. R.M. Youngson*	£2.95

ORDER FORM

All these books are available at your book shop or newsagent, or can be ordered direct from the publisher. Just tick the titles you want and fill in the form below.

Transworld Publishers, Cash Sales Department,
61–63 Uxbridge Road, Ealing, London, W5 5SA

Please send cheque or postal order, not cash. All cheques and postal orders must be in £ sterling and made payable to Transworld Publishers Ltd.

Please allow cost of book(s) plus the following for postage and packing:

U.K./Republic of Ireland Customers:
Orders in excess of £5; no charge
Orders under £5; add 50p

Overseas Customers:
All orders; add £1.50

NAME (Block Letters) ....

ADDRESS ....

....